MW00824455

A WEAVER'S BOOK OF
8-SHAFT PATTERNS

FROM THE FRIENDS OF HANDWOVEN

EDITED BY CAROL STRICKLER

To the memory of

Marguerite Porter Davison and Mary Meigs Atwater,

in gratitude for their pioneering works.

Interweave
An imprint of Penguin Random House LLC
penguinrandomhouse.com

Copyright © 1991 by Interweave
Penguin supports copyright. Copyright fuels creativity, encourages
diverse voices, promotes free speech, and creates a vibrant culture.
Thank you for buying an authorized edition of this book and for
complying with copyright laws by not reproducing, scanning, or
distributing any part of it in any form without permission. You are
supporting writers and allowing Penguin to continue to publish
books for every reader.

Printed in China
11

ISBN 978-0-934026-67-3

Cover photography by Joe Coca
Black and white photography by Dick Kezlan
Cover design by Signorella Graphics; cover fabric by Susan Wilson

Contents

Acknowledgments

A Weaver's Book of 8-Shaft Patterns was conceived as a simple idea: Interweave Press would ask weavers to send in samples woven on 8-shaft looms. We'd choose the best of these and publish black-and-white photos of them in a pattern book. Weavers with 8-shaft looms would be able to use it the way 4-shaft weavers have long used Marguerite Davison's "Green Book", *A Handweaver's Pattern Book,* as a draft resource.

Three years and thousands of working hours later, our naiveté is gone. We now realize that 8-shaft patterns can be considerably more complex and varied than 4-shaft ones, requiring more explanation and space. Hence, the simple idea became this major undertaking.

I offer my heartfelt thanks to the following persons:

to Stew Strickler, who carried innumerable boxes back and forth innumerable times, who talked me through things when I agonized, and who lived with THE BOOK all over the bedroom and living room for nearly two years;

to Ronnine Bohannan, who sifted, organized, and responded to the hundreds of original participant proposals;

to Karen Evanson and Bonnie Hoover, who received and logged samples and kept the paperwork in order;

to Ardis Dobrovolny, who helped me sort and review and choose the samples, and who was my "devil's advocate" when choosing got tough;

to the "conscripts" who wove samples to order when I thought something was needed;

to Yezhen Li, who patiently entered and checked and corrected and reformatted thousands of drafts on the computer (and assisted the photographer in her "spare time");

to Janet Strickler Johnston, who was my "alter ego" in checking those drafts against the samples;

to Linda Ligon and Madelyn van der Hoogt, who edited the manuscript again and again, paring and shaving, teaching me to say what I mean;

to Jane Patrick, who Put It All Together!

to prayer supporters all over the world, who kept me going;

and, above all and through all, to the hundreds of Friends of HANDWOVEN (the roster is listed below), who lent thousands of samples of their best 8-shaft weaving for this book.

Carol Strickler
September 1991

Participant list

All the individuals listed here submitted samples to this project. Unfortunately, we weren't able to use all the swatches submitted. Some samples were duplicates; other samples weren't included here due to space constraints. Some of the samples not included in the book will appear at a later date in HANDWOVEN magazine.

Betsy Abromaitis, Conestoga, PA
Patricia Adams-Langlois, Fontenelle, Quebec, Canada
Sharon Alderman, Salt Lake City, UT
Leslie Alperin, Pepper Pike, OH
Andrea Anderson, Menomonee Falls, WI
Mary Anderson, Los Altos, CA
Charlene Anderson-Shea, Honolulu, HI
Jean Anstine, Boulder, CO
Diane Ayers, Arroyo Grande, CA
Jean E. Babb, Belvidere, IL
Renee Badertscher, Lapeer, MI
Joyce Bahrenfus, Boone, IA
Kay Baranowski, Florissant, MO
Barbara Barnes, London, Ontario, Canada

Anna Rose Barry, Mesquite, TX
Monica Barry, Plattsburgh, NY
Joy Batchelder, Salisbury, NC
Barbara Batson, Madison, AL
Lynne A. Beck, Neshkoro, WI
Sue Beevers, Clinton, NY
Anita Bell, Lubbock, TX
Julia E. Benson, Woodstock, GA
Mary Bentley, N. Vancouver, British Columbia, Canada
Joy Berg, Roanoke, VA
Laurie Bernstein, Grapevine, TX
Gayle Bingham, Pflugerville, TX
Judith Blackmer, Pownal, VT
Helen Bobisud, Moscow, iD

Ann Bodine, San Jose, CA
Yolande Bolduc, St. Redempteur, Quebec, Canada
Pat Boswell, San Antonio, TX
Carol Leigh Brack-Kaiser, Columbia, MO
Kathleen Bradford, Port Townsend, WA
Susan Bradshaw, Watsonville, CA
Karen Braun, Errington, British Columbia, Canada
Gretchen Brinckerhoff, New Milford, CT
Jan Brown, London, Ontario, Canada
Ulla Bruhns, Fallbrook, CA
Nancy V. Bucci, Exeter, RI
Helen Budd, London, Ontario, Canada
Liv Bugge, Neenah, WI
Kim Marie Bunke, Madison, WI

Betty Burrill, Bethesda, MD
Sandy Cahill, Prairie Village, KS
Beth Carroll, Apex, NC
Evelyn Cartier, London, Ontario, Canada
Deborah Chandler, Houston, TX
Jill Coghlan, North Adams, MA
Patricia Cole, Garden City, MI
Nettie J. Conrad, Lansdale, PA
Debbie Cooper, Milford, MI
Jean Cornish, St. Thomas, Ontario, Canada
Betty Creamer, Estes Park, CO
Margaret Creon, Hadlock, WA
Cate Crissey, Irving, TX
Gloria Cyr, Boulder, CO
Adele DeVries, Wautoma, WI
Terry Deacon, Davisburg, MI
Sybil Deschaines, Huntsville, AL
Catherine Devine, Ithaca, NY
Frangoise Deygout, Merignac, France
Ardis Dobrovolny, Boulder, CO
Janet M. Drexel, Cambria, CA
Connie Dunn, Dodge City, KS
Richard Dye, Federal Way, WA
Judie Eatough, Provo, UT
Susan Ehrlich, Bryn Mawr, PA
Jan Reynolds Eubank, Flagstaff, AZ
Karen Evanson, Loveland, CO
Hazel Everingham, Leicester, NC
Gisela Evitt, Stanford, CA
Diane Ferguson, Stafford, TX
Beverly Fitzgerald, Hilton Head Island, SC
Donna Fleming, London, Ontario, Canada
Kate Foreman, Buffalo, MN
Denise Forrest, Milford, MI
Pamela Franck, Williamsburg, VA
Trudy Fratschko, London, Ontario, Canada
Jan Frazee, Oceanside, CA
Laurel Frazer-Allen, Darwin, Northern Territory, Australia
Verna Gabourie, Ohaton, Alberta, Canada
Jane Garrett, Bothell, WA
Lorinda Gayle, Cambridge, MA
Margaret Gaynes, Cupertino, CA
Terri Gehman, London, Ontario, Canada
Linda Gibbs, Auburn, AL
Louise Giddings, Leonardo, NJ
Marguerite Gingras, St. Foy, Quebec, Canada
Elmer Gobruegge, Laguna Hills, CA
Joanne Golden, Lethbridge, Alberta, Canada
Barbara Goonan, Ridgewood, NY
Judith Gordon, Chicago, IL
Dorotha Grandstaff, Walla Walla, WA
Leigh Grench, Salt Lick, KY
Phyllis Griffith, Grand Junction, CO
Sallie Guy, Murray, KY
Bianca Haglich, Tarrytown, NY
Roslyn Hahn, Warren, OH
Susan & Martin Hall, Painesville, OH
Gaye Hansen, N. Vancouver, British Columbia, Canada
Maisie Harris, Warrnambool, Victoria, Australia
Mary Hartman, Mt. Clemens, MI
Aletha Hay, W. Burlington, IA
Dianne K. Heidersbach, San Luis Obispo, CA
Eileen Hett, Edmonton, Alberta, Canada
June Hillyer, Asheville, NC
M. Lynette Holmes, Littleton, CO
Nancianne Horton, Keizer, OR
Cathy Huckins, Columbia, MO
Teresa Imobersteg-Carlson, Boll, Switzerland
Judy Ede Jackson, W. Jordan, UT
Sheila Jacobson, Lethbridge, Alberta, Canada
Esther James, Hickory Corners, MI
Nadine Janke, Hancock, MI
Dorothy Jennings, Hermann, MO
Joan Jensen, Chalfont, PA
Shirley Jensen, Santa Maria, CA
Betty Johannesen, S. Bend, IN

Trudi Johnson, Highland, MI
Janet Strickler Johnston, Kansas City, MO
Berta Jones, Monterey, CA
Dee Jones, Nevada City, CA
Tracy Kaestner, Pearland, TX
Louetta Kambic, Pittsburgh, PA
Liena Kaugara, Kalamazoo, MI
Manuela Kaulitz, Louisville, KY
Doramay Keasbey, Bethesda, MD
Virginia Kellogg, Jensen Beach, FL
Jacquie Kelly, Sierra Vista, AZ
Beverly Kent, Poway, CA
Marge King, Ashland, OR
May Kingman, Thousand Oaks, CA
Betty Burian Kirk, Sauk Village, IL
Judy Kleeves, Holly, MI
Ruth Kleinfeldt, Mundelein, IL
Jean Korus, Moscow, ID
Sandra Kragelj, 100 Mile House, British Columbia, Canada
Jeanne Young Kudlicki, Dallas, TX
Donna LaVallee, Newport, RI
Robert Lees, Don Mills, Ontario, Canada
Joyce Lemin, Shell Beach, CA
Dorothy Lenz, Sedona, AZ
Wanda Leonard, Killington, VT
Erika Lewis, Athens, GA
Yezhen Li, Beijing, Peoples Republic of China
Addie Lienau, Huntsville, AL
Linda Ligon, Loveland, CO
Delores Lindeman, Milk River, Alberta, Canada
Gail Liston, Raleigh, NC
Karen Lohry, Neshkoro, WI
Priscilla Lynch, Ada, MI
Ena Marston, San Luis Obispo, CA
Marilyn Mason, Houghton, MI
Vere May, Mesa, AZ
Marjorie McCann, Philadelphia, PA
Barbara McClanathan, Portland, OR
Joan McCulloch, Campbellford, Ontario, Canada
Carole McCullough, Cambridge, MA
Christine McKeeman, Manchaca, TX
Sue McKenzie, Montreal, Quebec, Canada
Barbara Meier, Boulder, CO
David Merrill, Loveland, CO
Barbara Miller, Pisgah Forest, NC
Susan Millikan, Coquitlam, British Columbia, Canada
Sue Minter, Billings, MT
Nancy Mitchell, Union, WV
Ruth Mitchell, Warrnambool, Victoria, Australia
Alison Nelson, McCall, ID
Betty R. Nelson, Decorah, IA
Camille Nelson, San Luis Obispo, CA
Sally Nielsen, Delavan, WI
Mary Oehler, Portland, OR
Georgia Olson, Kaysville, UT
Julie Owens, Estacada, OR
Sherron Pampalone, Crown Point, IN
Jane Patrick, Boulder, CO
Carol Pavlovic, Willits, CA
Roberta Pease, Lutz, FL
Sue Peters, Midland, MI
Sharyl and Bob Peterson, De Pere, WI
Marcy Petrini, Jackson, MS
Ann Pettit, Pacific Grove, CA
Arlene Post, Shelton, WA
Avie Powell, Iron River, MI
Dorothy M. Powell, Philadelphia, PA
Amy Preckshot, Columbia, MO
Margaret Prime, Abbotsford, British Columbia, Canada
Lorraine Ransome, Princeton, WI
Esther Reigel, Kalamazoo, MI
Jeanne Richards, Estes Park, CO
Joyce Fisher Robards, Spencerport, NY
Winnie Robinson, Moscow, ID
Ann Rogers, Green Lake, WI
Sondra Rose, Bellingham, WA

Noreen Rustad, Prince George, British Columbia, Canada
Jo Anne Ryeburn, Lynden, WA
Judith Rygiel, Nepean, Ontario, Canada
Sarah Saulson, Syracuse, NY
Joyce Schatz, Rodeo, NM
Mickie Schneider, Orrtanna, PA
Sue Schroeder, Beaufort, SC
Frances Schultz, Monarch, Alberta, Canada
Sue Semrow, Coloma, WI
Eileen Shannon, Lac La Hache, British Columbia, Canada
Valerie Sharir, Elizabethtown, PA
Debra K. Sharpee, DeForest, WI
Marla Shelton, Pontiac, MI
Margaret Sheppard, Houston, TX
Jack Shipman, Bethlehem, PA
Lucille M. Shissler, Mentor, OH
Norma Smayda, Saunderstown, RI
Betty Hancock Smith, Marietta, GA
Dorothy N. Smith, Tulsa, OK
Mary Young Smith, Asheville, NC
Mimi Smith, Fairport, NY
Peggy Smith, Middletown, NJ
Rosemary Smith, Huntington Beach, CA
Susan E.A. Smith, Cornish, ME
Ilse Sonner, Chapel Hill, NC
Ann Spurlock, Estes Park, CO
Yvonne Stahl, Denver, CO
Cheryl Stegert, Appleton, WI
Judy Steinkoenig, Boulder, CO
Nancy Steward, Kennett Square, PA
Marguerite Stoiber, Joliet, IL
Kazuko Stone, Green Bay, WI
Carol Strickler, Boulder, CO
Jean Sucher, St. Simons Island, GA
Marjorie Sweigart, Montezuma, NM
Chris Switzer, Estes Park, CO
Jannie Taylor, San Luis Obispo, CA
Robert Teachout, Holly Hill, SC
Nina Tefft, Ely, MN
Don Tharp, Findlay, OH
Joann Tharp, Findlay, OH
Theo Thibado, Homosassa, FL
Marjie Thompson, Cumberland Center, ME
Mary Jane Thorne, Columbia, MO
Patricia Toczydlowski, Calumet, MI
Lindsay Topham, Kelowna, British Columbia, Canada
Dianne Totten, Marietta, GA
Jennifer Trepal, Mason, OH
Sandra Url, Danville, WA
Suzanne Urton, E. Stroudsburg, PA
Agnes Vallely, DeLand, FL
Jette Vandermeiden, Midhurst, Ontario, Canada
Bev Viner, Hillsboro, OR
Linda Waid, Brandywine, MD
Sharon Walker, Markham, Ontario, Canada
Jennifer Weber, Green Bay, WI
Susan Wellnitz, Medford, MA
Kathryn Wertenberger, Golden, CO
Cheryl Wesseling, Fridley, MN
Lucille Whalen, Nakusp, British Columbia, Canada
Susan E.J. White, Orofino, ID
Emily Whittier, Decatur, AL
Karen Wiley, Arroyo Grande, CA
Susan R. Wilson, Moscow, ID
Mary Wright, Franklin, NC
Marie Wynne, Wembley, Western Australia, Australia
Judith Yamamoto, Chicago, IL
Jan Youd, Milford, MI
Nell Znamierowski, New York, NY
Mariah Zust, Unionville, MO

PREFACE

Collections of weave drafts form the backbone of our library at Interweave Press; they are among the books we turn to again and again. They range from Johann Kirschbaum's 18th century German record book of laboriously penned coverlet patterns, to late 19th century industrial references such as Oelsner's *A Handbook of Weaves,* to later classics such as Marguerite Davison's indispensible *Handweaver's Pattern Book.*

These and other similar volumes are inexhaustible sources of ideas and inspiration, but they are more, too. Beyond giving us more weave structure ideas than we can use in a lifetime, they tell us much about weavers and weaving in past eras. For instance, Kirschbaum's book contains a considerable repertoire of blanket weaves; this is a clue that European handweavers in the 1770s tended to specialize. Oelsner's extensive compendium leans toward those weaves most suitable for mechanized production; indeed, there was little handweaving being done in this country in 1915, when the book was translated into English. Marguerite Davison's drafts, on the other hand, are eclectic and largely from historical sources; handweavers of the 1940s were recreating the craft and rediscovering their roots, processes that remain compelling today.

I've occasionally wondered, over the many months *A Weaver's Book of 8-Shaft Patterns* has been in the making, what place it will take in the literature as years go by, and what it will tell about the state of handweaving in the developed world on the verge of the 21st century. Here's what I predict. It will speak of a large and committed weaving community: more than 250 weavers contributed samples for us to select from. It will speak, too, of a technically sophisticated body of weavers—weavers with multishaft looms and even computers to facilitate design, weavers with the skill and training to engage in creative exploration. It will document a healthy respect for our weaving heritage in the traditional patterns that have been lovingly recreated or imaginatively quoted.

More important than its possible historical value, however, is its immediate, practical intent. At a point in history when many weavers have more creative energy and desire to weave than they have time to devote to the craft, this book has been planned to serve as a constant guide, a source of inspiration, and a convenient bridge between the urge to weave and the satisfaction of watching fabric come to life on the loom.

Use it, and enjoy.

Linda Ligon
publisher

INTRODUCTION

This is a *pattern* book. It says so right there in the title. The book is based on the assumption that you know how to weave and you simply want to pick a pattern *to* weave. Additional information is included for the expert weaver who wants to experiment.

All of these patterns can be woven on an 8-shaft loom. (A few require only 5, 6, or 7 shafts.) All are loom-controlled patterns with selvedge-to-selvedge wefts. (There are none using inlay, pickup, doups, special heddles, shaft-switching, or other hand manipulations.) Some show color-and-weave effects—apparent pattern formed by the interaction of color sequences and interlacement.

The samples shown here were chosen to illustrate weave structure and pattern and color-and-weave effects. For your particular purpose the drafts might need to be woven in yarns that are finer or coarser, harder or softer, shinier or fuzzier, darker or lighter, more or less contrasting, washable or not.

Weaving on eight shafts can be quite a bit more complex than weaving on four. With four shafts there are 14 possible combinations of raised and lowered shafts. With eight shafts there are 254 up/down combinations! The complexity can be bewildering, especially since on any particular threading most of these 254 possibilities won't be practical or useful. Many of the drafts given here include more than one tie-up or treadling to help you get started without being overwhelmed.

Many of the 8-shaft weaves are based on familiar 4-shaft weaves. Some (such as summer & winter) use the same structural unit; additional shafts simply enable you to weave more elaborate patterns in the same interlacement. Other weaves (such as overshot) can be expanded from four to eight shafts in any of several ways, resulting in several different related weaves. And there are some weaves which can be woven *only* on more than four shafts. Because of this complexity it is usually better to learn something about the underlying weave structure or threading principles before attempting to modify a particular pattern. Therefore many of the chapters of drafts in this book begin with an introduction to the threading principles of that chapter's patterns.

Planning

The motto of every weaver should be Plan Ahead. Weaving samples before embarking on a project will help uncover any unpleasant surprises and prevent headaches. Planning and sampling are even more important when the weave is complex or the pattern fancy, as is the case with many 8-shaft weaves. Such planning should include counting the number of threads to be carried on each shaft (to see if heddles need to be shifted from one shaft to another, a task usually easier to do before you begin threading). If you are using a floor loom with treadles and plan to use a pattern with an unbalanced tie-up, you may need to rearrange the tie-up so that the heaviest loads are on the center treadles where you have better leverage. In cases where every shed involves lifting more than half the shafts, you may find it easier to weave the fabric face down. These are some of the details that should be considered when you plan an 8-shaft project.

Drafts

The parts of a draft are the threading, the tie-up, and the treadling. When the interaction of these elements is mapped on paper or computer screen, the resulting picture of the fabric is the "drawdown" or "fabric diagram". A *thread-by-thread* draft gives the complete, detailed threading, tie-up, and treadling order required to weave a given fabric. But there is another type of draft, the *block* or "profile" draft; it is like a shorthand in which each symbol represents a group of warp threads to be threaded, tied, and treadled by some formula.

The elements of the drafts in this book are laid out to correspond to fabrics as they

I.1

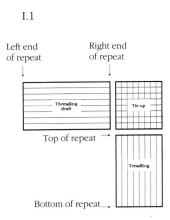

Left end of repeat

Right end of repeat

Threading draft

Tie-up

Top of repeat →

Treadling

Bottom of repeat →

I.2a

Examples of thread-by-thread drafts

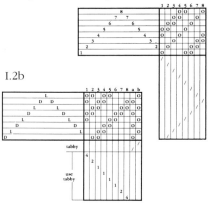

I.2b

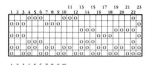

I.3 Example tie-up from a 7-shaft piqué (from #698)

Skeleton of the same (use two or three treadles at a time)

In the original = treadle #		In the skeleton treadle #'s
1	=	1-2-3
2	=	2-3
3	=	1-3
4	=	1-2-4
5	=	2-4
6	=	1-4
7	=	1-2-5
8	=	2-5
9	=	1-5
10	=	1-2-6
11	=	2-6
12	=	1-6
13	=	1-2-7
14	=	2-7
15	=	1-7
16	=	1-2-8
17	=	2-8
18	=	1-8
19	=	1-2-9
20	=	2-9
21	=	1-9
22	=	1-2-10
23	=	1-2-3

I.4 Example of a profile draft:

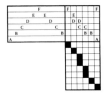

appear in their photographs: the left end of the threading is the left side of the repeat in the photo, and the bottom of the treadling is the bottom of the repeat. So to weave as shown, read the threading in the same direction as you thread (looking at the front of the loom) and follow the treadling from bottom to top. If you thread in the opposite direction, follow the treadling from top to bottom (see figure I.1).

In *thread-by-thread* drafts, each shaft is represented by a horizontal row in the threading and tie-up. Each thread in the threading sequence is positioned on its correct row, and is designated by the shaft's number as well. In some colored fabrics, the numbers are replaced by letters such as D, M, and L for dark, medium, and light. In the tie-up of a thread-by-thread draft, the O's in the grid represent the shafts (horizontal rows) that should be lifted for each shed (vertical column, i.e. treadle). In the treadling, each treadle is represented by a vertical column. Slash-marks (/) indicate individual picks of a single weft; their position in the columns indicates the sequence of treadles to be used. In some treadlings there are letters such as D, M, and L denoting dark, medium, or light color of weft. In some treadling sequences there are numbers instead—indicating that a shed (treadle) is to be used that number of times in succession (usually with a tabby pick after each pattern pick). Figures I.2a and I.2b show two example thread-by thread drafts.

Sometimes a pattern requires more than ten treadles. When this is the case, the tie-up has been written out in full. Table-loom and dobby-loom weavers can usually use such a full tie-up and treadling "as is". A weaver using a treadled floor-loom may need to rewrite it as a "skeleton tie-up" which requires pushing two or more treadles at the same time (use figure I.3 for an example).

In a *profile* draft, each block is represented by a horizontal row in the threading and tie-up, and each letter represents a group of threads, a unit or block of that weave structure. Letters in the profile tie-up signify blocks that weave together (or separately) as pattern. (In the spot and lace chapters, some tie-ups use symbols instead to signify blocks that weave as warp floats and weft floats.) The squares in the profile treadling stand for the order in which the blocks or block combinations are woven, each square representing a group of picks (treadling unit) of that weave (see figure I.4).

Many patterns are treadled "as-drawn-in" (or "trompt as writ", as they used to say). This means that the treadling follows the same order as the threading. In this book, there are two different forms of "as-drawn-in". In the thread-by-thread or *literal* form, the treadling exactly follows the threading. (That is, if the threading is shafts 1, 2, 3, 2, 3, 4, 5 then the treadling uses treadles 1, 2, 3, 2, 3, 4, 5.) In the *block* form, pattern is woven in blocks in the same order and proportion as the blocks or units are threaded. Chapter texts will provide more information in weaves where profile drafts have been used or block treadling is appropriate.

Other Considerations

Most of the patterns in this book are for balanced fabrics. That means the warp threads are set so that, when woven, there are as many weft picks per inch as there are warp ends per inch in a one-weft weave, or as many pattern picks per inch as ends per inch in a pattern-and-tabby "supplementary weft" weave. With the same yarn, threading, and treadling, however, a tie-up with fewer warp/weft intersections requires a closer sett or thicker weft unless it is to become weft-dominant and unbalanced. On the other hand a compound-weft weave may require a wider-than-normal sett and/or finer wefts to remain balanced.

Unless otherwise noted, the colors of the samples are assumed to be light warp and dark weft, or light warp and tabby or ground weft with dark pattern weft.

To determine if plain weave is possible on any pattern, look at the threading. If every second thread always falls on particular shafts and no others do, then lifting those shafts for one shed, and all other shafts for the other shed, will result in plain weave or tabby. (For example, in an unbroken twill the tabbies might be formed by 1-3-5-7 vs 2-4-6-8. In summer & winter they might be 1-2 vs 3-4-5-6-7-8. In spot Bronson they might be 1 vs 2-3-4-5-6-7-8.) In some weaves no true or perfect plain weave is possible because there are breaks or shifts in the draft that make it impossible to lift or lower alternate threads.

See the chapter text for such information about a particular weave.

Chapter 1
STRAIGHT TWILL, CREPE, AND DICE WEAVES

STRAIGHT TWILL

Threading

Twill, plain twill, straight twill, direct twill, straight draw—whatever you call it, it's the threading on which all twills and twill derivatives are based. Warps threaded on all shafts successively in unbroken order from bottom to top or top to bottom, repeating over and over without reversing or varying—that's a straight twill threading (figure 1.1).

1.1

Dull and boring, you say? Not so. Eight-shaft twill has a wealth of tie-up and treadling possibilities.

Tie-ups

Plain weave on a straight twill threading on an even number of shafts (6, 8, etc.) is woven by lifting the odd-numbered shafts vs the even-numbered shafts. No true plain weave is possible on a twill threading that uses an odd number of shafts (5, 7, etc.); it will always have 2-thread skips where 1 and 5 or 1 and 7 are adjacent in the threading.

For weaving *as* twill, with diagonal lines, the tie-up for a straight twill is usually a systematic one, with a particular arrangement of up/down shafts that advances one shaft per treadle, as shown in figure 1.2.

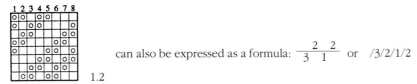

can also be expressed as a formula: $\dfrac{2\quad2}{3\quad1}$ or /3/2/1/2

1.2

In such a formula the horizontal line or the slash marks represent a weft which goes "over three, under two, over one, and under two warp ends". Notice that for each treadle the over/under sequence is the same but is shifted one shaft higher than for the previous treadle.

If the tie-up deviates from this straight progression, it is sometimes called a "fancy twill". Example:

1.3

Sometimes the twill is divided into smaller units in the tie-up, the treadling, or both (as in crepe, waffle, and dice weaves). These weaves and patterns have their own different tie-ups (and sometimes the threadings are modified as well, which puts them into a different category from straight twill). In this book, crepes and dice weaves have been included here under straight twill; waffle weave is a later chapter, and there are additional straight twill threadings in the Twill Gamps and "As If's" chapters.

Treadling Orders

The treadling orders for a straight twill threading can also vary. A treadling sequence can be in straight order (advancing one treadle in succession from treadles 1 to 8 or 8 to 1 over and over). When used with a formula tie-up this results in a fabric with unbroken diagonal lines. The treadling order can also be pointed, broken, manifold, etc. (echoing those threadings), or it may be specific to a form for some particular pattern. A pointed treadling on straight threading results in vertical zigzags.

Variations

To enlarge or reduce a straight twill threading, simply add or subtract complete repeats. (Breaking the twill, or repeating just part of it in some way, changes the *threading* from straight twill to something else.) You *can* change the tie-up or the treadling or both (see the Twill Gamps, "As If's", and Waffle Weave chapters for additional examples of this).

Straight twill can also be varied by using color sequences in both warp and weft, for a color-and-weave effect. Several such patterns are shown here and in the Twill Gamps chapter.

CREPE AND DICE WEAVES

These weaves are usually woven on a straight twill threading, but lack the diagonal appearance of a straight twill.

According to *A Handbook of Weaves* by G. H. Oelsner, crepes (also called "oatmeal weaves") are "weaves in which the warp and filling are interlaced so as to give the cloth a mixed or uniformly mottled appearance". The warp and weft floats in the weave are usually very short and varied in length. Crepe is sometimes drafted by choosing two formula tie-ups and alternating treadles from them. Sometimes it is drafted by dividing the tie-up into quadrants, designing one quadrant and then rotating or inverting or reversing it into the other three sections. This is often done in such a way that there are clean breaks between the quadrants (that is, treadle 5 lifts the opposite shafts from treadle 4, and shaft 5 is always lifted or lowered the opposite of shaft 4).

In *The Weaver's Book of Fabric Design*, Janet Phillips defines dice weaves as "small repeating patterns that are constructed on a checkerboard arrangement whereby two opposing squares on a weave diagram are identical to each other and the other two are a damask [reversed negative] of the first". (Emery says that "the alternation of the two faces of a *satin weave* in squares" is "a weave-pattern combination sometimes described as 'dice weave' ".)

Marge King, who wove many of the crepe samples included here, offers the following weaving notes: "Two things characterize all these weaves—excessive weft draw-in, and a tendency to beat into bands of two, four, or eight picks. Both problems seem to be helped by using yarns that have 'tooth' and are *not* hard or slick, and by trying a wider sett." Crepe and dice fabrics are often woven with warp and weft of the same size but subtle color differences. Because of the short floats and tiny pattern the fabrics are ideal for clothing.

#1 & #2
by Gretchen Brinckerhoff
Stripes on straight twill.

1

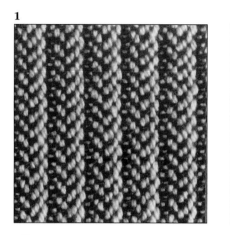

2

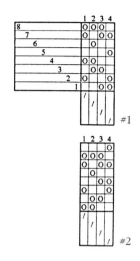

#3
by Camille Nelson
Whipcord from *Manual of Swedish Handweaving* by Ulla Cyrus-Zetterström

3

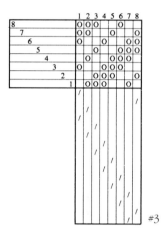

#4
by Winnie Robinson
Satin woven on a dark warp, from *Contemporary Satins,* Shuttle Craft Guild
Monograph 7 by Harriet Tidball.

4

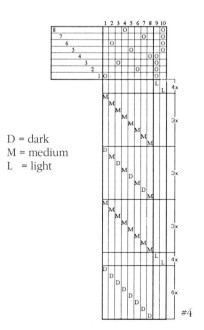

D = dark
M = medium
L = light

#5–12
by Betty Burian Kirk

Undulating treadlings on a straight twill. Some of these patterns are taken from or inspired by *The Weaving Book* by Helene Bress, *Weaving Techniques for the Multiple-Harness Loom* by Pierre Ryall, and undulating twill workshop notes by Karen Selk. For more information about undulating twills, see the text in the Broken Twill chapter.

Note: Most of these require floating selvedges because of successive weft picks in the same shed.

#13–15
by Ann E. Spurlock
*Irish Poplin from "Mrs. Maddox's coat fabric".
+A Mary Meigs Atwater pattern.
#"Smock" from *The Key to Weaving* by Mary Black.

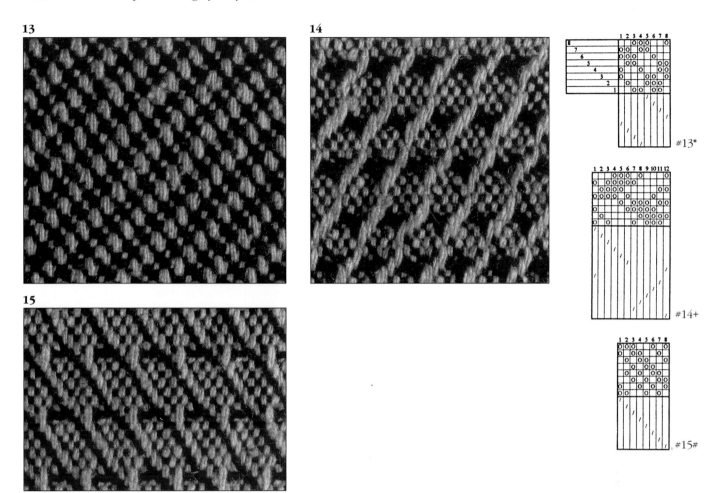

13

14

15

#13*

#14+

#15#

#16 & #17
by Berta Jones
Tricot from *A Handbook of Weaves* by G.H. Oelsner. *Note:* This sample has a light weft and a dark warp. With the right yarns and setts, these lengthwise or crosswise ribs have a slight stretch and imitate knitted ribbing.
*back rib—warp and weft are the same color   **face rib—contrasting weft

16

17

#16

#17

#18–20

by Jan Reynolds Eubank

Straight twill. *Note:* These samples have a light weft and a dark warp. At this sett and with this tie-up, they are all weft-dominant on the back.

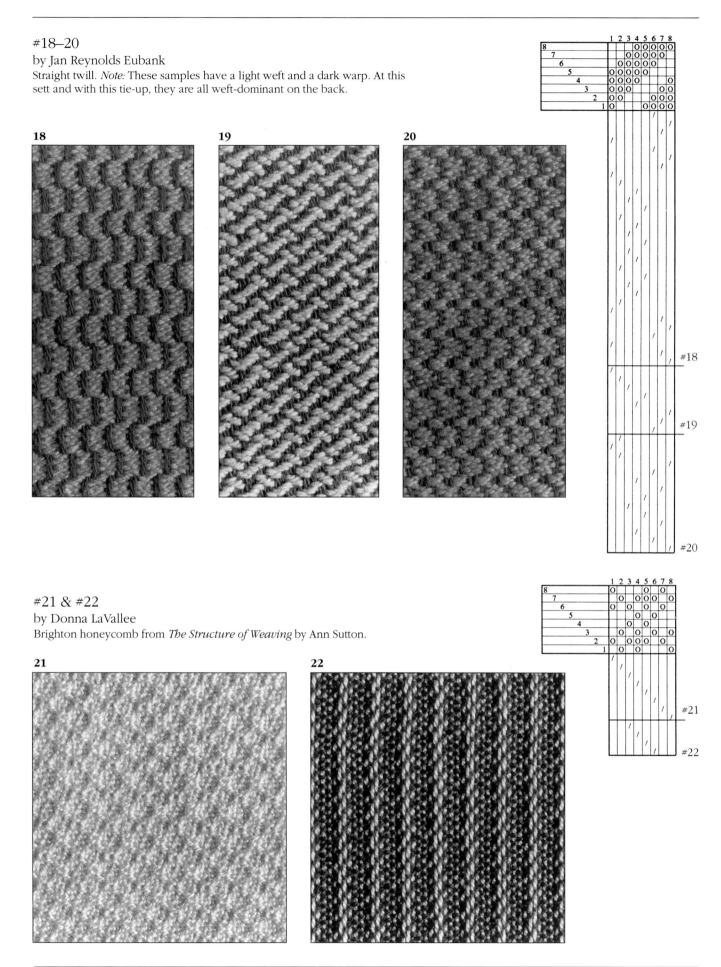

18

19

20

#21 & #22

by Donna LaVallee

Brighton honeycomb from *The Structure of Weaving* by Ann Sutton.

21

22

#23–34

by Marge King

Crepe and interlocking twills from *A Handbook of Weaves* by G.H. Oelsner.
Many of these fabrics look quite different on the back.

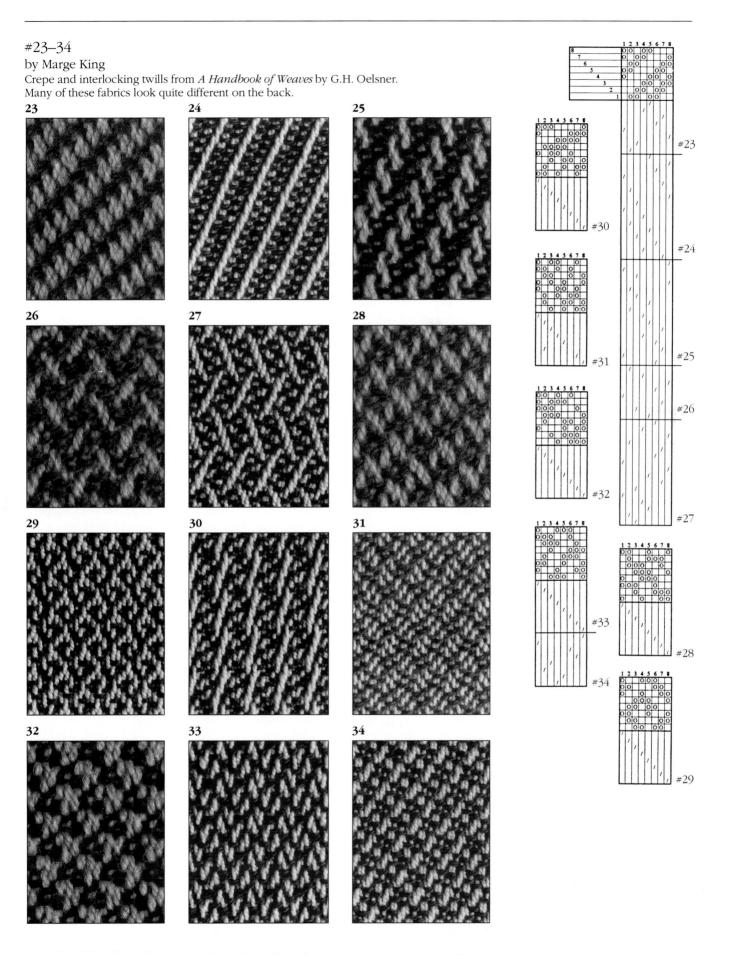

23

24

25

26

27

28

29

30

31

32

33

34

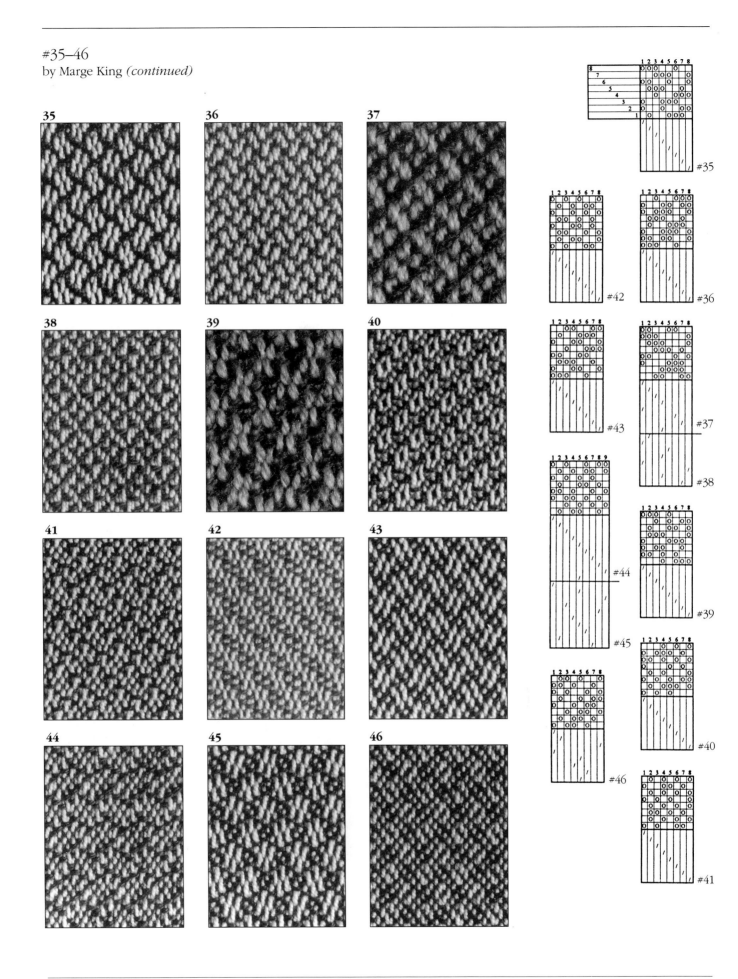

35

36

37

38

39

40

41

42

43

44

45

46

#47
by Diane Ferguson
"Breaks and recesses" from *A Handbook of Weaves* by G.H. Oelsner. *Note:*
This weave looks its best when the warp and the weft are identical yarns.

47

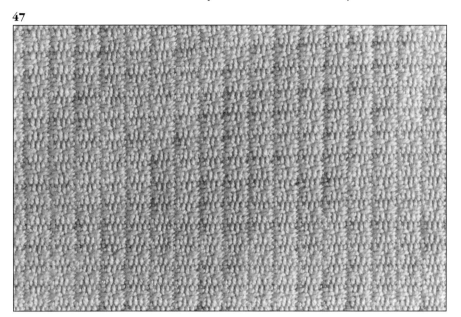

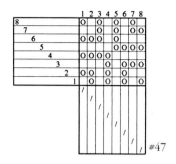

#48 & #49
by Jean E. Babb
Crepe from *A Handbook of Weaves* by G.H. Oelsner.

48   **49**

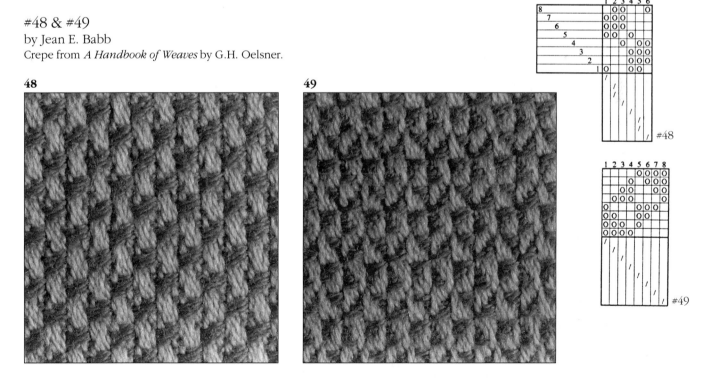

#50–54

by Laurel Frazer-Allen

Straight twill from *Weaving Techniques for the Multiple-Harness Loom* by Pierre Ryall.

Note: With these yarns, at this sett, this fabric is weft-dominant on both faces.

50

51

52

53

54

#50

#51

#52*

#53

#54

#55 & #56
by Joyce Lemin
Color-and-weave crepe.

55

56

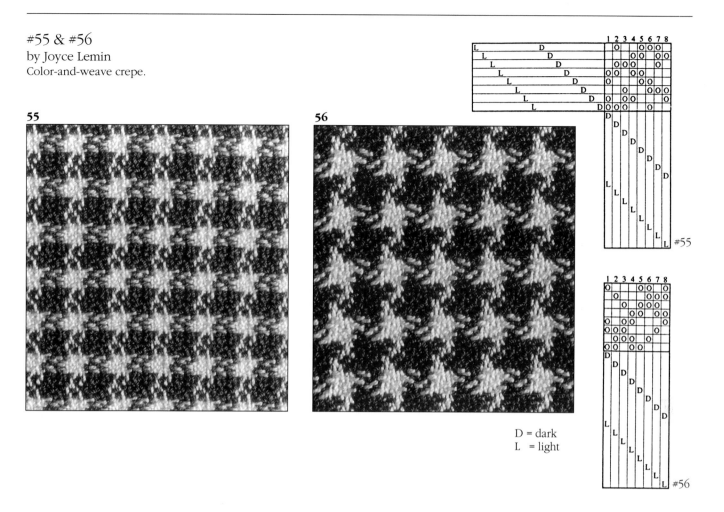

D = dark
L = light

#55

#56

#57
by Nancy V. Bucci
Color-and-weave from *Color-and-Weave* by Margaret and Thomas Windeknecht.

57

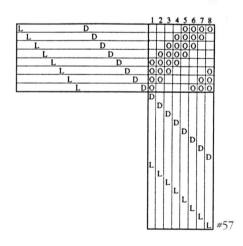

#57

#58 & #59
by Pat Boswell

Color-and-weave on straight twill. *Use a solid light warp and a solid dark weft. *Note:* These two samplers are identical except for color. One has a solid light warp and a dark weft; the other has eight dark and eight light color order in both the warp and the weft. All samples have a straight twill threading and treadling. Only the tie-ups change from sample to sample. The samples at the left show structure only; the ones on the right show color-and-weave.

    Some of the tie-ups have two or more identical treadles in order to keep the same straight twill treadling. Use floating selvedges, because these repeated ties will sometimes cause two or more successive weft picks in the same shed.

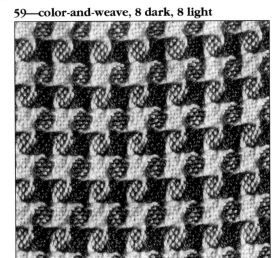

58—solid warp and weft

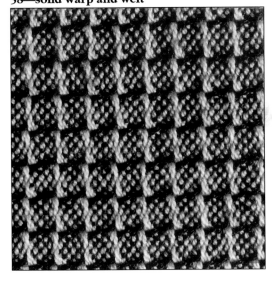

59—color-and-weave, 8 dark, 8 light

#58*
#59

#60 & #61
by Pat Boswell *(continued)*

*Use a solid light warp and a solid dark weft.

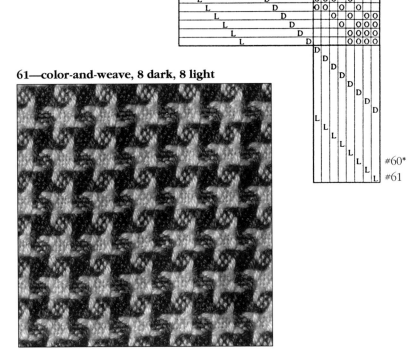

60—solid warp and weft

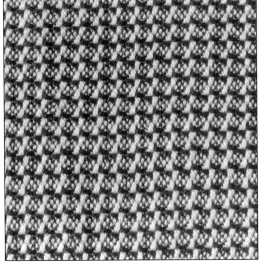

61—color-and-weave, 8 dark, 8 light

#60*
#61

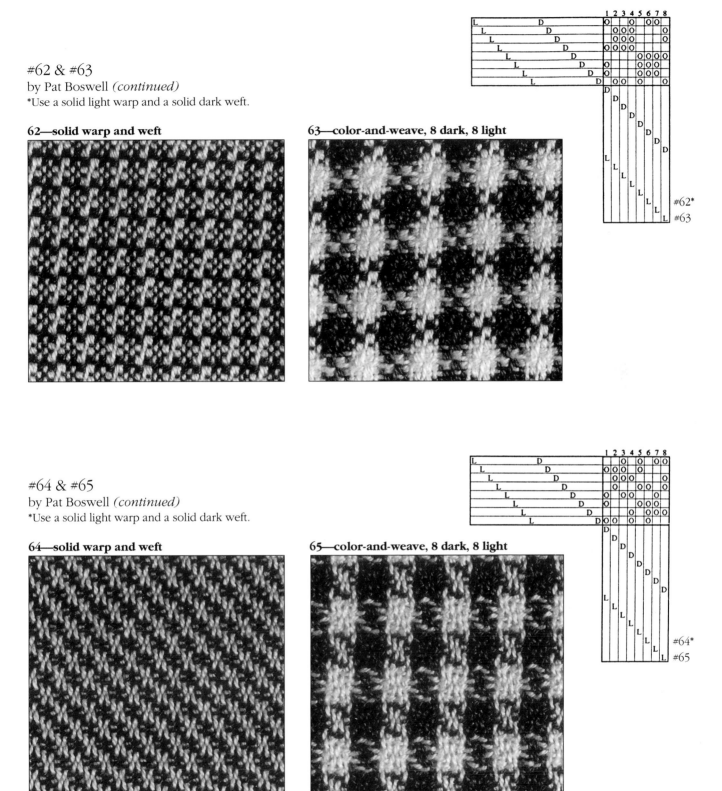

#62 & #63
by Pat Boswell *(continued)*
*Use a solid light warp and a solid dark weft.

62—solid warp and weft

63—color-and-weave, 8 dark, 8 light

#62*
#63

#64 & #65
by Pat Boswell *(continued)*
*Use a solid light warp and a solid dark weft.

64—solid warp and weft

65—color-and-weave, 8 dark, 8 light

#64*
#65

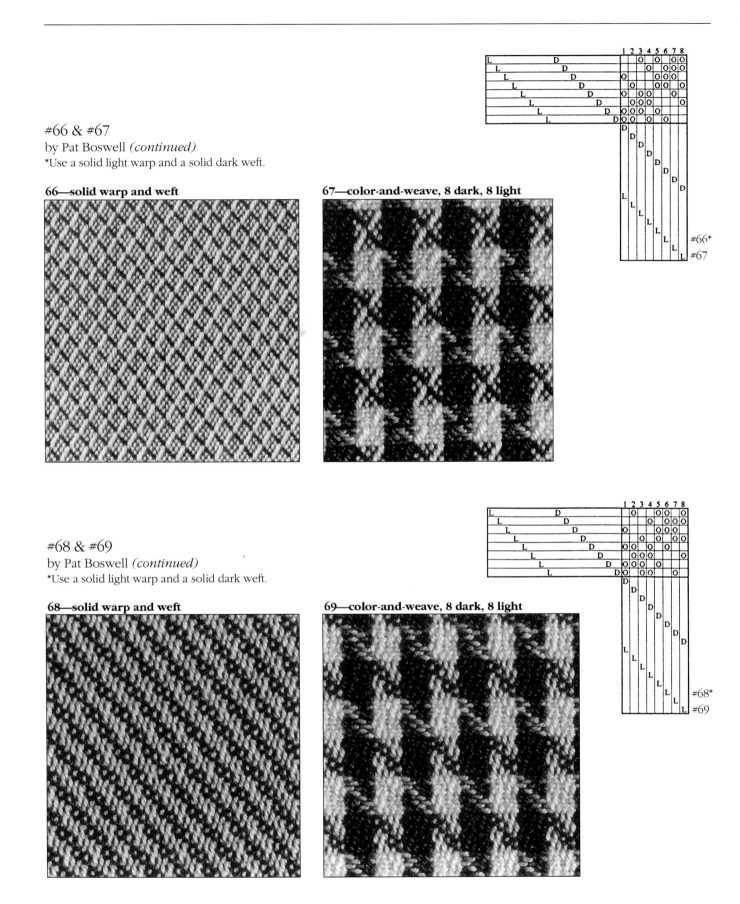

#66 & #67
by Pat Boswell *(continued)*
*Use a solid light warp and a solid dark weft.

66—solid warp and weft

67—color-and-weave, 8 dark, 8 light

#68 & #69
by Pat Boswell *(continued)*
*Use a solid light warp and a solid dark weft.

68—solid warp and weft

69—color-and-weave, 8 dark, 8 light

#70 & #71
by Lucille Shissler
Color-and-weave on straight twill.

70

71

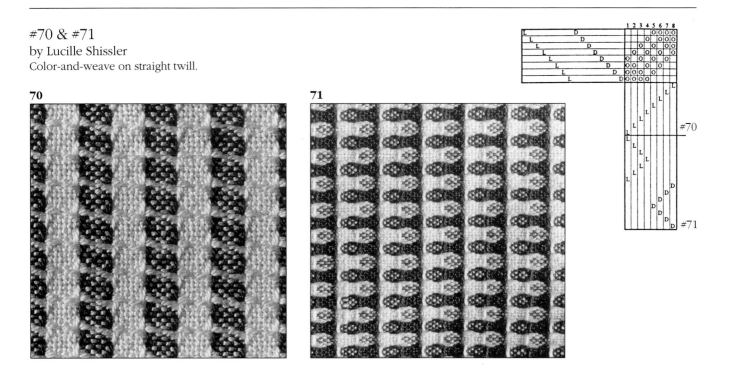

#72 & #73
by Marie Wynne
Color-and-weave on straight twill.

72

73

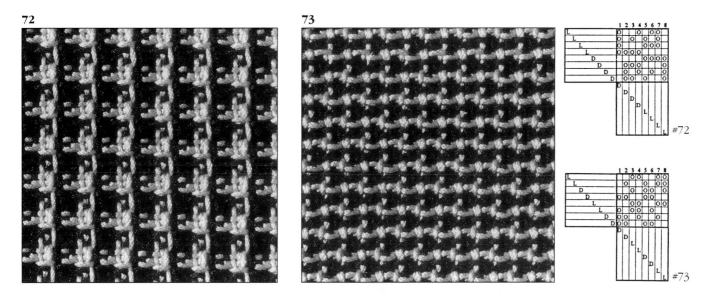

#74–81

by Judith L. Blackmer

Color-and-weave on straight twill. *Note:* Many of these color-and-weave samples have different and equally interesting backs.

74

75

76

77

78

79

80

81

Chapter 2
POINT TWILL

A *point twill*, sometimes called a "return" or "waved" twill, is a straight twill that reverses direction at intervals. The intervals may be alike (a symmetrical point) or different (an asymmetrical point). Threads at reversal points are counted as part of both the ascent and the descent (but are not repeated).

Threading

Ordinary point twill (with as many threads in each direction as there are shafts) is a symmetrical point (figure 2.1). "Rosepath" is a symmetrical point twill that progresses one shaft beyond the total number of shafts used; it accomplishes this by returning to the beginning of its sequence before reversing. Thus an 8-shaft rosepath is a symmetrical point with nine threads in each direction (including the reversals)—see figure 2.2.

Further extensions of these basic symmetrical point twills to ten or eleven threads in each direction are sometimes called "Bird's Eye" or "Goose Eye" because of the dot-centered diamond figures that they form when treadled as-drawn-in (figure 2.3).

Asymmetrical point twills (such as in Figure 2.4) are less common than symmetrical ones because their patterns are unbalanced or zigzagging. (Note that these are sometimes called even and uneven twill, but some authors, including Irene Emery, use the term "uneven twill" to mean one that is warp-dominant or weft-dominant, unbalanced in the over/under interlacement.)

The arms of a point twill can be repeated or shortened; the result is sometimes called an "extended point twill". Most of the so-called "M & W" twills fall in this category (such as in figure 2.5).

2.5

(8 ascending, 4 descending, 4 ascending, 16 descending,
4 ascending, 4 descending, 8 ascending)

There is another, rarer, *block* form of "M & W"-type of design; each block is a small point twill which shares one shaft with the next block. Originally German linen patterns requiring 10 or more shafts for three or more 4-shaft blocks, some of these patterns can be adapted to seven shafts by using three shafts per block. In her article "Seventeenth and Eighteenth Century Twills: The German Linen Tradition" (*Ars Textrina 3,* 1985) Patricia Hilts describes the original forms as a type of *Gebrochene Arbeit* (literally "broken work"); here they are called "overlapping block point twills". Figure 2.6 is an example of such a pattern.

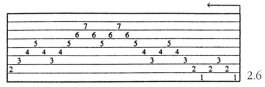

2.6

(Block A = point twill on shafts 1,2,3; Block B = point twill on shafts 3,4,5;
Block C = point twill on shafts 5,6,7)

All of the above point twills are unbroken. That is, every thread is preceded and followed by a thread on an adjacent shaft. To visualize this, consider the twill as numbers from 1 to 8, spaced around the rim of a circle (figure 2.7—on next page).

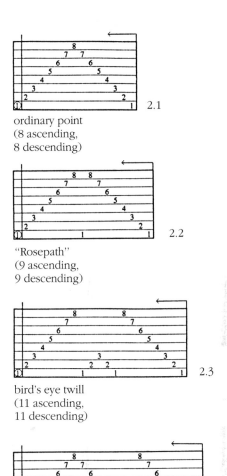

ordinary point
(8 ascending,
8 descending)

"Rosepath"
(9 ascending,
9 descending)

bird's eye twill
(11 ascending,
11 descending)

Asymmetrical point twill
(16 ascending, 8 descending)

2.7

Notice that 1 and 8 are adjacent (just as 8 follows 1 when a straight twill is repeated). A straight twill is just 'round and 'round the circle with no change. A point twill is back and forth, reversing directions but staying on the rim and taking no shortcuts. (Broken twills, which *do* take shortcuts across the circle, are considered in the next chapter.)

Tie-ups

If the odd-even alternation of shafts is maintained in the threading of a point twill, plain weave is achieved by weaving the odd shafts vs the even.

Tie-ups for point twills can be the same systematic formula-type ones as for straight twills. Some points can also be tied up to weave like 2-block twills. Fancy tie-ups and treadlings can be designed that weave the ordinary symmetrical point twill like an 8-pointed star or some other motif.

Treadling Orders

The treadling on a point twill can be simple or fancy. The twill is usually a one-shuttle weave, with the sequence moving from treadle to treadle in unbroken order. With a formula tie-up, a straight treadling will commonly result in horizontal zigzags and a point treadling will weave some form of diamonds. An "as-drawn-in" treadling is usually a literal (not block) copy of the threading; that is, the treadles are used in the same order as the shafts are threaded. The "overlapping-block point twill" can also be treadled like overshot or like crackle (both of these with supplementary and tabby wefts) or like a 2-block or 3-block twill.

Variations

There are several ways to enlarge or reduce a point twill design. If the threading is just a symmetrical point, the intervals between reversals can simply be lengthened or shortened. If the threading is fancier, as in the "M & W" patterns, the intervals can be lengthened or shortened, and small or large sections of the design can also be repeated or eliminated. In the "overlapping-block" designs, repeats of the blocks can be added or eliminated, but the 3-shaft point twill nature of the blocks should not be altered.

Tie-up and treadling can be varied to treat the point twill like an overshot, with some pattern sheds repeated two or more times, woven with tabby.

Some point twills (such as "rosepath") work well with tie-ups and treadlings that create small figural motifs or "ethnic" borders, often on a plain-weave ground created by weaving alternate tabby picks between the pattern picks (see samples #104–144). Color-and-weave effect can also be used on point twills. In this book, some point threadings are also shown in the Twill Gamps and Waffle Weave chapters.

#82 & #83

by Linda J. Waid

Point twill, by Margaret and Thomas Windeknecht *Color-and-Weave*. *Note:* The backs (not shown) of these samples are different and equally interesting.

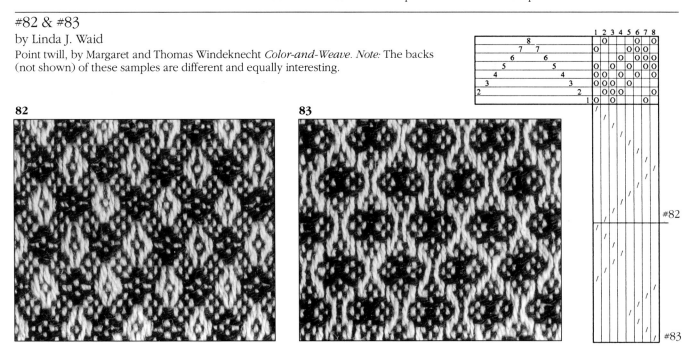

82

83

#84–91

by Anita Bell

Point twill, color-and-weave effect by Jim Pouton which appeared in the Winter 1981 issue of *Weavers Journal. Note:* The backs of these fabrics are sometimes very different from the faces.

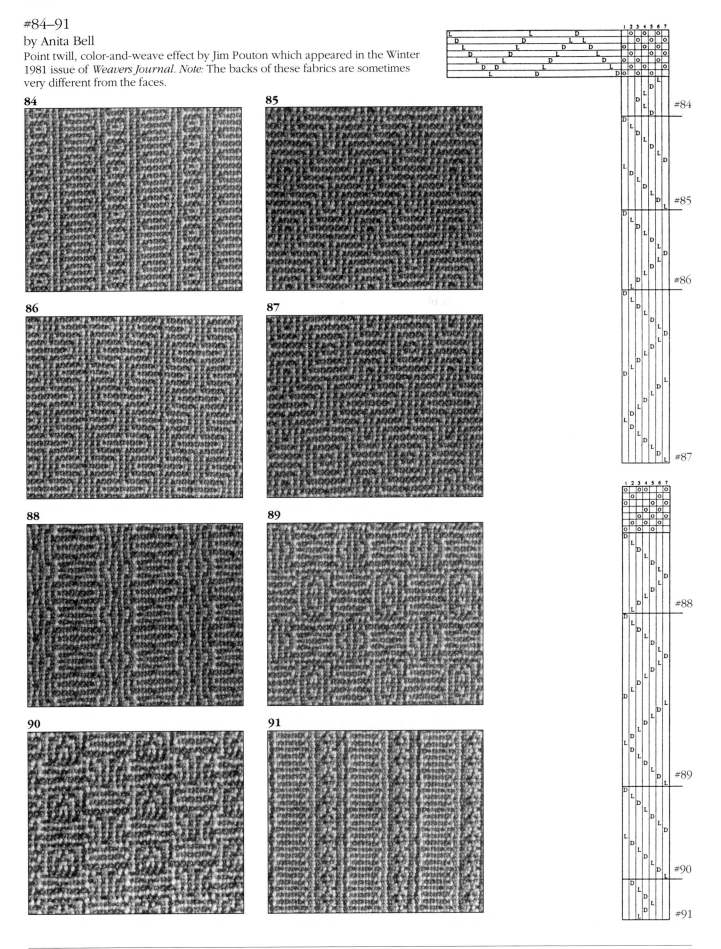

84

85

86

87

88

89

90

91

#92 & #93
by Joy E. Berg
Point twill. *Note:* These samples have a light pattern weft and a dark warp and tabby.

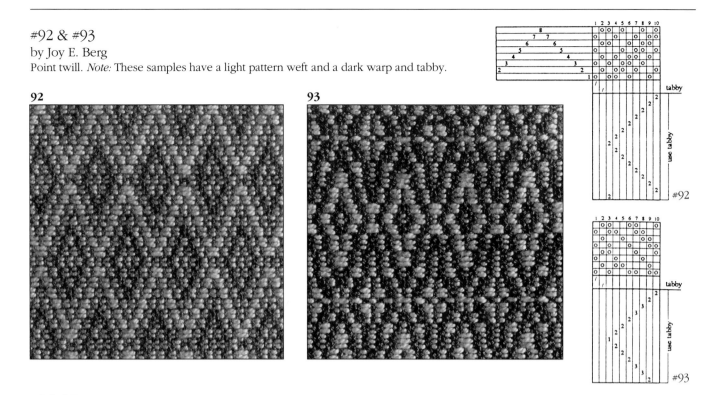

92

93

#94–97
by Marjie Thompson
Point twill from *A German Weaver's Pattern Book 1784–1810* by Christian Morath. *Note:* Each sample is treadled both straight and point twill. The backs are equally attractive.
p = point; s = straight.

94

95

96

97

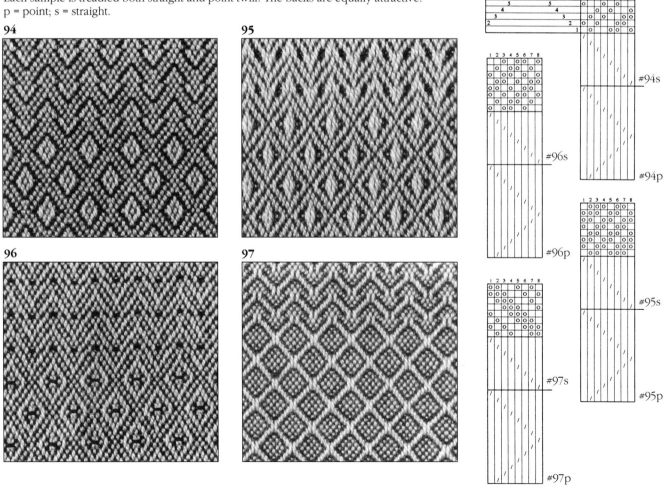

#98

by Marjie Thompson

This is an uneven point twill from *A German Weaver's Pattern Book 1784–1810* by Christian Morath.

#99–103

by Betty Creamer

Rosepath. *Beat lightly; +waffle variation.

98

99

100

101

102

103

#104–112
by Sally Nielsen

Rosepath. These borders are representative of the incredible variety of motifs which can be woven on a rosepath threading. For the samples which require more treadles than available, use a direct or skeleton tie-up and push two or more treadles at a time (see page 8 for notes on how to do this).

Use tabby with all of these treadlings. Gaps in the pattern treadling for a particular border indicate one or more extra tabby picks at that point to separate parts of a motif. The **treadlings** "read" in the same direction as the photos. To weave these motifs right-end-up follow the treadlings from bottom to top.

Note: Some motifs have long pattern-weft skips on the back.

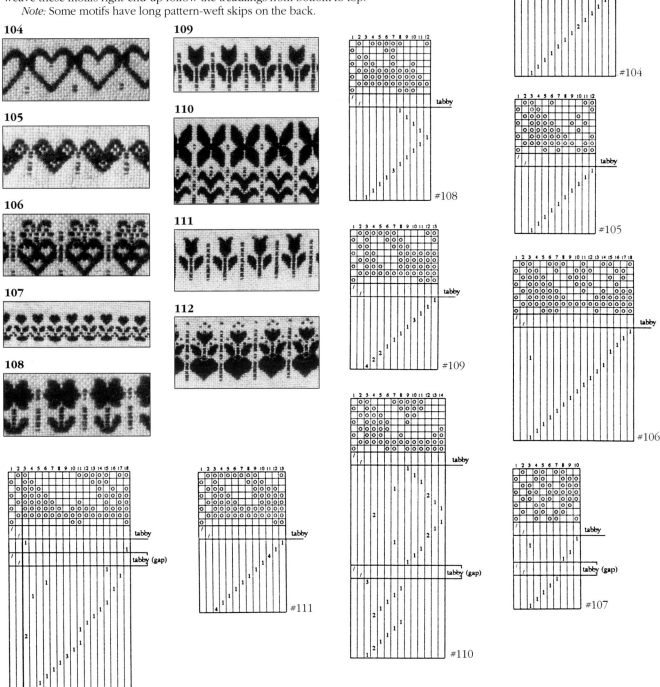

104

105

106

107

108

109

110

111

112

#104

#105

#106

#107

#108

#109

#110

#111

#112

#113–122
by Sally Nielsen (continued)

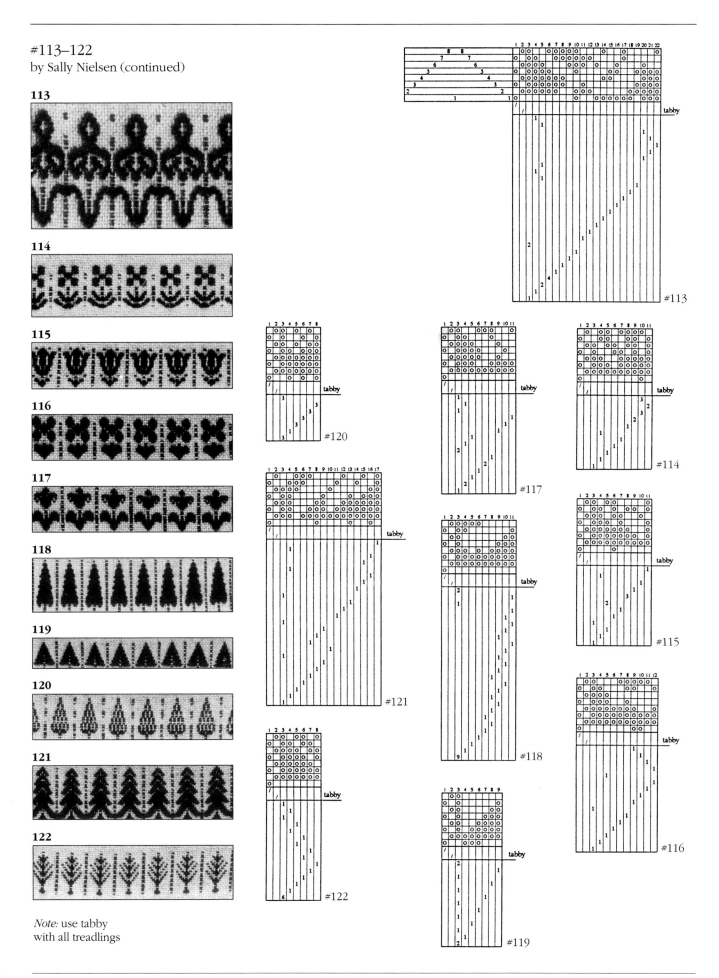

113

114

115

116

117

118

119

120

121

122

Note: use tabby
with all treadlings

#123–133
by Sally Nielsen (continued)

123

124

125

126

127

128

129

130

131

132

133

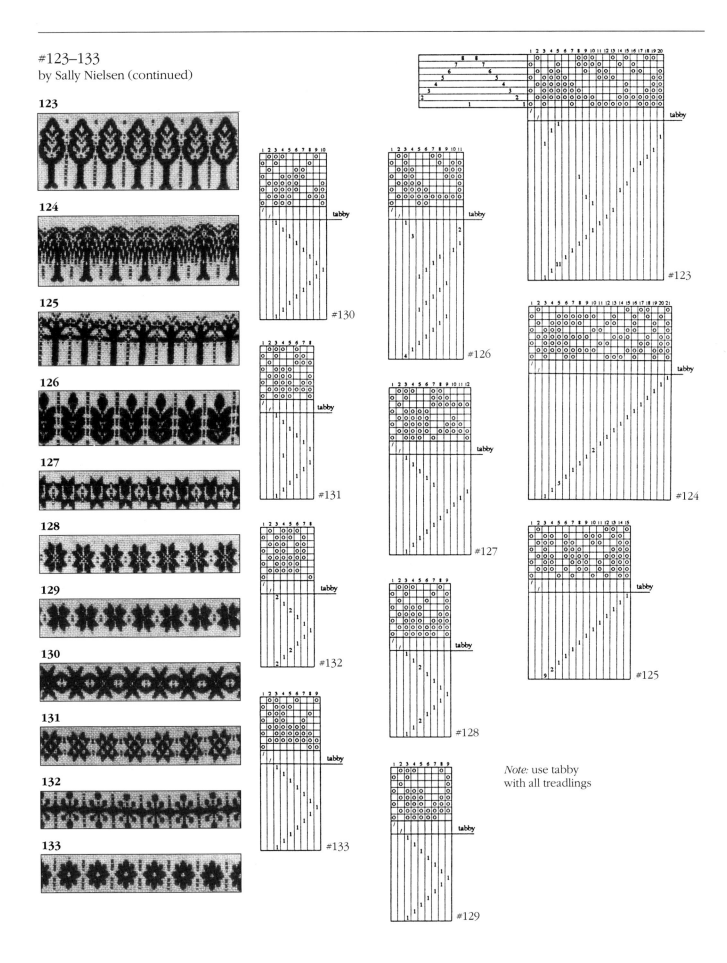

#123

#130

#131

#132

#133

#126

#127

#128

#129

#124

#125

Note: use tabby
with all treadlings

#134–144
by Sally Nielsen (continued)

134

135

136

137

138

139

140

141

142

143

144

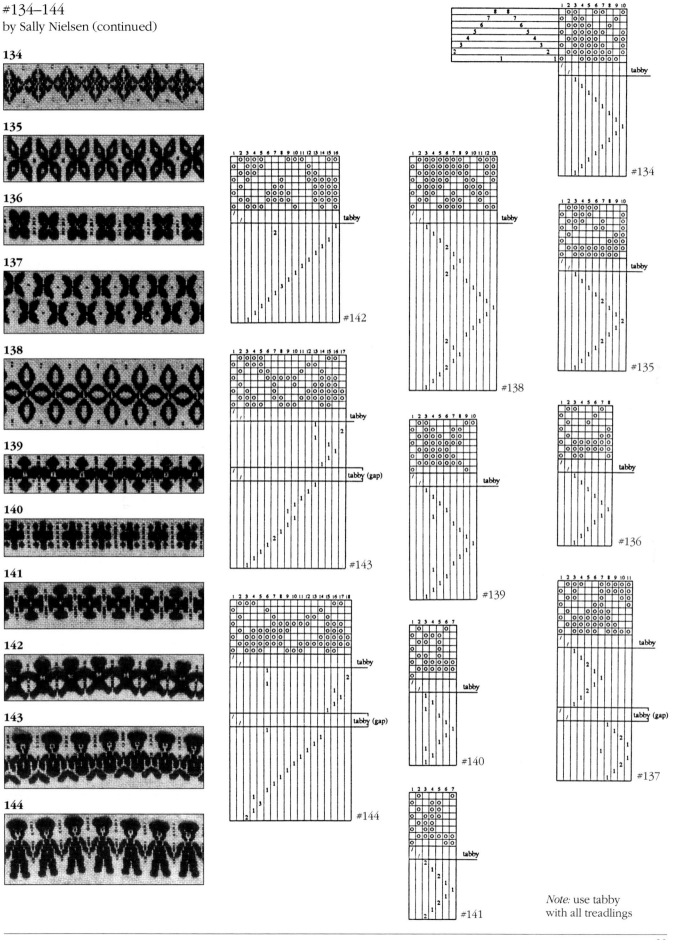

Note: use tabby
with all treadlings

#145–148

by Joyce Fisher Robards

A lace-fashion treadling with light weft.
*"Monk's belt" treadling.
+A honeycomb treadling. H = heavy, F = fine.
/A lace-fashion treadling.

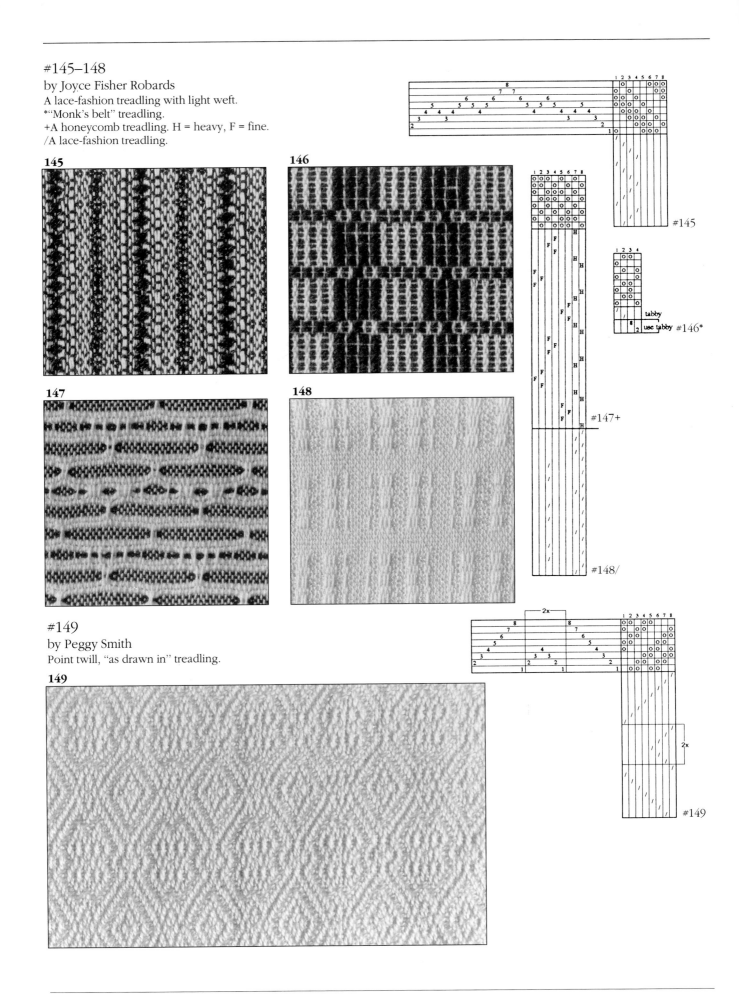

145

146

147

148

#145

#146*

#147+

#148/

#149

by Peggy Smith

Point twill, "as drawn in" treadling.

149

#149

#150–153

by Theo Thibado
Point twill, a "shared-leg M & W".
*This tie-up is slightly changed from a regular $\dfrac{2 \quad\quad 2}{\ 1 \quad 3\ }$ formula.

+This tie-up is slightly changed from a regular $\dfrac{1 \quad 1 \quad 2}{\ 1 \quad 1 \quad 2\ }$ formula.

150

151

152

153

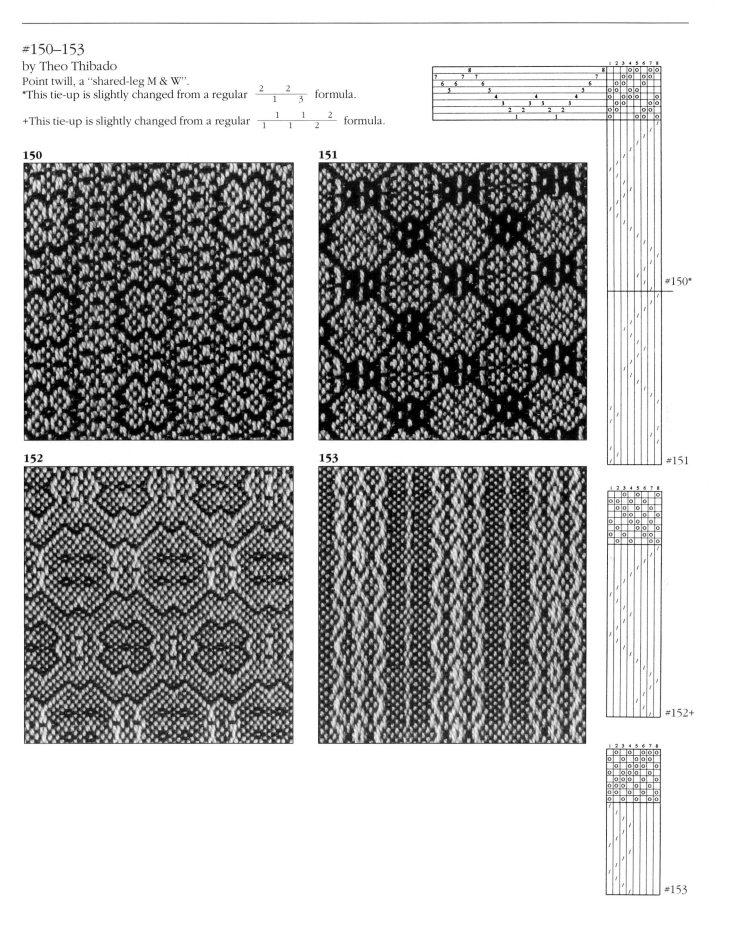

#154
by Yvonne Stahl

Point twill, an elaborate "shared-leg M & W". *Note:* The M
or W which is weaving with longer skips forms a lacy area.

154

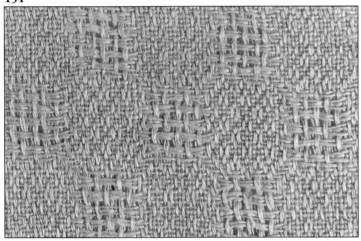

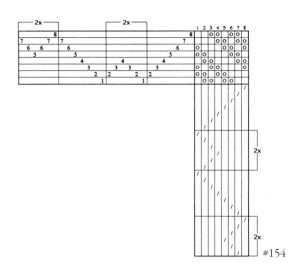

#155–157
by Roslyn J. Hahn

Point twill, "separate-leg M & W" from Black's *Key to Weaving*.

155

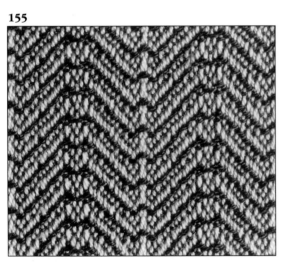

156

157

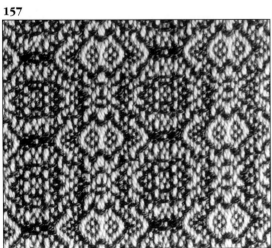

#158–163
by Patricia Cole
Point twill, "separate-leg M & W".

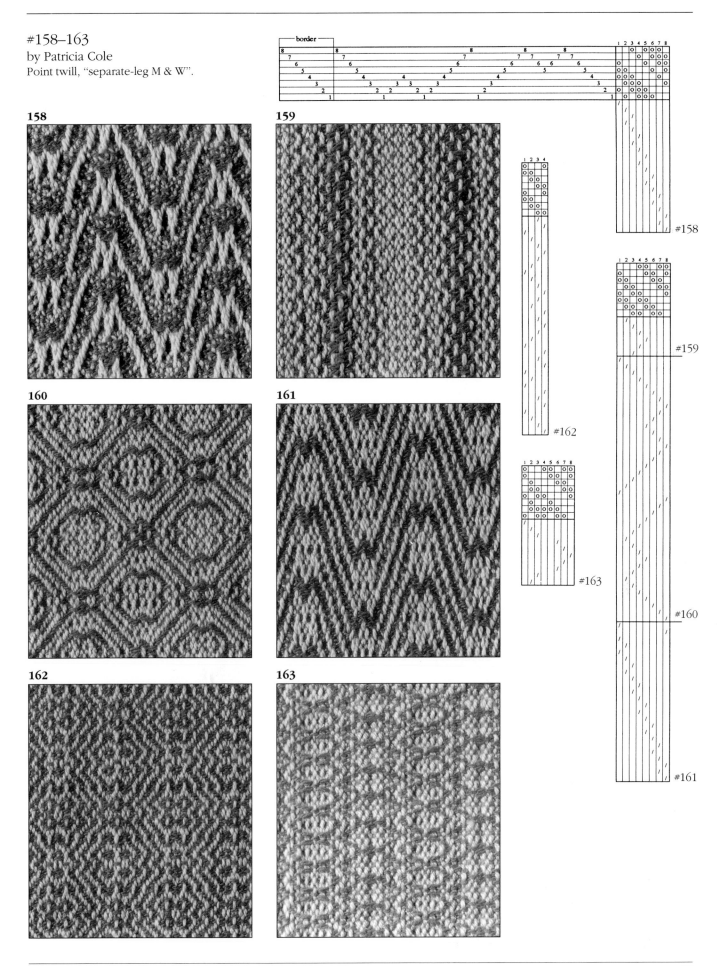

#164–167
by Sue Beevers
An elaborate (2-block) point twill.

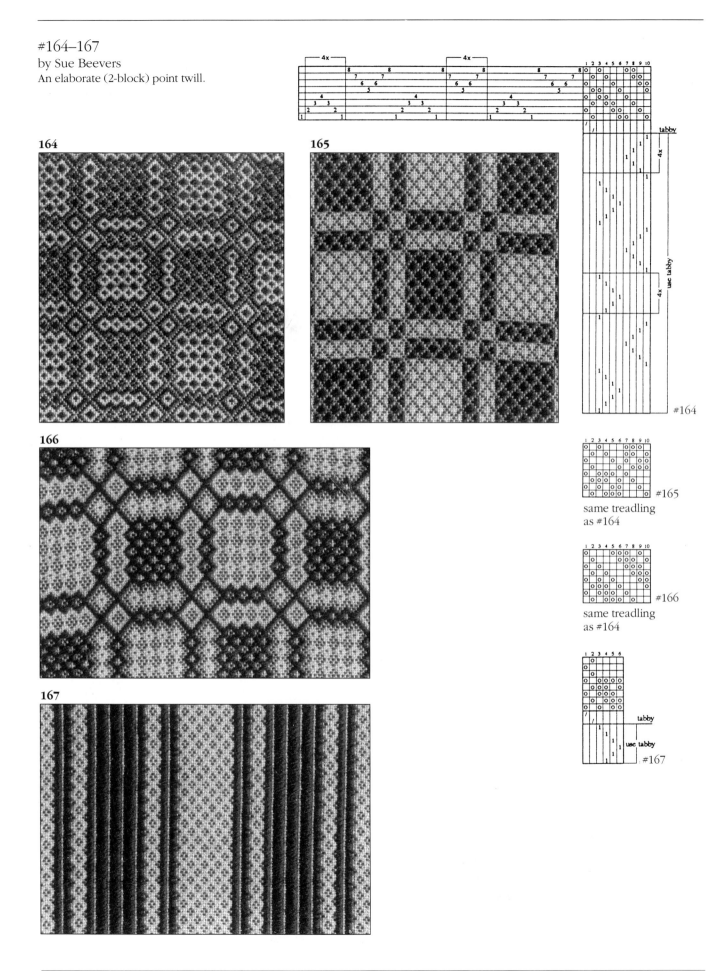

164

165

166

167

#164

#165
same treadling
as #164

#166
same treadling
as #164

#167

#168–170
by Sue Beevers
An elaborate point twill.

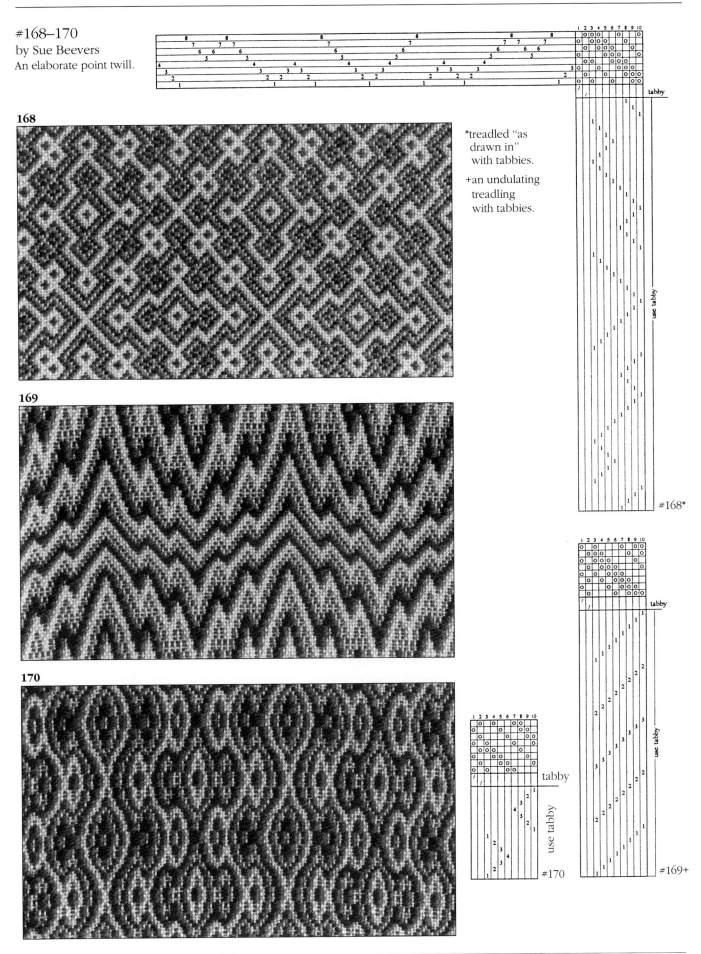

168

169

170

*treadled "as drawn in" with tabbies.

+an undulating treadling with tabbies.

#168*

#169+

#170

#171 & #172

by Yvonne Stahl

This 3-division 16-shaft twill from Patricia Hilts, draft 19 *(Ars Textrina 3),* was adapted to 7 shafts by Carol Strickler.

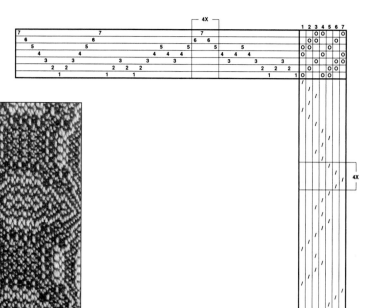

171

#171

#172

same treadling as #171

172

#173 & #174

by Yvonne Stahl

"Bethlehem star", a 3-division 16-shaft twill from Patricia Hilts, draft 18 *(Ars Textrina 3)*, adapted to 7 shafts by Carol Strickler.

*treadling is crackle-fashion.

Note: A true tabby is not possible on this threading because of the adjacent 1's and 7's.

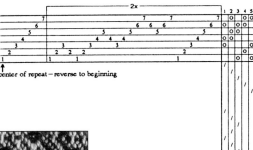

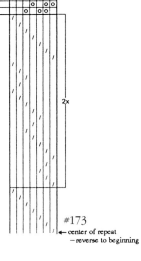

center of repeat – reverse to beginning

#173
← center of repeat
– reverse to beginning

173

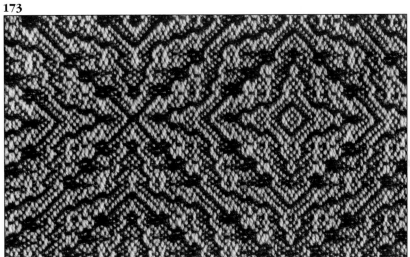

tabby

use tabby

#174*

174

3.1 broken point twill

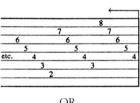

OR

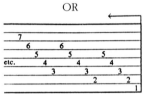

intermittent straight

intermittent point

3.2

Chapter 3
BROKEN & UNDULATING TWILLS

Broken twills are threadings in which the succession of adjacent shafts in the threading is broken by the addition or subtraction of one or more shafts of the sequence. Because of the breaks, true plain weave is usually impossible to weave on a broken twill threading.

Threading

Broken point twill (often called "herringbone" or "dornick") is probably the most common form of broken twill. The break consists of the omission of a number of shafts from the regular sequence. That number is usually one fewer than half the shafts of the twill, so in an 8-shaft dornick three shafts are skipped. The breaks are almost always at the reversing points of the twill. In figure 3.1, a typical example, there are 8 threads ascending, 3 skipped, 8 descending, and 3 skipped.

A broken point twill can be symmetrical (with as many ascending as descending threads, as in the above example) or asymmetrical. The break usually makes the warp threads on either side of it take opposite paths, eliminating the longer weft skips that straddle the point in ordinary point twill.

Another form of broken twill is an *intermittent twill*, in which several shafts are omitted at regular intervals but the twill continues in the same direction and is unbroken at the points if it does reverse. This makes an intermittent draft look like overlapping segments of twill (thus sometimes called "offset twill"). Intermittent twills are almost always very regular, with segments of equal length and breaks of equal size. Examples are shown in figure 3.2.

Sometimes twills are broken by omitting one or two shafts after each thread to make the twill line tilt more vertically; these are called *steep twills*. If, on the other hand, a shaft is repeated two or more times in succession, the twill line is *flattened*. When steep twills, straight twill, and flattened twills are combined in the threading, the result is an *undulating twill* threading. (As was seen in the Straight Twill chapter, the undulation can actually be in the treadling or the tie-up instead of the threading. The samples in *this* chapter have undulating *threadings*.) Examples (figure 3.3):

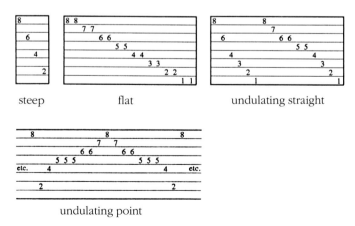

steep   flat   undulating straight

undulating point

3.3

The disadvantage of putting undulation in the threading is that in the flattened areas two or more warp threads will always act together as thicker warps throughout the length of the fabric, creating a weaker structure. Plain weave cannot be woven on these threadings.

The ultimate broken twill threading is *satin* (sometimes called "scattered twill") with a break after every thread. A true satin threading requires at least five shafts, so that the threads can be scattered as widely and as uniformly as possible. Examples (figure 3.4):

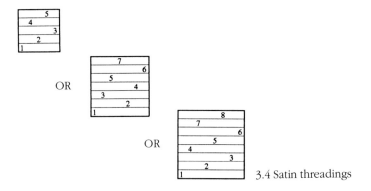

OR

OR

3.4 Satin threadings

There are no satin threadings in this book. There is one satin tie-up/treadling in the Straight Twill chapter, and there are several examples of 8-shaft "false damask" in the Block Twills and other chapters.)

Braided twills may also be drafted on a threading that looks like broken twill; a few of those are included here, and the rest are in the chapter of Plaited Twills (page 100).

Tie-ups & Treadling Orders

Broken point twill (dornick) *can* be tied up and treadled like any twill, but it is *usually* woven with a formula tie-up and straight treadling which creates vertical stripes of reversing diagonals with well-defined edges. With the exception of a "literal as-drawn-in" treadling, other forms tend to look like mistakes.

The tie-up for an intermittent or offset twill is usually a half-and-half tie-up (sometimes called "batavia") in which half of the shafts are up and the other half down (4/4), but other formula tie-ups can also be used. Either straight or "literal as-drawn-in" treadlings are most effective, because they result in a less cluttered design.

For an undulating twill threading the tie-up can be any formula type that has fairly small divisions (such as 3/1/2/2). A tie-up with skips of four or more shafts can be used but it tends to create very long weft floats where the twill line is flattened. The treadling can be straight twill or it can undulate to enhance or counteract the undulation of the threading.

Variations

A broken point twill can be varied by shortening or lengthening the ascending and descending sections of the threading. (Extremes should be avoided, though; a pattern with many short unequal sections will look "choppy," and a pattern with very long unbroken sections may look flawed.) Tie-ups and treadlings can also be changed.

An intermittent straight twill can be altered by lengthening or shortening the sections of twill or the size of the breaks. An intermittent point twill can also be enlarged or reduced by increasing or decreasing the number of segments between reversing points.

To vary an undulating twill threading try shortening the flat part and lengthening or shortening the straight and steep parts. (Lengthening the flat part or increasing the repeats of a shaft will make the fabric looser and sleazier.) The steep parts of an undulating twill can also be made even steeper by skipping more shafts in the breaks.

#175–177
by Jill Coghlan

A crepe threading from *A Handbook of Weaves* by G.H. Oelsner.
Note the difference between the face and the back of each of these samples. Many other tie-ups and treadlings are possible on this threading.

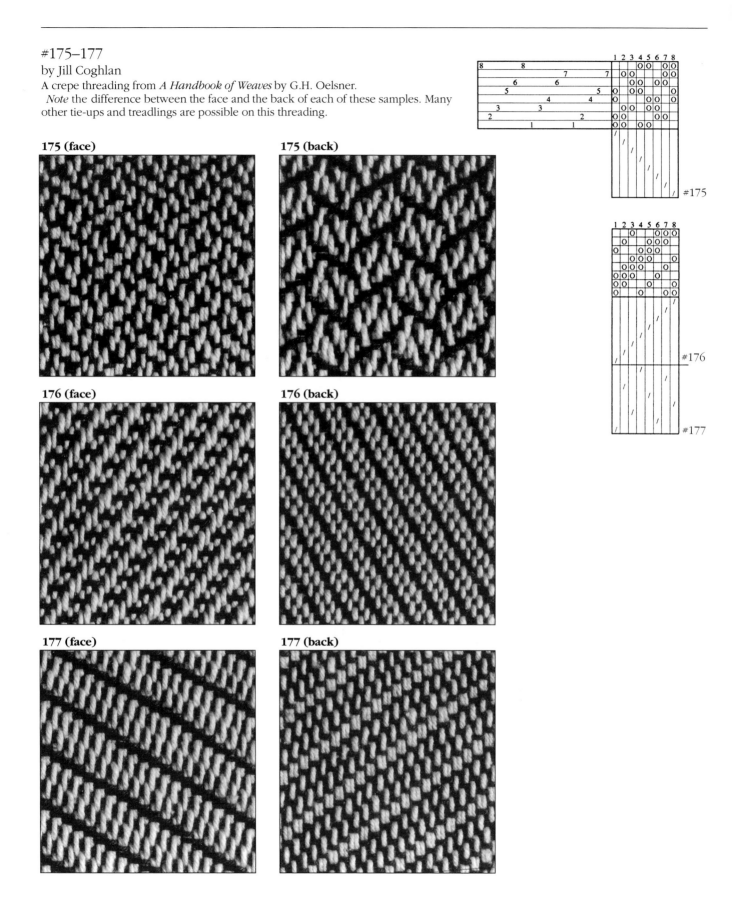

175 (face)

175 (back)

176 (face)

176 (back)

177 (face)

177 (back)

#178–180

by Betty Burrill

An intermittent twill from *A Handbook of Weaves* by G.H. Oelsner.

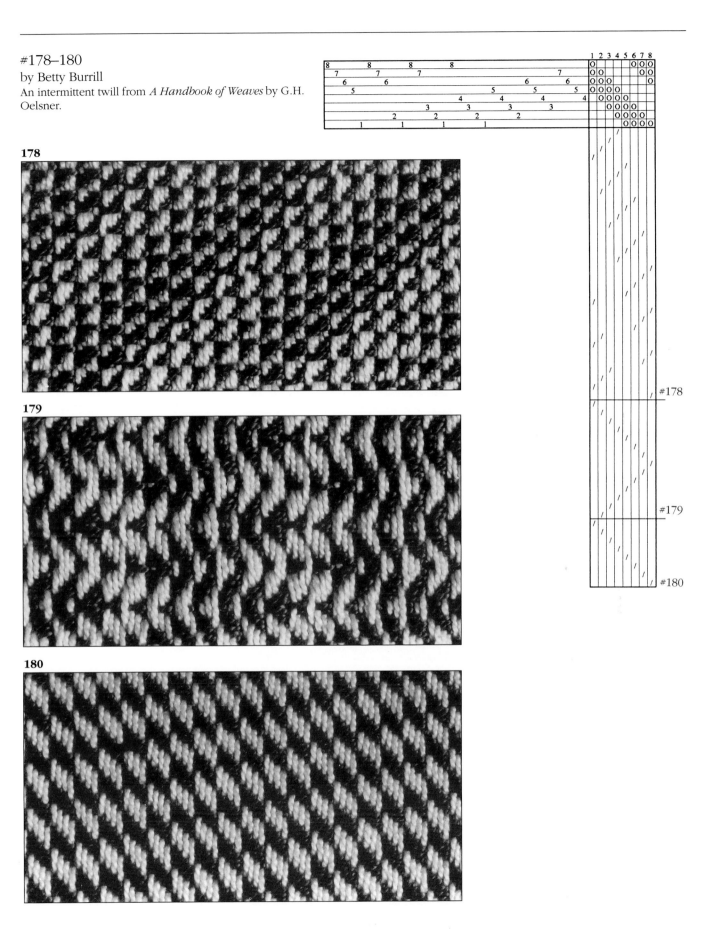

178

179

180

#181–186
by Kathleen Bradford
A braided twill.

181

182

183

184

185

186

#181

#182

#183

(4-shaft imitations)

#184

#185

#186

#187–190

by Betty Hancock Smith

Herringbone Plaid.

Note: These samples are all woven with "as-drawn-in" treadlings; only the tie-ups change. #188 uses floating selvedges because two shots fall in same shed.

187

188

189

190

Use treadling #187 for these tie-ups.

#188

#189

#190

#191–194
by Dianne Ney Totten
Herringbone Plaid (same
threading as #187–190).

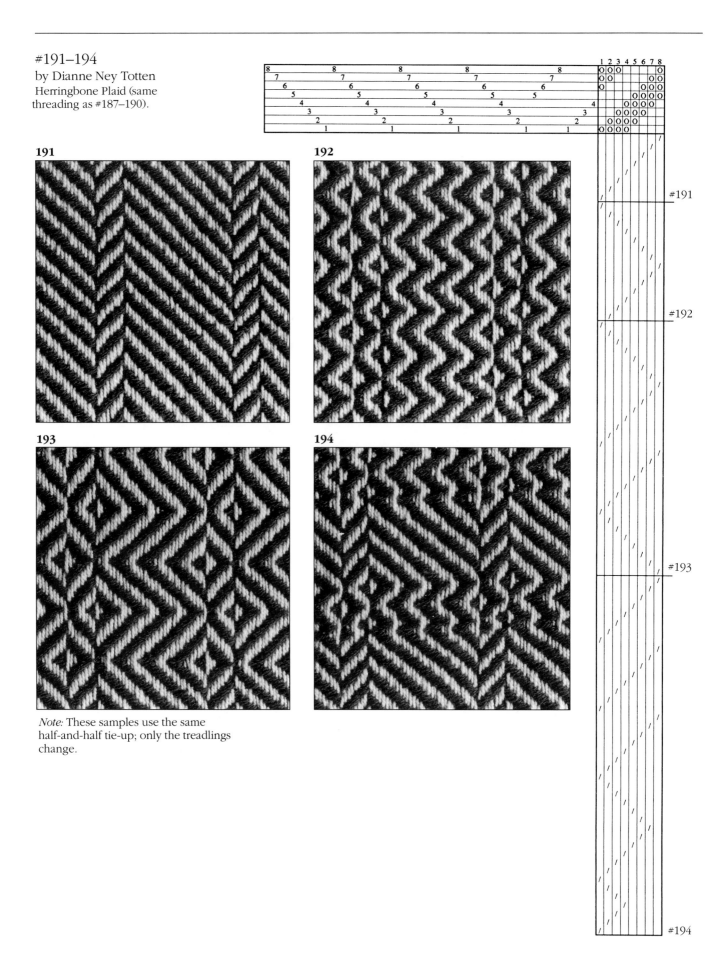

191

192

193

194

Note: These samples use the same
half-and-half tie-up; only the treadlings
change.

#195–200

by Dee Jones

Dornick threading. *Note:* Any of these treadlings (straight, point, "as-drawn-in")
 can be combined with any of these tie-ups for interesting designs.

195

196

197

198

199

200

#201–203
by Dee Jones
Dornick twill.

201 **202** **203**

#204 & #205

by Barbara M. Goonan
An undulating twill threading (steep and straight). *Note:* These
samples have a light weft and a dark warp.

204 **205**

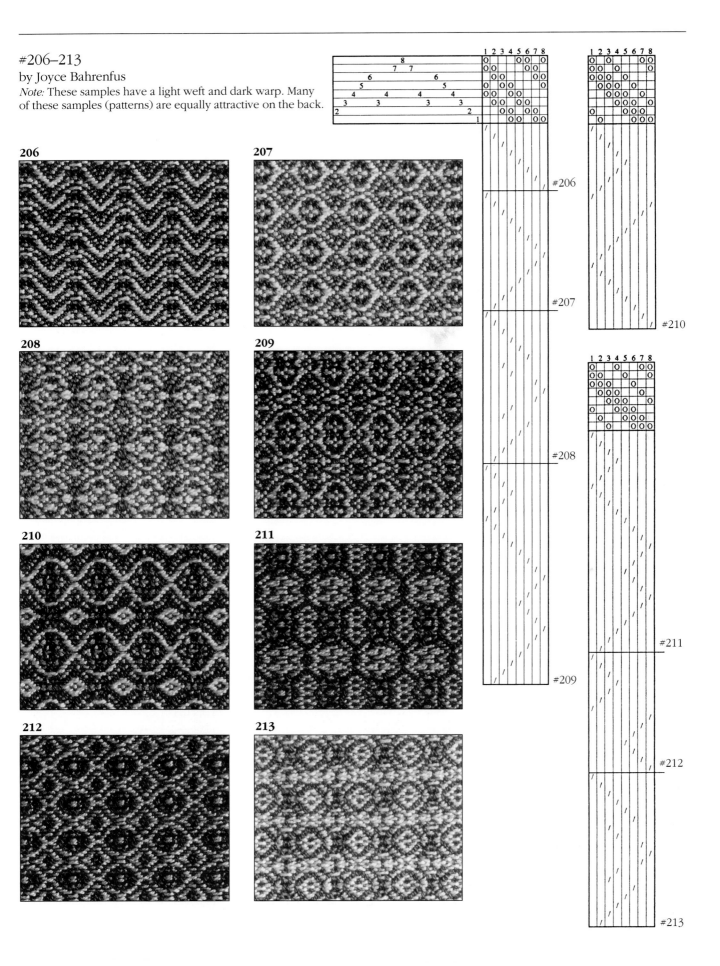

#206–213

by Joyce Bahrenfus

Note: These samples have a light weft and dark warp. Many of these samples (patterns) are equally attractive on the back.

206

207

208

209

210

211

212

213

#214–224

by Joan Jensen, Judy Kleeves, Trudy Johnson
(North Oakland Weavers' Guild Twill Study Group)
An undulating twill (from "Twills with Twist", Nov/Dec '85 HANDWOVEN).
*#217, #221, and #223 use floating selvedges (because of repeated weft shots).

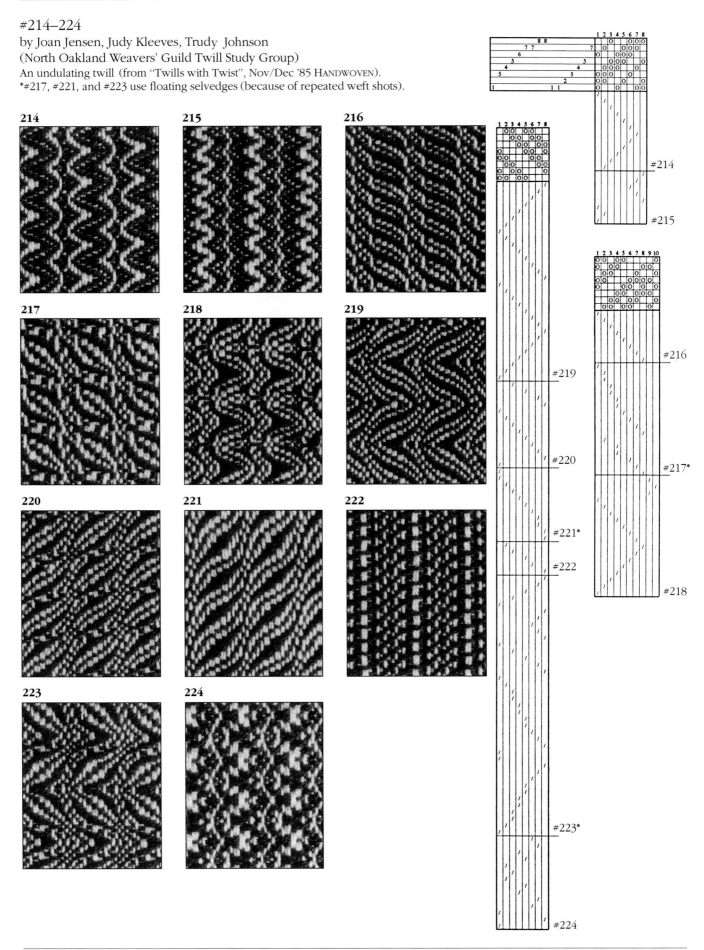

214

215

216

217

218

219

220

221

222

223

224

Chapter 4
BLOCK TWILL

When the threads of one weave are carried on one set of shafts and the threads of another weave are carried on a different set, Oelsner said, the threading is called a *Grouped Draft.* Today, when the two weaves are both twill the weave is commonly called *block twill, double twill,* or *turned twill.* (Sometimes it is called "double-faced twill", a confusing misnomer.)

Blocks are groups of threads that behave alike by virtue of their threading, tie-up, and/or treadling. On 8 shafts the most common form of block twill weave is two blocks, one block consisting of straight twill threaded on shafts 1-4 and the other straight twill on shafts 5-8. If either the threading, the tie-up, or the treadling causes the blocks to weave as 4-shaft broken twill, the result is sometimes called "false damask", "false satin", or "double broken twill".

Threading

When the pattern is a 2-block threading and the units are always the same, the threading can be written as a profile (A and B blocks) with a "key" that indicates what threading sequences or units to use in place of each letter. For example, if the key is:

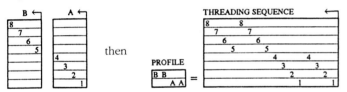

4.1

In occasional cases the twill key is a point twill which needs slight adjustments; the final "pivot point" thread needs to be added at the end of each *series* of identical blocks. For example, if the key is:

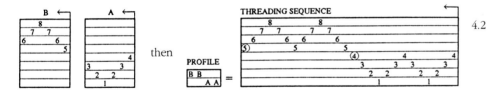

4.2

The blocks *can* use different keys (such as A = straight twill and B = rosepath) but such combinations are not as versatile as the ones where both blocks are the same twill, and they are therefore seldom used.

In this book many of the threadings are given as profile drafts with relevant keys. Others that are not "standard" are given as thread-by-thread drafts.

Tie-ups

If the odd-even alternation of shafts has been maintained in the threading of the block twill, plain weave is woven by lifting odd shafts vs even shafts. If not (as in a broken twill threading) there may still be a combination of shafts that will raise or lower alternate threads.

The tie-up for 8-shaft 2-block twill is usually divided in half horizontally so that shafts 1-4 can do one thing while shafts 5-8 do another. If the interlacement frequencies of the two blocks are the same, the stripes of warp will have equal takeup and the fabric

4.3a

4.3b

A weft-dominant
B warp-dominant

A warp-dominant
B weft-dominant

4.3c

4.3d

both
weft
dominant

both
warp
dominant

4.4 You can use:

but *not*:

because the latter has some treadles which would cause entire sections of warp to be raised or lowered where a 4-shaft block has been repeated in the threading.

selvedges will be straight. (Examples of this include 1/3 and 3/1, as in blocks of weft-dominant vs warp-dominant twill, or 2/2 vs 2/2, as in blocks of twill vs basketweave.) If, on the other hand, the interlacements are extremely different the warp tension may become uneven or the selvedges wavy. (An example of such inequalities would be 1/3 and 1/1/1/1, as in weft-dominant twill vs plain weave; plain weave has more interlacement than the twill and will force threads apart where the twill lets them relax or collapse.)

When the tie-up treats the blocks independently, there are four different ways that two blocks can be put together in the tie-up. For example, if both blocks are being treated as unbalanced twill the tie-ups can be as shown in figure 4.3.

It is usual for the warp-twill line to run opposite to the weft-twill line (figures 4.3a and 4.3b). The result is smooth lines of twill where blocks adjoin and clean breaks where they oppose. These four tie-ups in combination are the ones most commonly used on 2-block straight twill threadings.

In the above figure, every 4-shaft section weaves either 1/3 or 3/1 straight twill. Other possibilities for the sections include such tie-ups as 2/2 straight twill, 1/3 or 3/1 broken twill, 2/2 basket weave, plain weave, or double weave. Tie-up sections can be "stacked" one atop one other, so that while the A block is weaving one structure the B block can produce the same or another. There are examples of this in the "As If's" chapter of this book.

Any 8-shaft formula tie-up that includes at least one shaft from each block on every treadle can be used with a 2-block 8-shaft twill. For an example see figure 4.4.

Treadling Orders

In 8-shaft 2-block 1/3–3/1 twill the treadling order is usually "block as-drawn-in", producing pattern in the blocks in the order in which they were threaded. This form of block twill is usually woven with one color warp and a contrasting color weft, to show the structural pattern of warp-dominant and weft-dominant blocks to best advantage.

The treadling can be divided into 4-treadle units as shown in figure 4.5:

4.5

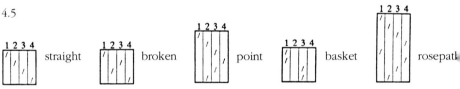

straight broken point basket rosepath

These units can be repeated or combined as desired. The treadling can be varied to weave stripes (by repeating one 4-treadle unit over and over) or bands (by tying and treadling "both blocks alike" followed by an opposite or different "both alike"). Or the treadling can be any ordinary 8-treadle twill such as straight or point or rosepath; some are more successful than others. The possibilities are numerous.

Variations

Structural stripes are widened or narrowed by adding or subtracting units of threading. (It is usually best to add or subtract full units so that the pattern junctions are not broken.) Tie-up sections can be combined in different ways, keeping in mind that using different interlacements may cause scalloped selvedges or uneven warp tension. Treadling can be varied as desired, although the most effective designs are the ones that are either straight and simple or closely related to the threading.

There is no law that says that the "groups" of shafts in a block twill must be equal. For example, one block can be threaded straight on three shafts and the other straight on five shafts, treated in tie-up and treadling as 3-end twill and 5-end satin. The problem with such unbalanced fabrics, though, is that different interlacements have different rates of take-up in both warp and weft. Such fabrics *might* require a loom with double warp beam, and they would *certainly* require careful designing and experimentation with yarns and sett!

There are other successful block twill patterns in the Twill Gamps and "As If's" chapters of this book. Block twill threadings that are tied up and treadled as double cloth are in the Block Double Weave chapter.

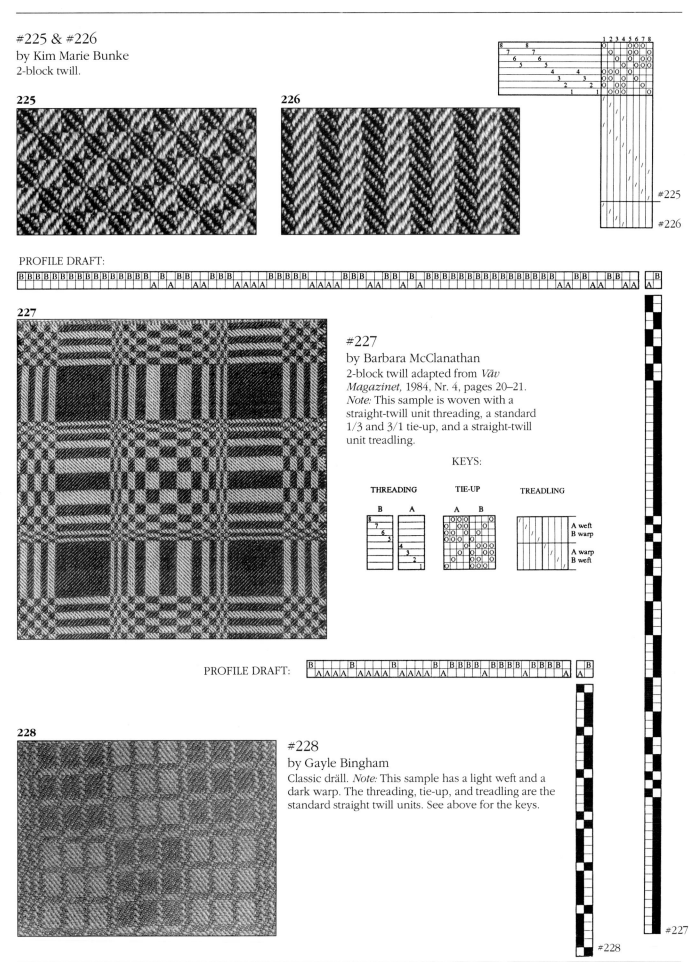

#225 & #226
by Kim Marie Bunke
2-block twill.

225

226

#225

#226

PROFILE DRAFT:

227

#227

by Barbara McClanathan
2-block twill adapted from *Väv Magazinet*, 1984, Nr. 4, pages 20–21.
Note: This sample is woven with a straight-twill unit threading, a standard 1/3 and 3/1 tie-up, and a straight-twill unit treadling.

KEYS:

THREADING   TIE-UP   TREADLING

B   A   A   B

A weft
B warp

A warp
B weft

PROFILE DRAFT:

228

#228

by Gayle Bingham
Classic dräll. *Note:* This sample has a light weft and a dark warp. The threading, tie-up, and treadling are the standard straight twill units. See above for the keys.

#227

#228

#229–234
by Judith Rygiel

The threading is straight twill units (see key). Because some of the tie-ups and treadlings differ from the standard, they are listed individually. Sample #234 uses "as-drawn-in" profile treadling. *A block = plain weave; B block = 2/2 twill. **This sample uses tie-up and treadling key to follow as-drawn-in profile treadling.

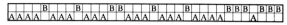

#229–234

Threading key:

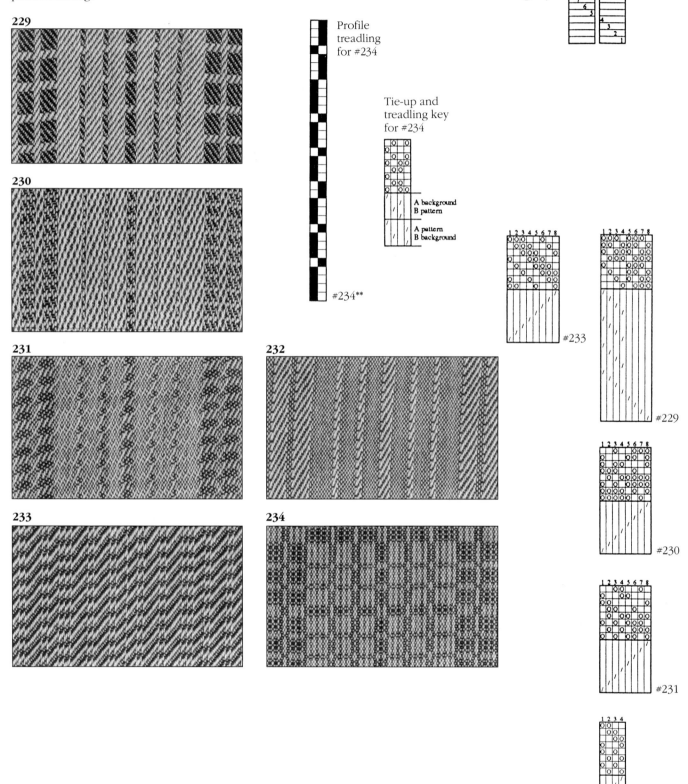

Profile treadling for #234

Tie-up and treadling key for #234

A background
B pattern

A pattern
B background

#234**

229

230

231

232

233

234

#233

#229

#230

#231

#232*

#235–237
by Sue Beevers

The threading is standard straight twill units (see key). Treadle ADI profile for #235 and #236; follow treadling key for #237. *This sample is woven face down.

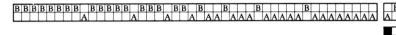

235

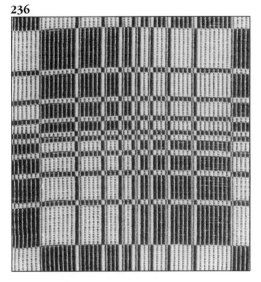

Threading key:

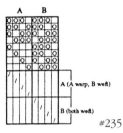

Tie-up and treadling key for #235

A (A warp, B weft)

B (both weft)

#235

#235 &
#236

236

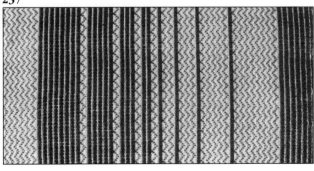

Tie-up and treadling key for #236

tabbies

B pattern &
A background
(use tabbies)

A pattern &
B background
(use tabbies)

#236*

237

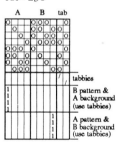

Tie-up and treadling key for #237

tabbies

A 3/1 twill
B 1/3 columns
(use tabbies)

#237

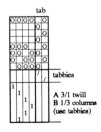

#238–240
by Sharon Walker

Use threading, tie-up, and treadling keys. *Stripes of block A = 2/2 twill; block B = plain weave. +As-drawn-in profile treadling. #As-drawn-in profile treadling with optional sequin insertion in double weave pockets. Face all sequins the same way in the pockets (that is, concave or convex side up). Do not over press the sequined cloth as too much heat may melt them, and too much pressure reduces their reflectivity.

Profile threading   #238–240

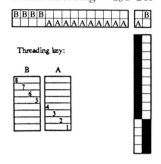

Threading key:

238

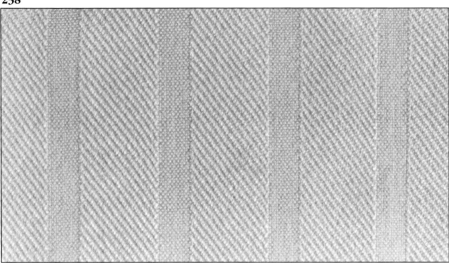

Profile tie-up
and treadling
for #239 & #240

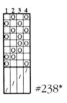

#238*

239

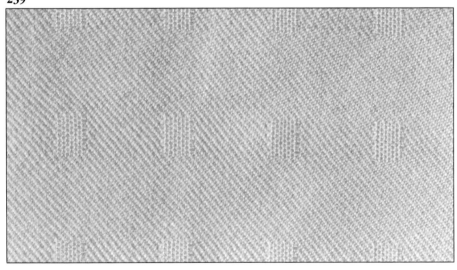

Tie-up and
treadling key
for #239

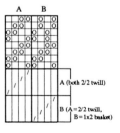

A (both 2/2 twill)

B (A = 2/2 twill,
   B = 1x2 basket)

#239+

240

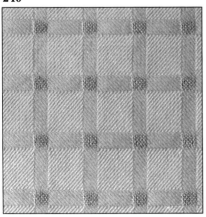

Tie-up and
treadling key
for #240

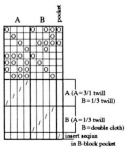

A (A = 3/1 twill
   B = 1/3 twill)

B (A = 1/3 twill
   B = double cloth)

/ insert sequin
   in B-block pocket

#240#

#241–244
by Yvonne Stahl
2-block twill from Worst, *How to Weave Linens.*

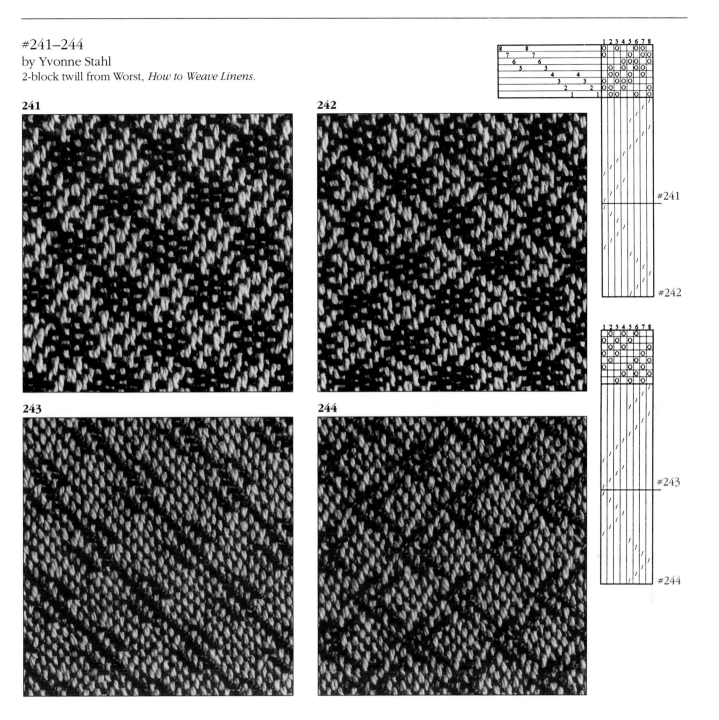

241

242

243

244

#245
by Gayle Bingham
2-block twill, "korndräll".

245

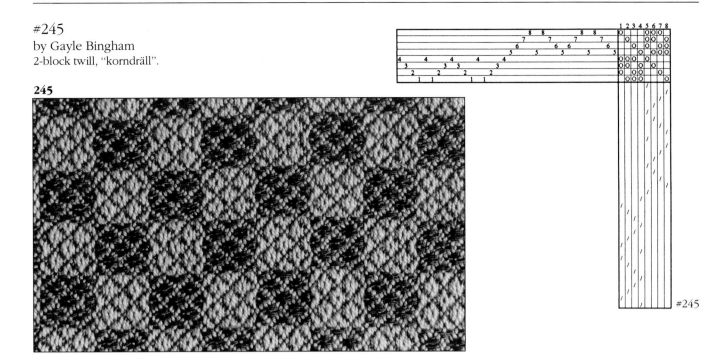

#245

#246
by Marjie Thompson
False damask check from a linen towel, Holland, 1931, published in the Central Ohio Weavers Guild Newsletter, 1980.

246

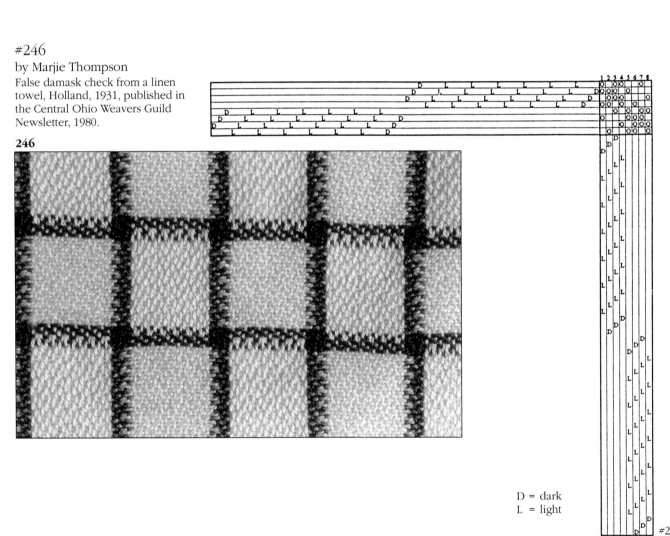

D = dark
L = light

#246

#247 & #248
by Judy Steinkoenig

Color-and-weave block houndstooth from Hulda Peters, *Vavbok*. This threading is standard straight twill units. Use threading, tie-up, and treadling keys. Notice L (light) and D (dark) designations in profile threading and treadling.

247

248

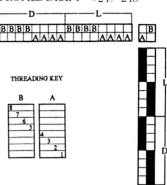

THREADING KEY

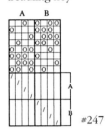

Tie-up and treadling key

#247

Tie-up for #248 (same treadling as #247)

Chapter 5
MANIFOLD/CORKSCREW TWILLS

A *manifold twill* or *corkscrew twill*, sometimes called "interlocking twill", is one in which two or more twills are merged by using threads alternately from each, usually beginning them on shafts as widely separated as possible. Two parallel straight twills alternated this way in the threading, tied in a standard manner, and treadled literally as-drawn-in produce a fabric with two parallel diagonal lines closely interlocked. The design is especially prominent when the two twills are different colors (that is, when dark and light alternate in both warp and weft). If the corkscrew twill uses an odd number of shafts (such as 7 instead of 8), adjacent warp floats overlap and interlock even more.

Threading

For a manifold twill, any two or more twills can be interlocked (alternated). The simplest 8-shaft corkscrew is two straight twills, one beginning on the fourth shaft above the other (figure 5.1). If *three* straight twills are interlocked on 8 shafts, the result might be as shown in figure 5.2. In this example, one repeat is 8 threads if the warp is solid color or 24 threads if each twill is a different color.

Twills other than straight and identical can also be interlocked. In the example in figure 5.3, two repeats of straight twill are interlocked with one repeat of an undulating twill.

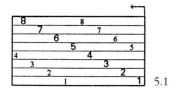

5.1

(The separation between the two twill lines can also be smaller or larger.)

5.2

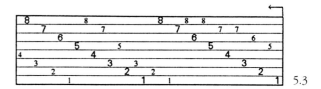

5.3

Tie-ups

When a manifold twill is threaded as above with maximum separation between the lines, the usual tie-up is half-and-half (half up/half down, as 3/3 on 6 shafts, 4/3 on 7 shafts, 4/4 on 8 shafts—sometimes called "batavia").

Treadling Orders

Normally a manifold twill is treadled literally as-drawn-in (with the treadles used in the same order as the shafts are threaded). An 8-pick or 16-pick straight manifold treadling order can also be used on other manifold twill threadings.

Variations

Manifold twills are not easily modified. Threadings *can* be reduced slightly by being redrafted on fewer shafts. New twills can be drafted "from scratch". Twills that individually use fewer than the total number of shafts can be combined. (One such sampler in this chapter alternates a 3-shaft straight twill with a straight twill on the other five shafts.)

Addition of color is perhaps the biggest variation that can be made in a manifold twill. This is often done by threading each of the original twills in a different color.

Extended Manifold Twills

A 20th-century weaver, William G. Bateman, devised threadings he called *extended manifold twills* in which he extended each pair of threads of an ordinary manifold twill into threading units on several shafts. Dr. Bateman's draft extensions are varied and numerous; for a complete explanation of his designing process and drafts, see *Extended Manifold Twill Weaves*, Shuttle Craft Guild Monograph 40, edited by Virginia I. Harvey.

#249 & #250
by Nancianne Horton

7-shaft corkscrew twill from *More Than Four* by Mary Elizabeth Laughlin. *Note:* These samples have a light weft and a dark warp. The tie-up uses eight treadles and is slightly irregular.

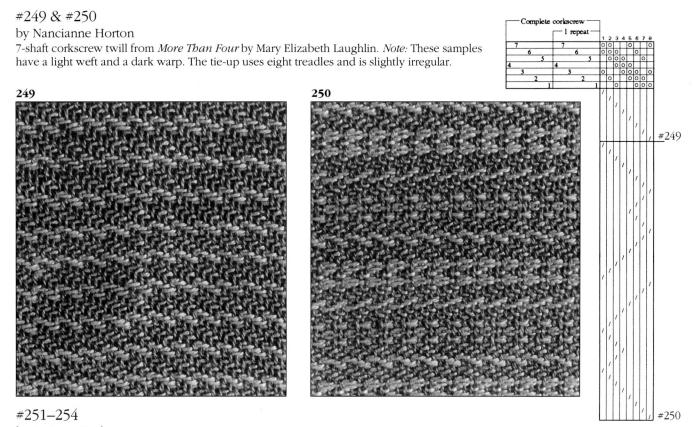

249

250

#251–254
by Jo Anne Ryeburn

7-shaft corkscrew twill. *Note:* In some of these samples, the back is strikingly different from the face.

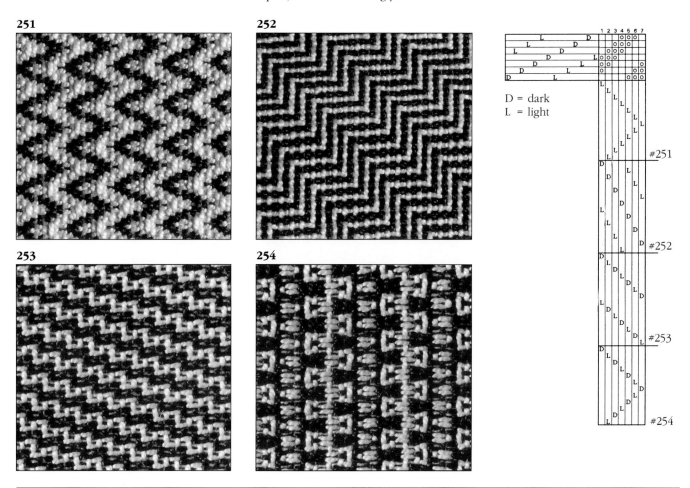

251

252

253

254

D = dark
L = light

#255–260
by Kathleen Bradford

2-line manifold twill from *A Handbook of Weaves* by G.H. Oelsner.
Note: Uses 9 of the 10 treadles.

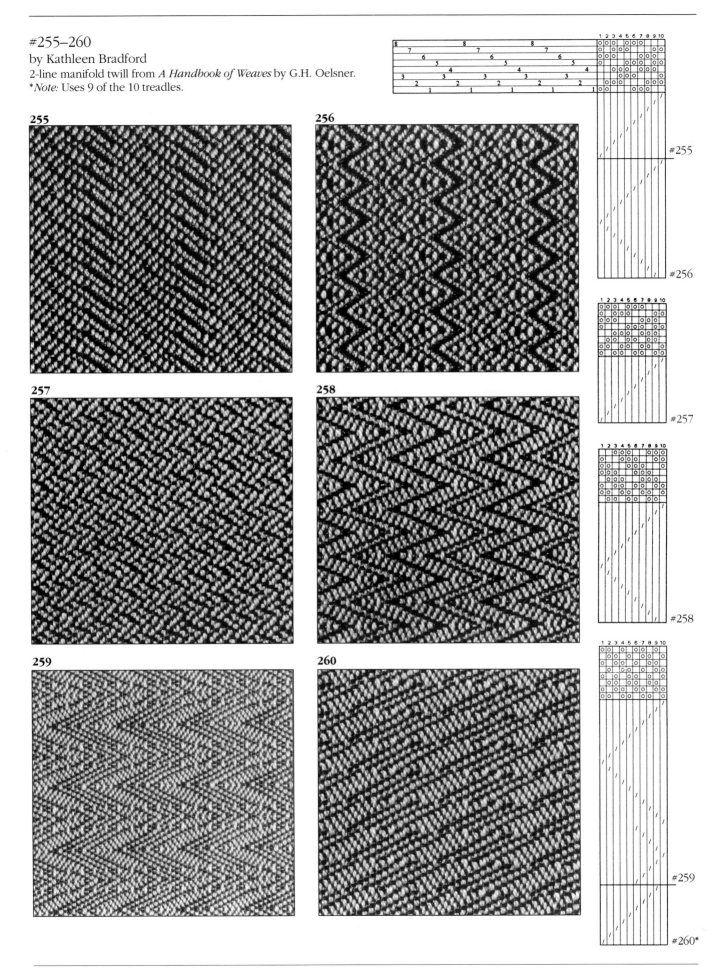

255

256

257

258

259

260

#261 & #262

by Jeanne Young Kudlicki

4-line manifold twill adapted by Carol Strickler from a sample by Nerma Lee Hill. *Note:* The original sample (two lines straight and two lines undulating) had each line of the manifold threaded and treadled in a different color in closely related tones for a shimmery effect. Here, light and dark are alternated. There is one place in the threading and treadling (*) where there are two threads (a dark and a light) next to each other on shaft or treadle 3. There is one place in the threading and treadling where two threads have been omitted from the sequence to prevent long skips.

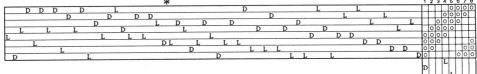

261

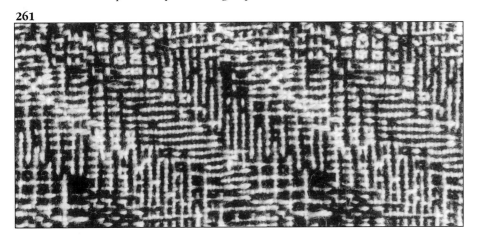

262

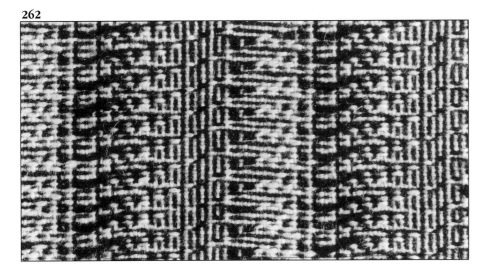

#263–268

by Julie Owens (Tweavers Study Group)

Bateman's extended manifold twill, draft #201 from *Extended Manifold Twill Weaves: Shuttle Craft Guild Monograph 40* by Virginia Harvey.

Note: Samples #263 and #264 have identical treadlings—the first one uses dark and light pattern wefts as designated in the treadling, while the second one uses all dark pattern weft.

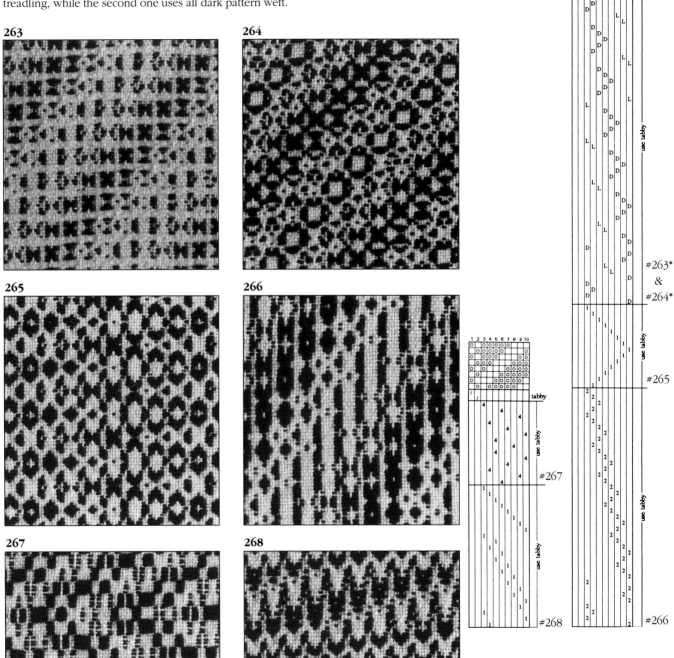

263

264

265

266

267

268

Chapter 6
SHADOW WEAVE

As Mary M. Atwater introduced *shadow weave* in the 1940's and as Harriet Tidball perpetuated it, each dark/light pair from two interlocked straight twills is treated as a repeatable unit. (Other authors have since devised other threading formulas for weaving the same fabric.) The structure is basically plain weave, with small skips where some blocks adjoin.

Shadow weave is usually a balanced weave (e.p.i.=p.p.i.) that has alternating dark and light (or sometimes alternating heavy and fine) threads in warp and weft. The resulting fabric has blocks of warpwise and weftwise pinstripes. Because each block is plain weave, the shaft-pair of a block can be repeated many times in succession in both threading and treadling without weakening the structure of the fabric.

In addition to the samples in this chapter, some "parallel shadow weave" threadings based on other weaves are shown with the threadings (such as crackle and huck) to which they are related.

Threading

In the Atwater method of threading shadow weave, the basic pattern is drawn on alternate threads and then the "shadow" threads are filled in on the "opposite" shaft. On eight shafts this results in the key shown in figure 6.1.

Shadows *follow* patterns when the block twill line is ascending A toward H, but *precede* them when descending. If the profile draft has reversing points, one thread can be added or subtracted at each point to maintain the pattern/shadow alternation and make the design symmetrical.

Four of the blocks are opposites of the other four. For example, blocks A and E are both threaded on shafts 1 and 5 but with the pattern thread on shaft 1 in A and on shaft 5 in E. The same is true of blocks B and F, C and G, and D and H. Thus when pattern threads are raised in any block, shadow threads are raised in the opposite block; when any block is weaving warpwise stripes its opposite block is weaving weftwise stripes.

The other methods of threading shadow weave (such as Marian Powell's) differ only in the shaft numbers used for each block in threading, tie-up, and treadling; the principle is the same and the resulting fabric is the same. In the Powell method, each block is threaded on *adjacent* shafts, resulting in the key shown in figure 6.2. The same blocks are still opposites.

There are subtly different ways of treating pointed drafts, some of which make not-so-subtle differences in the resulting pattern. If the blocks are in broken twill order or the block draft has some other oddity, there are sometimes places in the threading where two successive ends (one pattern, one shadow) are threaded on the same shaft. Or sometimes the color sequence shifts and two pattern or two shadow threads are adjacent to each other.

Tie-up And Treadling Orders

If the threading is Atwater method,
the tie-up is half-and-half (figure 6.3):

6.1

Atwater method

6.2

Powell method

Treadling key

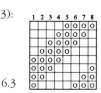

6.3

The treadling pairs are "literal as-drawn-in" (see figure 6.3). Treadling block A (alternating treadles 1 pattern and 5 shadow) weaves blocks A, B, C, and D as weftwise stripes and the other four blocks as warpwise stripes. Treadling block B makes B, C, D, and E weftwise, etc. As in the threading, shadows *follow* patterns when blocks are ascending (A toward H) and *precede* them when blocks are descending (H toward A). Blocks that are warpwise stripes on the face of the fabric are weftwise stripes on the back, and vice versa. The *structure* of the fabric is plain weave except for two-thread skips where certain blocks adjoin. Usually no completely true plain weave is possible.

If the threading is Powell method, the principle is the same. The tie-up and treadling are rearranged so that the pairs of treadles for each block are adjacent (just as the shafts are in the threading). The structure of the fabric is the same (figure 6.4).

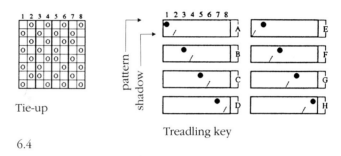

Tie-up

Treadling key

6.4

The keys above show all eight blocks that are possible on eight shafts. In either system it is possible to use only the first four blocks (A, B, C, and D) of threading and treadling for a 4-block profile in 8-shaft shadow weave. In that case, the blocks can be controlled independently and made warpwise or weftwise as desired, since each block is on a separate pair of shafts.

Variations

Shadow weave has many possibilities for variation. Patterns can be altered by adding or removing threads at reversing points in the threading and treadling. A design can be enlarged or reduced by repeating the threading for each block more or fewer times. The underlying block design can be modified by removing or adding entire blocks. It can also be reduced to a less complex 6-shaft (6-block or 3-block) pattern.

Using different treadling orders offers a wide range of possibilities for variation on a shadow weave threading. As long as the pairs of alternating opposite-shed wefts are maintained, any twill sequence can be used as block treadling. Or the treadling can be modified to weave the fabric as "shadow huck", where some parts weave as blocks of warp and weft skips on a pinstriped plain-weave ground. Other variations are possible by exchanging the positions of the pattern and shadow wefts.

Color and yarn choices also make great differences in a shadow weave pattern. The classic form of shadow weave is two contrasting (but not clashing) colors of the same smooth fine thread for pattern and shadow warps and wefts, with sett and beat producing balanced fabric. The greater the contrast in value (darkness and lightness) of pattern and shadow colors, the stronger the resulting pattern. Conversely, the closer the two are in value, the subtler the pattern. If the two are shiny and dull yarns of identical hue, the pattern will be subordinate to color and texture in the fabric. Hue is important too; analogous colors tend to blend and soften the pattern, whereas, depending on their intensities, complementary colors can range from a shimmering to a vibrant to a muddy visual effect.

The two wefts can also be heavy and fine (rather than identical in size); if they also contrast in color or value, the heavy thread will dominate. Different effects result when the wefts are all one color. Most of the samples here are the classic form of shadow weave, dark/light smooth threads in 50/50 weave.

#269 & #270
by Jannie Taylor (Central Coast Weavers)
Straight and point shadow weave, Atwater method.

269

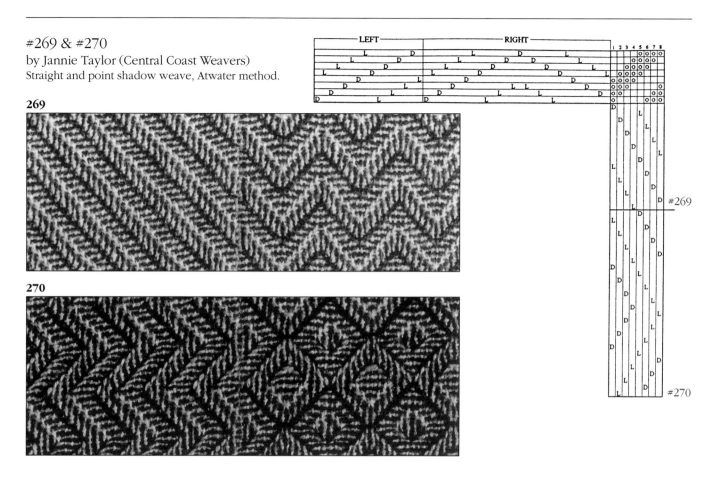

270

#269

#270

#271
by Lorinda Gayle
"Gothic Cross", Powell method.

271

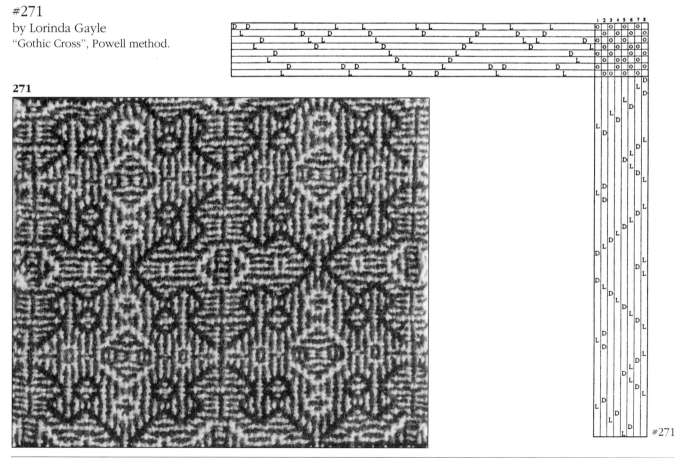

#271

by Dorothy M. Powell
Extended point shadow weave, Powell method.

272

273

274

275

#272

#273

#274

#275

#276–281

by Anita Bell

Triple diamonds, #8–22 from *1000(+) Patterns in 4, 6, and 8 Harness Shadow Weaves* by Marian Powell.

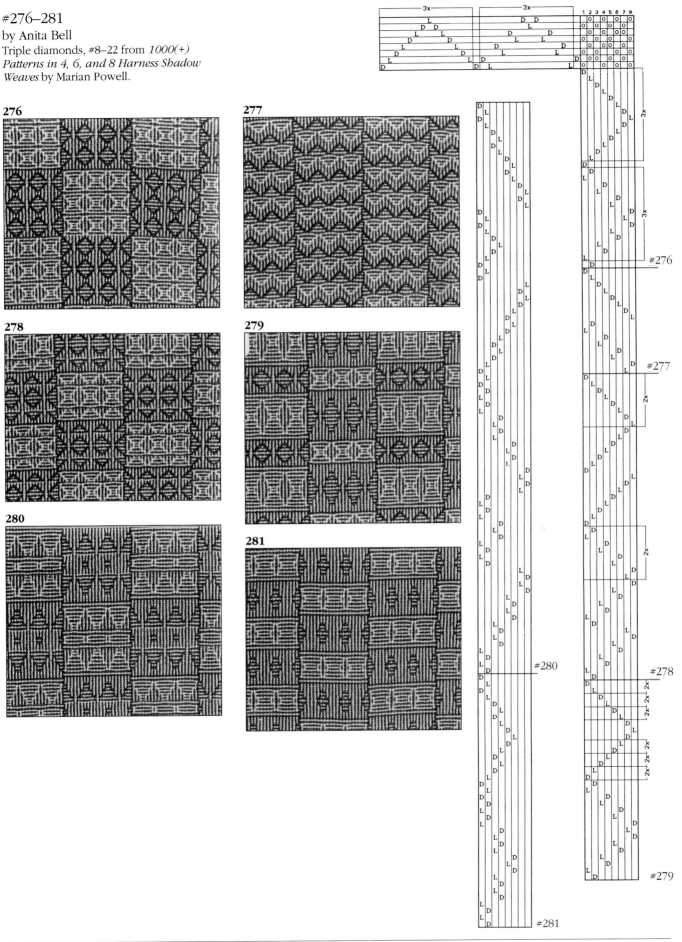

276

277

278

279

280

281

#282–285

by Anita Bell

Broken point blocks, #8–19 from *1000(+) Patterns in 4, 6, and 8 Harness Shadow Weaves* by Marian Powell. *Note:* This threading (and the treadling for #282) has two threads in succession on the same shaft (and treadle) at the center and at the ends of the repeat. #285 is sometimes called "shadow huck".

282

283

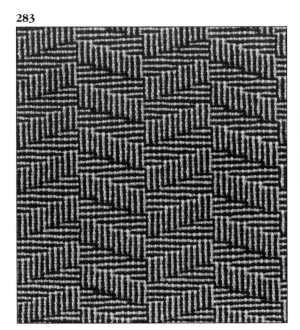

284

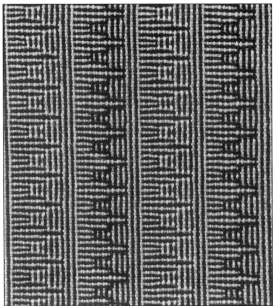

285

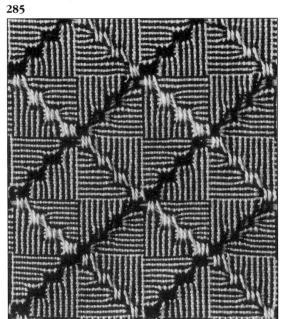

#286–289
by Nettie Conrad
Undulating point twill blocks, Powell method.

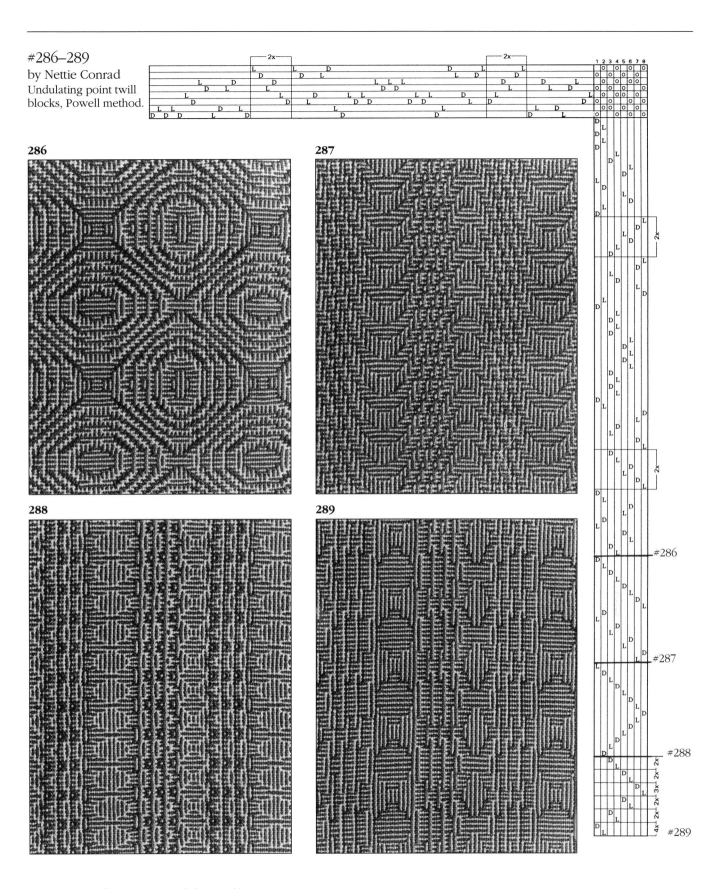

286

287

288

289

Threading profile, showing undulation of blocks

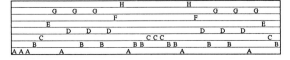

#290–293
by Susan Ehrlich
An adaptation of #8–14 from *1000(+) Patterns in 4, 6, and 8 Harness Shadow Weaves* by Marian Powell.

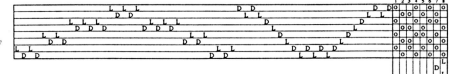

290

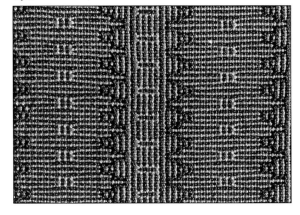

291

293

292

#294–296

by Marla Shelton (North Oakland Handweavers Guild)
"Light and Dark" from *200 Patterns for Multiple-Harness Looms* by Russell E. Groff, page 75, Powell method.
Note: There are two dark threads together at the beginning and end of the repeat partway through the repeat in the threading. This tie-up differs slightly from the standard (with shaft 8 missing from the sixth treadle) creating huck-like skips in the fabric.

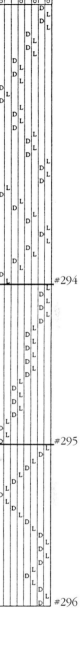

294

295

296

#297–300
by Debbi Cooper (North
Oakland Handweavers
Guild)
"Monday blue" from
200 Patterns for Multiple-Harness Looms by Russell E. Groff, page 120, Powell method.
*#300 is the same treadling order as #297 but with all light weft.

297

299

298

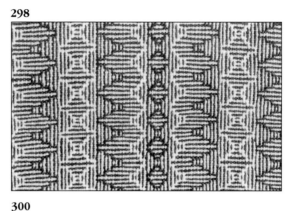

300

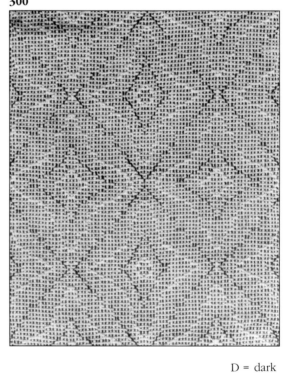

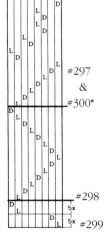

#297
&
#300*

#298

#299

D = dark
L = light

#301–304
by Ardis Dobrovolny

Undulating twill shadow weave designed by Carol Strickler, Atwater method.

301

303

302

304

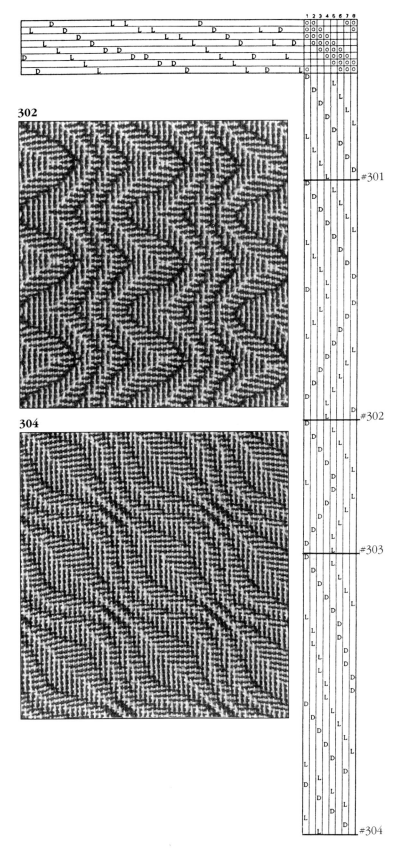

#301

#302

#303

#304

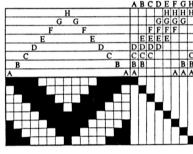

7.1

Chapter 7
WARP REP

Block warp rep is sometimes called *ripsmatta* (which means "rep rug"), *mattor* ("rugs"), or just *rep* ("ribbed"). This warp-faced weave, of Scandinavian origin, may have been the actual inspiration for Atwater's shadow weave. It is usually woven with a warp of alternating dark and light ends of a smooth, relatively thin yarn at a very close sett. The weft is usually alternating picks of heavy and fine yarns; the heavy is almost always at least four times the diameter of the fine, and both are usually straight and smooth. The structure is basically plain weave.

Threading

Warp rep is threaded the same way as shadow weave, with alternating pattern and shadow threads on pairs of shafts, except that the warp is crammed at a warp-faced sett. One slight difference, though—usually in rep the "shadow" thread follows the "pattern" thread and nothing is added or subtracted at the points of a reversing design.

Because warp rep has units of threading that can be used without alteration in a profile draft, the weave is written as a block pattern. Each letter in the profile threading represents a specified number of warp ends and each mark in the profile treadling represents a specified number of picks. (Those numbers differ with the sett and size of the warp and the thickness of the heavy weft.)

On eight shafts, a warp rep design can be an *8-block* pattern, with four blocks automatically the opposites of the other four (A vs E, B vs F, C vs G, and D vs H). In such 8-block designs the blocks always combine or overlap, as shown in figure 7.1.

When ABCD weaves as pattern, EFGH automatically weaves as the opposite color, etc. The threading key for an 8-block 8-shaft rep is (figure 7.2):

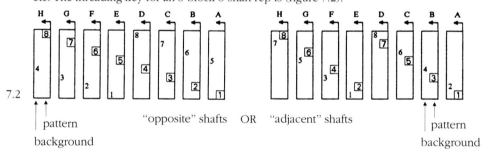

7.2

More often, 8-shaft rep is a *4-block* design (blocks A, B, C, D of the above keys). With a separate pair of shafts used for each block, the blocks can be woven independently or combined at will (see figure 7.3).

A 4-block pattern can also be woven as "all blocks" (pattern color on the face in every block) or "no blocks" (background color on the face in every block).

Tie-up

Each block combination is woven by alternating two treadles that lift opposite shaft combinations. For an 8-block threading, the tie-up (figure 7.4) is:

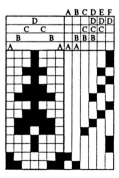

7.3

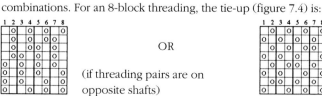

7.4

OR

(if threading pairs are on opposite shafts)

(if threading pairs are o adjacent shafts)

The first pair of treadles weaves blocks ABCD vs EFGH. Treadles 3 and 4 weave BCDE vs AFGH. Treadles 5 and 6 weave CDEF vs ABGH. Treadles 7 and 8 weave DEFG vs ABCH. Each block is plain weave within the block but there are always places at block joints where two warp ends rise or sink together. In 8-block warp rep, there is no pure plain weave.

For the more common 4-block warp rep, the tie-up can be drawn to control the blocks independently (figure 7.5):

opposite   adjacent

7.5

OR

(The left key is used if threading pairs are on opposite shafts; the right key is used if threading pairs are on adjacent shafts.) The treadles that weave "ABCD against none" produce true plain weave. The complete tie-up requires 16 treadles. An alternative is a skeleton tie-up and the use of two treadles at a time (figure 7.6).

Using such a skeleton tie-up makes it harder to keep the treadling error-free, but it *does* make it possible to weave all 16 block combinations with only eight treadles.

Treadling Orders

Block warp rep is usually woven alternating the two treadles of a block using two smooth straight wefts, one at least four times the diameter of the other. If the closely-set warp is kept at a relaxed tension and the wefts are laid firmly straight through each shed, the wefts will remain straight and the warps will do all of the bending in the interlacement. Blocks of pattern appear where one or the other warp color appears on the face of the heavy weft and behind the fine weft. The more extreme the size difference between the wefts, the more clearly the design will show. The opposite color appears on the back of the fabric in each block.

To weave a pattern "square", repeat the alternating heavy/fine weft sequence on the two treadles until the block being woven appears square (as high as it is wide). Where blocks shift in the treadling, some sections of warp go over or under both the final fine weft and the first heavy weft of the next block—not a mistake but inherent in the weave.

Variations

The design scale of a rep pattern can be enlarged or reduced by adding or subtracting pairs of warp ends in the threading blocks and by adding or subtracting pairs of heavy/fine weft shots in the treadling. Entire blocks can also be added or subtracted in the profile. (Most successful block designs are ones in which the blocks are threaded in unbroken twill order.)

Solid stripes can also be added to a design by threading areas of the warp in one color (instead of two) on any block. In the 4-block version, solid horizontal bands can be woven by repeating the "ABCD vs none" treadling unit.

Once the block design is established in the threading, the primary variation is treadling the blocks in a different order or combining them in different ways (easier with a 4-block than with an 8-block design). Different wefts also make a difference. (If a rigid weft, such as wooden doweling, is used for the "heavy thread", better coverage is achieved by substituting doubled half-size warp ends at the same sett. Two smaller threads lie side by side and flatten over the dowel better than a single heavier thread.) For another variation, using two wefts nearly alike in size or using just one weft, a fine one, makes the fabric look like warp-faced shadow weave composed entirely of weftwise pinstripes on both faces with subtle lines at the block shifts.

	1 2 3 4 5 6 7 8

7.6

Skeleton for 4-block "adjacent" tie-up. (There is no skeleton for "opposite".)

A warp rep fabric generally does not "drape"; it bends parallel to the weft but is less flexible in the warp-wise direction. (It's like a rag rug that can be rolled from end to end but does not easily fold selvedge to selvedge.) Because of this characteristic, the weave is most suitable for fabrics that are intended to be flat (such as rugs, placemats, wall hangings, etc.). With stiff or rigid wefts it can be used for rolled or nearly rigid objects (such as roller blinds).

#305–308

by Renée Baderstscher

"What's It Mattor?"

Threading color order key:

A = dark on shaft 1, light on shaft 2
B = dark on shaft 3, light on shaft 4
C = light on shaft 1, dark on shaft 2
D = light on shaft 3, dark on shaft 4
E = dark on shaft 5, light on shaft 6
F = dark on shaft 7, light on shaft 8
G = light on shaft 5, dark on shaft 6
H = light on shaft 7, dark on shaft 8

Note: In these samples, one heavy/fine repeat of treadling squares with each 11-end or 12-end block of the warp.

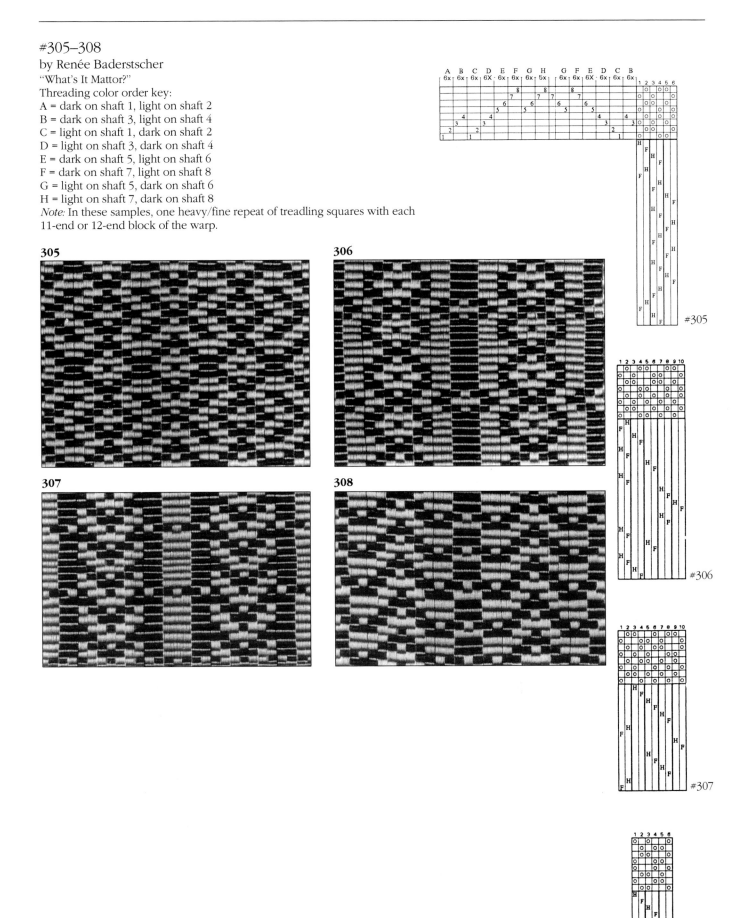

305

306

307

308

#305

#306

#307

#308

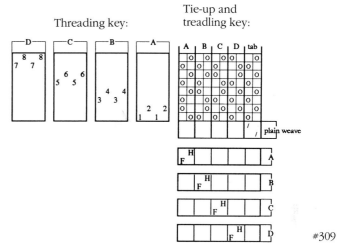

#309

#309
by Esther Reigel

"Moonbeamer's Friendship". *Note:* In the border, odd shafts are light and even shafts are dark. In repeats, colors are reversed. Treadle blocks in as-drawn-in order. In this sample, one repeat of heavy/fine is used to square a 4-end block. The sample is: 1 repeat + end + borders wide, and 1 repeat + end long.

309

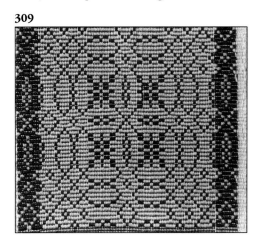

Threading key:

Tie-up and treadling key:

plain weave

#309

#310
by Liv Bugge

"Double Chariot Wheels", adapted from *Of Coverlets* by Sadye Tune Wilson and Doris Finch Kennedy. *Note:* In this sample, one heavy/fine sequence is used to square with each 8-end block (actually 16 ends doubled in the heddles). The sample is 1 repeat + end in width and length—the blocks are treadled in as-drawn-in order.

#310

310

Threading key:

Tie-up and treadling key:

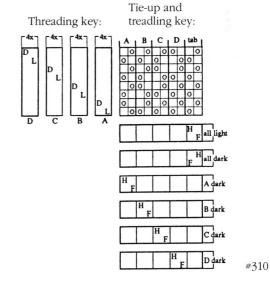

all light

all dark

A dark

B dark

C dark

D dark

#310

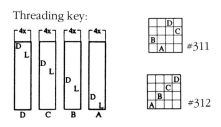

#311 & #312
by Liv Bugge
"Rose" adapted from
Praktisk Vavbok by Nina
Engeström. *Note:* In
these samples, one
heavy/fine sequence is used to square each 8-end block unit (actually 16 ends
doubled in the heddles). Both samples are 1 repeat + end in length and slightly
more than that in width. In #311, the larger parts of the small rose motifs are
repeated three times (instead of two times).

#311
&
#312

311

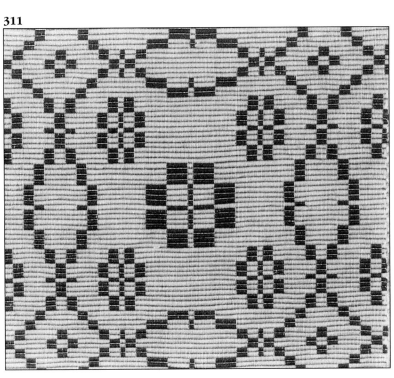

312

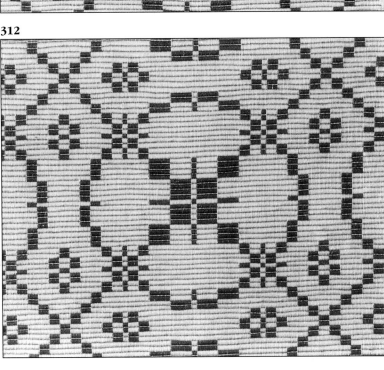

Threading key:

PROFILE TIE-UPS

#311

#312

Tie-up and
treadling key:

TREADLING PROFILE

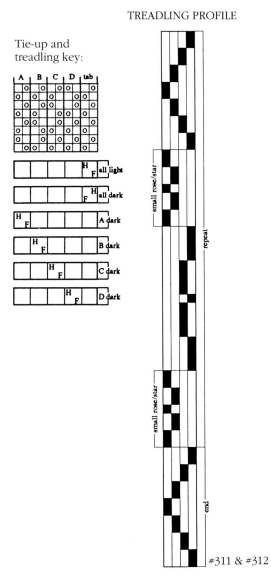

Chapter 8
TWILL GAMPS

A "gamp" or "sample blanket" is a piece of fabric in which warpwise stripes of different threadings or colors are crossed with weftwise bands of the same patterns or colors, usually in the same order. The result is an array of squares which show all the possible combinations of threadings and treadlings, or of colors, used. Note that one of the diagonal rows of squares shows each threading or color woven on itself (figure 8.1).

The samples in this chapter are selected from four twill gamps containing 883 different squares! All of the threadings are twills that have been described in previous chapters (straight, point, extended point, M and W, broken, 2-block, etc.). Each vertical column of samples is one threading. Each horizontal row of samples is one tie-up and treadling crossing all of the threadings. Some of the samples are structural patterns, while others show color-and-weave-effect patterns.

8.1

Threadings

	U	V	W	X	Y	Z
U	UU	VU	WU	XU	YU	ZU
V	UV	VV	WV	XV	YV	ZV
W	UW	VW	WW	XW	YW	ZW
X	UX	VX	WX	XX	YX	ZX
Y	UY	VY	WY	XY	YY	ZY
Z	UZ	VZ	WZ	XZ	YZ	ZZ

Treadlings

#313–317

by the Boulder "Octogang" Weaving
Group: Jean Anstine, Gloria Cyr, Ardis
Dobrovolny, Barbara Meier, and Carol
Strickler.
All tie-up/treadling combinations are used
across all six of these stripes.

313-1 **313-2** **313-3**

314-1 **314-2** **314-3**

315-1 **315-2** **315-3**

316-1 **316-2** **316-3**

317-1 **317-2** **317-3**

Boulder "Octogang" continued.

Boulder "Octogang" continued.

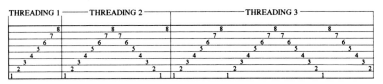

THREADING 1	THREADING 2		THREADING 3		

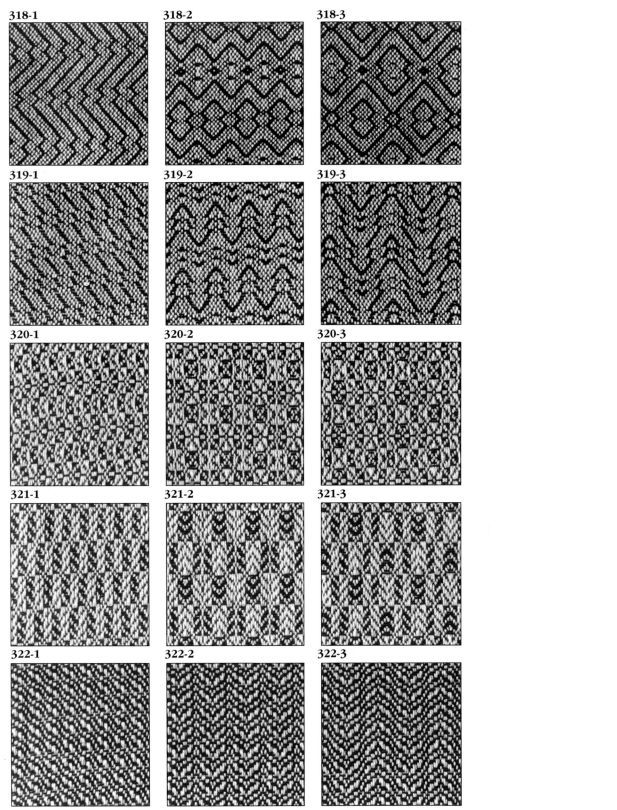

318-1 **318-2** **318-3**

319-1 **319-2** **319-3**

320-1 **320-2** **320-3**

321-1 **321-2** **321-3**

322-1 **322-2** **322-3**

Boulder "Octogang" continued.

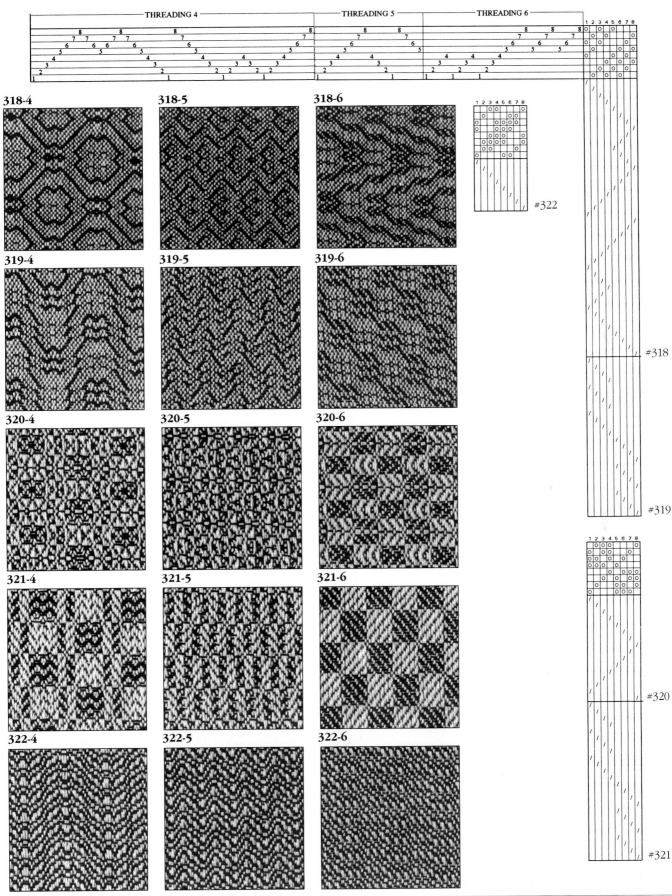

318-4

318-5

318-6

319-4

319-5

319-6

320-4

320-5

320-6

321-4

321-5

321-6

322-4

322-5

322-6

#322

#318

#319

#320

#321

#323–327
by Kim Marie Bunke

All tie-up/treadling combinations are used
across all six of these stripes.

THREADING 1 — THREADING 2 — THREADING 3

323-1   **323-2**   **323-3**

324-1   **324-2**   **324-3**

325-1   **325-2**   **325-3**

326-1   **326-2**   **326-3**

327-1   **327-2**   **327-3**

Kim Marie Bunke continued.

THREADING 4   THREADING 5   THREADING 6

323-4   323-5   323-6

324-4   324-5   324-6

325-4   325-5   325-6

326-4   326-5   326-6

327-4   327-5   327-6

#327

#323

#324

#325

#326

#328–332
Kim Marie Bunke continued.

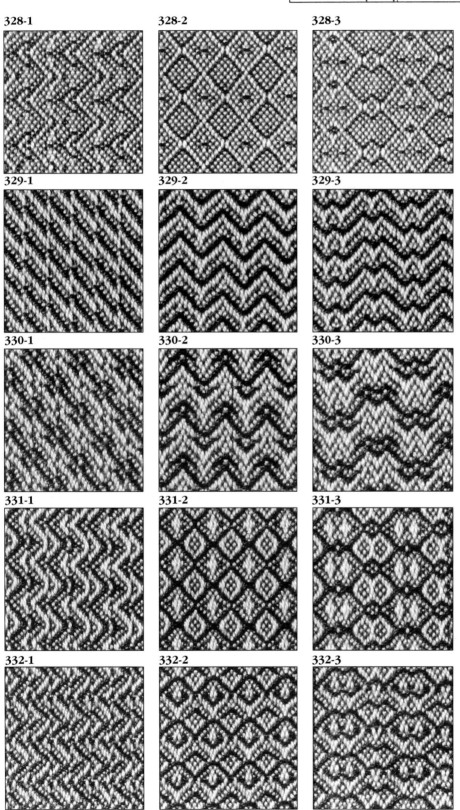

Kim Marie Bunke continued.

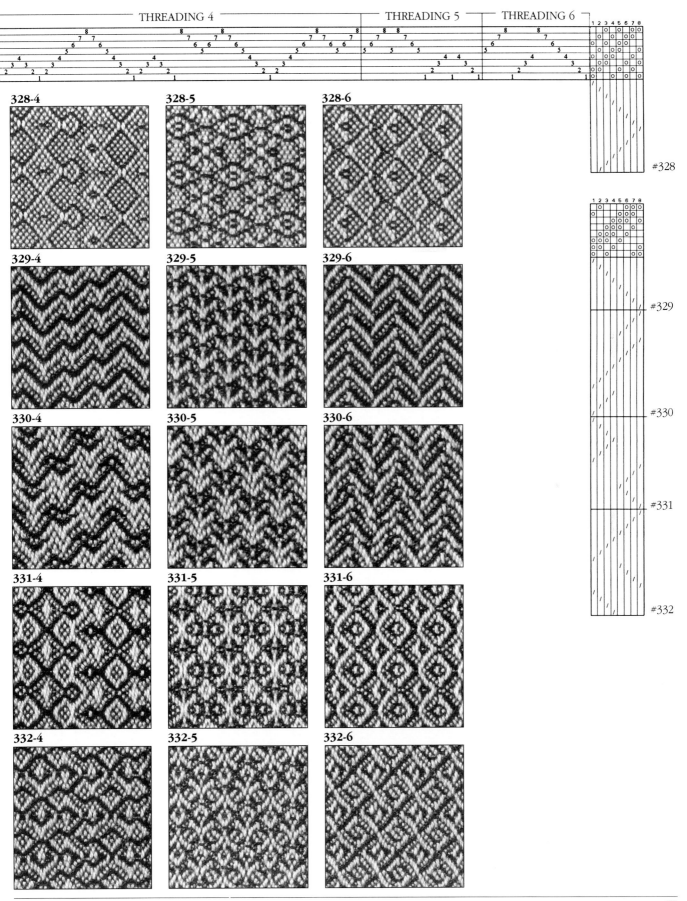

THREADING 4   THREADING 5   THREADING 6

328-4   **328-5**   **328-6**

329-4   **329-5**   **329-6**

330-4   **330-5**   **330-6**

331-4   **331-5**   **331-6**

332-4   **332-5**   **332-6**

#328

#329

#330

#331

#332

#333–337

by Barbara Meier

This color-and-weave-effect sampler was designed by Carol Strickler.

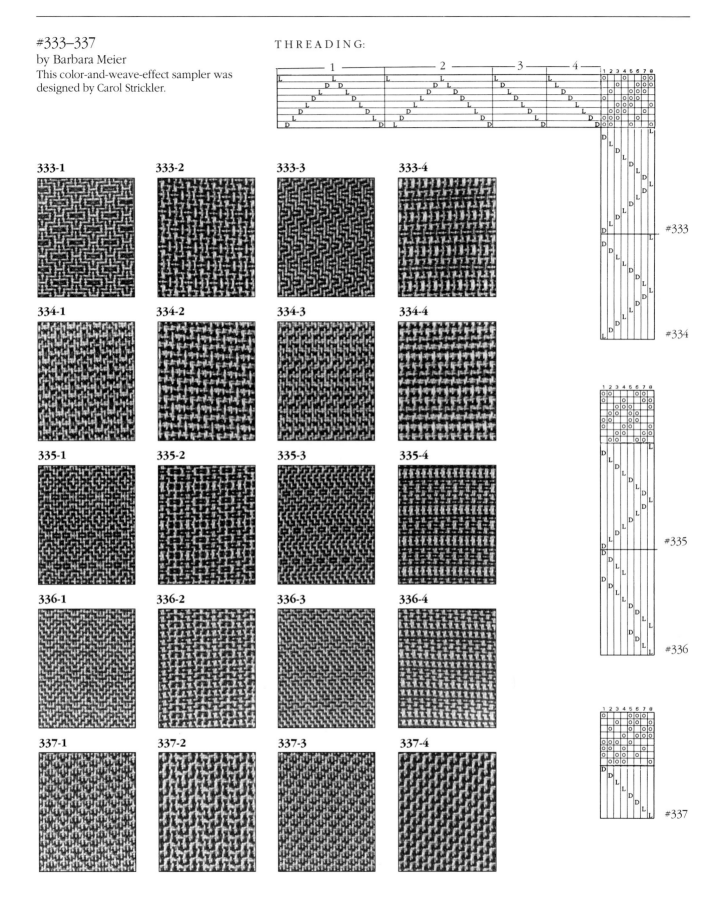

333-1 **333-2** **333-3** **333-4**

334-1 **334-2** **334-3** **334-4**

335-1 **335-2** **335-3** **335-4**

336-1 **336-2** **336-3** **336-4**

337-1 **337-2** **337-3** **337-4**

#338–342
Barbara Meier continued.

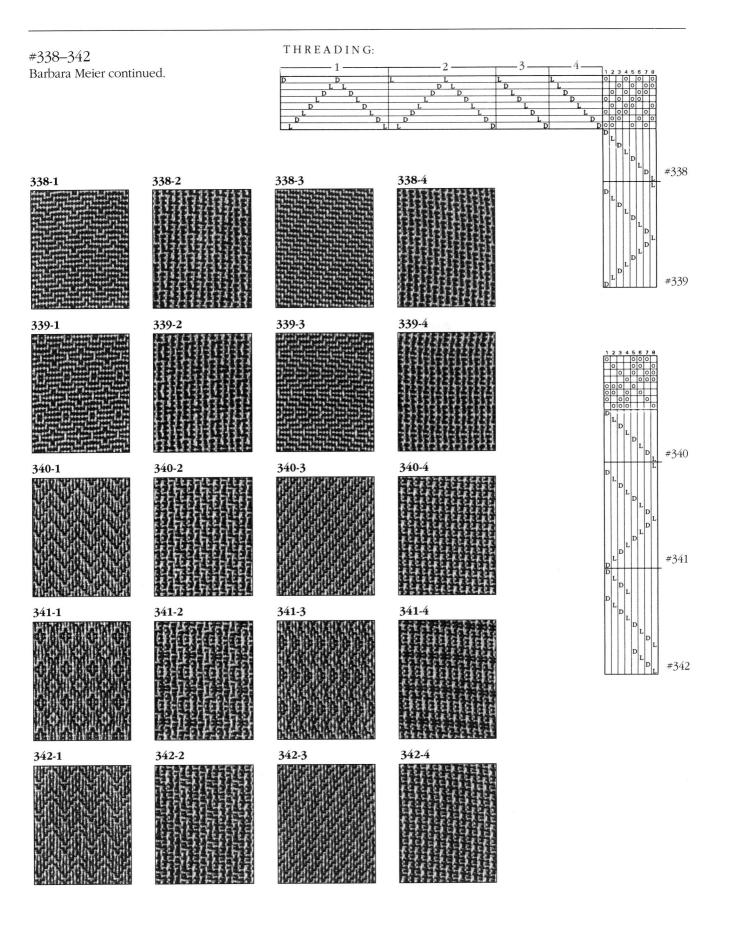

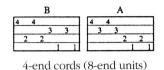

4-end cords (8-end units)

OR

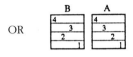

2-end cords (4-end units)

OR

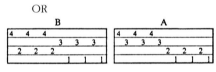

6-end cords (12-end units)

9.1

Chapter 9
M's & O's

The weave known, for some obscure reason, to today's weavers as *M's & O's* has also been called "poor man's huck", "jump twill", and "linen weave". In its original 4-shaft form the weave has two blocks, one based on straight twill and one on broken twill threadings. When one block weaves as plain weave, the other automatically weaves as unbalanced basket weave, forming warpwise cords (groups of warp ends acting as one) where the adjacent ends group together. No true plain weave all the way across the fabric is possible in the 4-shaft M's & O's; the closest structure is an all-over texture or basketweave variant. See the threading keys in figure 9.1.

Threading

There are two different ways that M's & O's is expanded to an 8-shaft weave—4-block and 3-block.

In the *4-block* form, the usual two blocks of 4-shaft M's & O's are threaded on shafts 1-4 and another two blocks are threaded in the same manner on shafts 5-8. Threading keys are shown in figure 9.2.

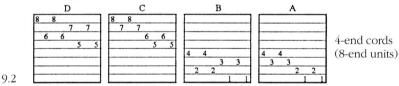

4-end cords
(8-end units)

9.2

Like the 4-shaft version, this weave has no true plain weave all the way across the fabric, but it can be woven with the texture all the way across. Blocks A and B are opposites, as are blocks C and D. That means that when one of the blocks is weaving cords its opposite is automatically weaving true plain weave.

In the *3-block* form of M's & O's, the 4-shaft draft is expanded to eight shafts in a somewhat different manner. The 1's and 2's are retained as a part of each unit, and two other shafts are used for each block of pattern. These units are rearranged slightly so that an odd-shaft/even-shaft alternation is maintained. Areas of true plain weave (1,2) can be threaded between motifs or as side borders, and true plain weave can be woven all the way across the fabric (see keys, figure 9.3).

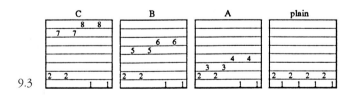

9.3

4-end cords (8-end units)

Most of the samples in this chapter use 4-end cords (8-end units). In one sample, half-units are used (making 4-end cords, 12-end units), and in another sample the threading does reverse like a point twill at the center of the middle block (making one 5-end cord amid the 4-end cords).

Tie-up

For the 4-block "grouped" M's & O's, the tie-up is attained by stacking two 4-shaft tie-ups in all their different combinations (see figure 9.4).

For 3-block M's & O's the tie-up is rearranged. If odd/even alternation has been maintained in the threading, plain weave is 1-3-5-7 vs 2-4-6-8. Within each block, 1-even vs 2-odd weaves cords, while 1-odd vs 2-even weaves plain weave. Because the 1's and 2's are in the same position in the threading of each block to stop the floats, blocks can be woven independently or combined as desired.

Treadling Orders

The usual way of weaving M's & O's is to use one weft (similar in size to the warp) and alternate the two treadles of a block or block combination until the block is square. (This is easier to measure in the plain weave squares than in the corded ones.) If the weft is all one color, the pattern is formed by sections of cords alternating with sections of plain weave. The two samples shown in figures 9.5 and 9.6 illustrate the cord and background textures of 4-block and 3-block M's & O's.

Variations

There are two ways to enlarge or reduce an M's & O's pattern. One is to repeat a block more or fewer times, making more or fewer cords. The other is to add or subtract pairs of threads from each cord. Two-end cords (4-end units) tend to make the pattern very subtle because they don't differ very much from the plain weave. Cords larger than 6 ends (12-end units) tend to distort the fabric because their intersecting ratio does differ so much from plain weave. The pattern in M's & O's is primarily textural, which means that the weave is usually unsuitable for elaborate designs.

Color effects can be introduced in warp and weft. For example, using a solid color warp and two alternating colors in the weft produces columns of color in the corded area and a salt-and-pepper effect in the plain weave. Heavier weft makes the plain blocks warp-dominant and the corded blocks balanced or weft-dominant. Finer weft and wider sett make the cords weft-faced and the plain blocks weft-dominant.

Other twill-type tie-ups and treadlings can sometimes be used for interesting results. The weave can also be treadled as a mock honeycomb, with heavy wefts that undulate around the plain blocks.

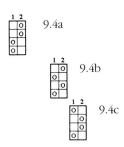

9.4 In each 4-shaft section, (a) weaves the "straight" block (A or C) as cords and the "broken" block (B or D) as plain weave, (b) weaves the "straight" block (A or C) as plain weave and the "broken" block (B or D) as cords, and (c) weaves both blocks as texture.

9.5. 4-block M's & O's showing textured and plain background blocks (by Virginia Kellogg).

9.6. 3-block M's & O's showing plain-weave background (by Susan A. Millikan).

9.5

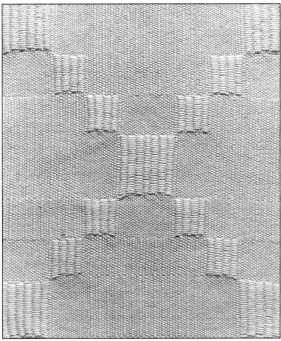

9.6

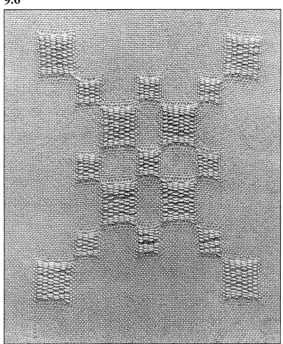

#343–345
by Nancy Mitchell

M's & O's adapted from "Green Fire", page 127, in *200 Patterns for Multiple-Harness Looms: 5 to 12 Harness Patterns for Handweavers* by Russell E. Groff. *Note:* This tie-up varies slightly from the conventional. The twill treadlings differ from the usual M's & O's treadlings.

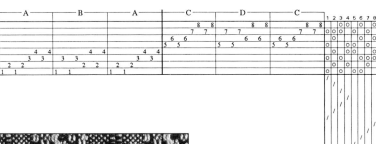

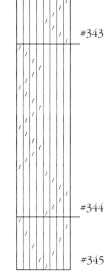

343

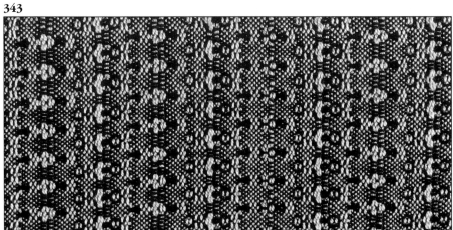

344

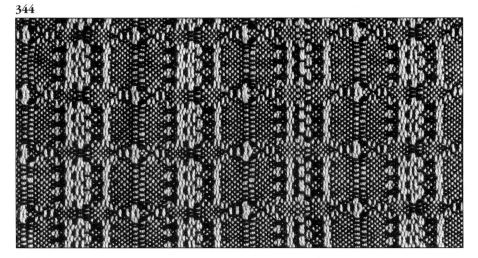

345

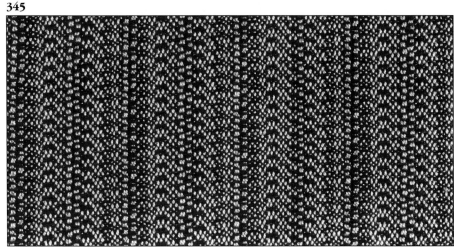

#346–348
by Ruth Mitchell

M's & O's from *More Than Four* by Mary Elizabeth Laughlin. Use profile draft and keys.

*In this treadling, both the C and the AB blocks are woven with alternating dark and light wefts.

+This is a honeycomb treadling using heavy outline weft and fine cell weft. The cells are blocks C and AB.

Threading key:

Tie-up and treadling key for #346 & #347.

#346

#347*

#348+

346

347

348

#349

by Julia Benson

Note: Threading *does* reverse at points (center of block A and center of block D). In the tie-up, the two right hand treadles weave pseudo-tabby. This sample has light weft and light warp.

349

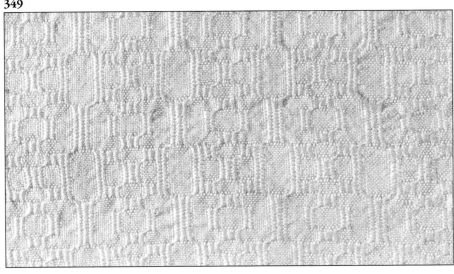

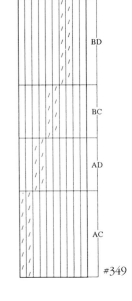

AD

BC

BD

BC

AD

AC

#349

#350

by Ulla Bruhns

Motifs on 3-block M's & O's. Use profile draft and keys.

350

Threading key:

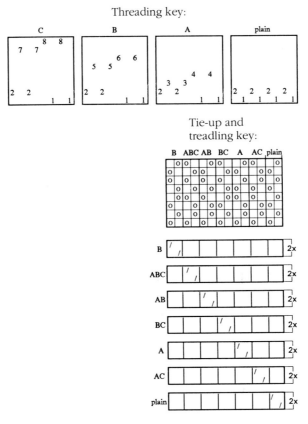

C

B

A

plain

Tie-up and treadling key:

| B | ABC | AB | BC | A | AC | plain |

B — 2x
ABC — 2x
AB — 2x
BC — 2x
A — 2x
AC — 2x
plain — 2x

PROFILE DRAFT

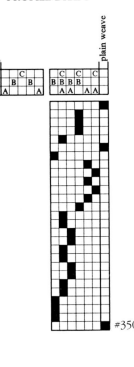

plain weave   plain weave

	C			C	C	C
	B	B		B	B	B	B
A		A		A	A	A	A

#350

#351 & #352
by Ulla Bruhns
Use profile draft and keys.

Threading key:

Tie-up and treadling key:

PROFILE DRAFT

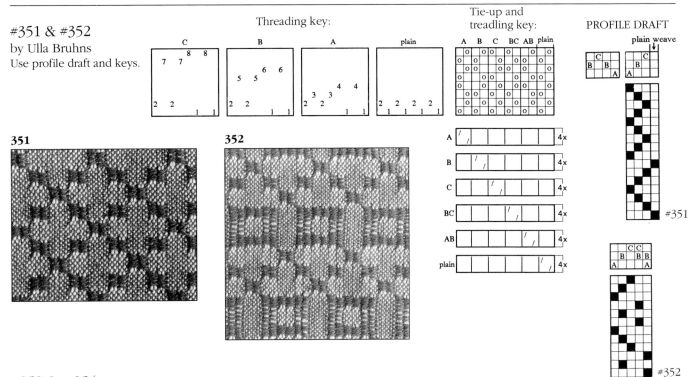

351

352

#353 & # 354
by Ulla Bruhns

M's & O's. Use profile draft and keys. Threading key is the same as that for samples #351 & #352.
*This tie-up and treadling weaves blocks like turned huck.

PROFILE DRAFT

353

Tie-up and treadling key

Tie-up and treadling key

354

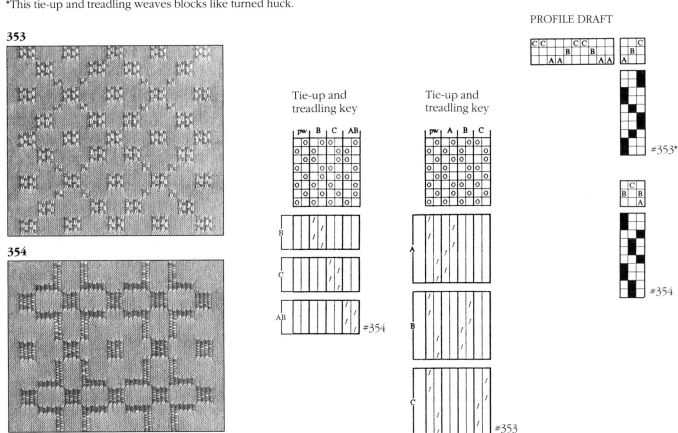

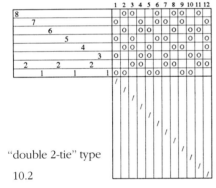

twill type
10.1

Chapter 10
PLAITED TWILLS

A *plaited twill* (or "braided twill") is a weave in which opposing diagonal lines seem to interlace or braid with each other. (Some crepes are actually very-small-scale plaited twills.)

Threading, Tie-up, and Treadling

Two different threading systems can produce a plaited twill. One is straight and broken twill (figure 10.1) and the other is based on a threading from the "double 2-tie" system (figure 10.2).

Variations

The threading of the twill type can be extended or reduced by adding or subtracting pairs of ends. In the "double 2-tie" type, the threading can be extended to more shafts or reduced (not very successfully) to fewer. Many tie-up and treadling variations are possible (see the samples in this chapter for suggestions).

"double 2-tie" type
10.2

#355 & #356

by Sondra Rose

A plaited twill from *A Handbook of Weaves* by G.H. Oelsner.

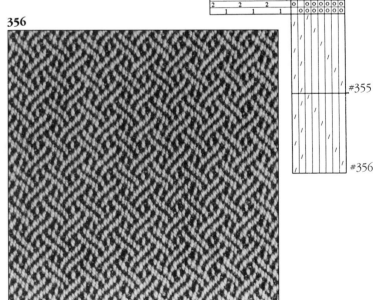

355

356

#357–360

by Sondra Rose

Plaited twills from *A Handbook of Weaves* by G. H. Oelsner. *Note:* #357 and #358 are very tiny plaited twills. They are actually crepes on a straight twill threading. For similar crepes see the Straight Twill chapter.

*6-shaft plaited twill.

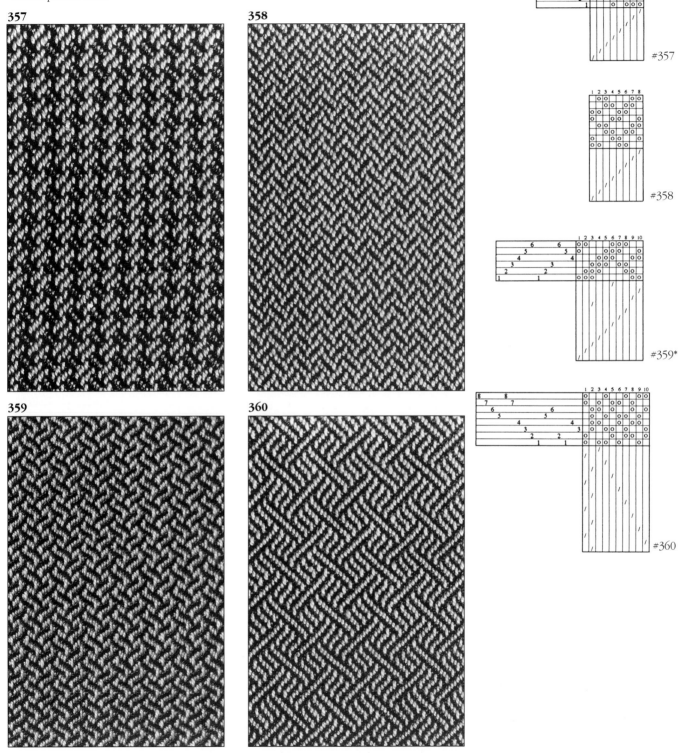

357

358

359

360

#361–368

by Doramay Keasbey

Note: Some of these plaited twills use more than 10 treadles and may require a skeleton tie-up (see the introduction for how to do this). These samples are light weft on dark warp.
*Because this treadling involves some doubled picks, floating selvedges are necessary.

361

362

363

364

365

366

367

368

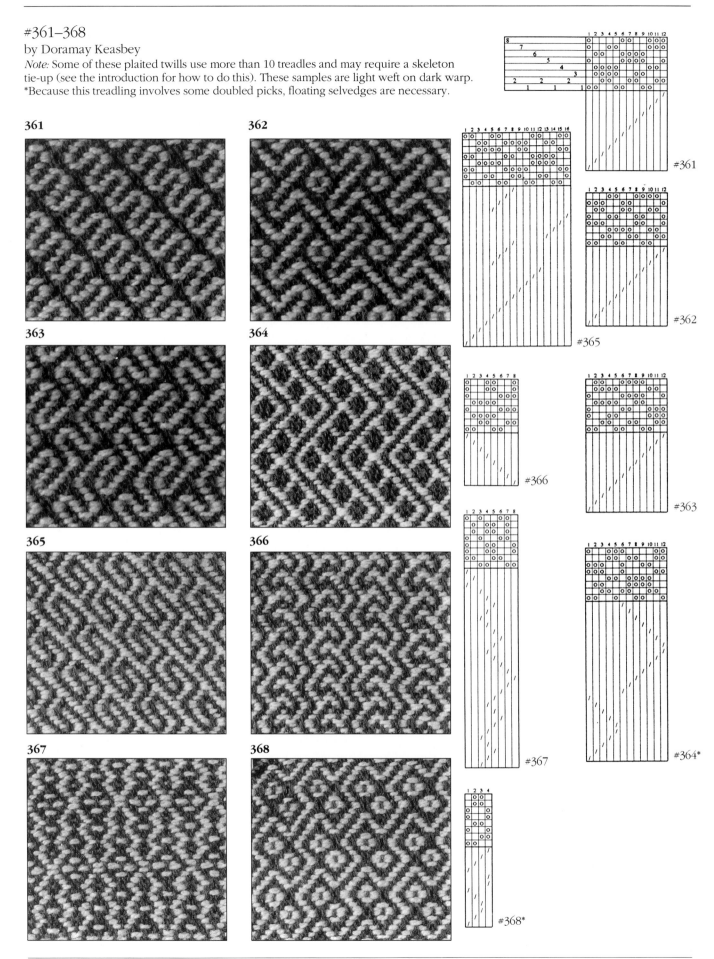

#369–371
by Barbara McClanathan

These plaited twills are from *Double Two-tie Unit Weaves* by Clotilde Barrett and Eunice Smith. *Note:* This sampler has a light weft on a dark warp.

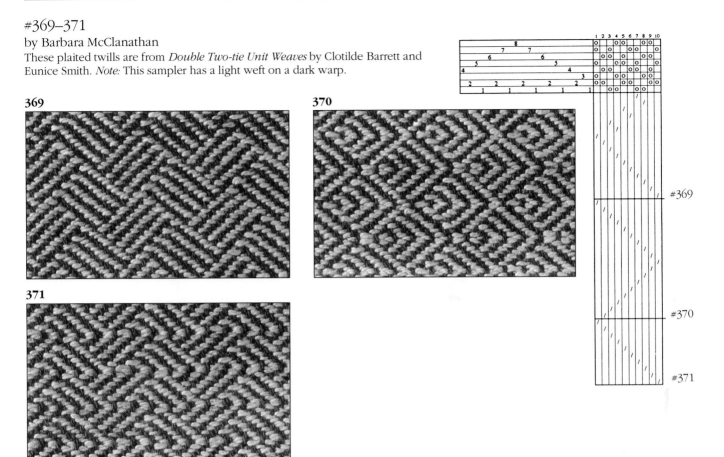

369

370

371

#372
by Mary Anderson

Note: Use the skeleton tie-up provided if you do not have enough treadles on your loom.

372

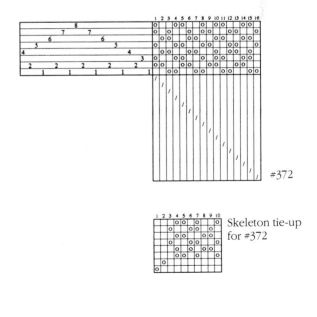

Skeleton tie-up for #372

#373–376
by Catherine Devine
Plaited twills.

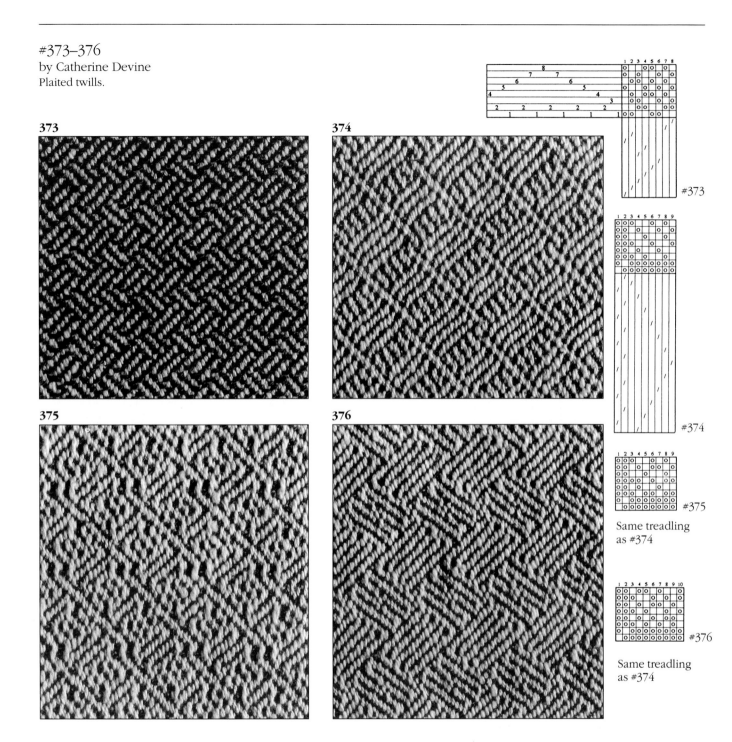

373

374

375

Same treadling
as #374

376

Same treadling
as #374

#373

#374

#377–380
by Marjorie Sweigart
Plaited twills.

377

378

379

380

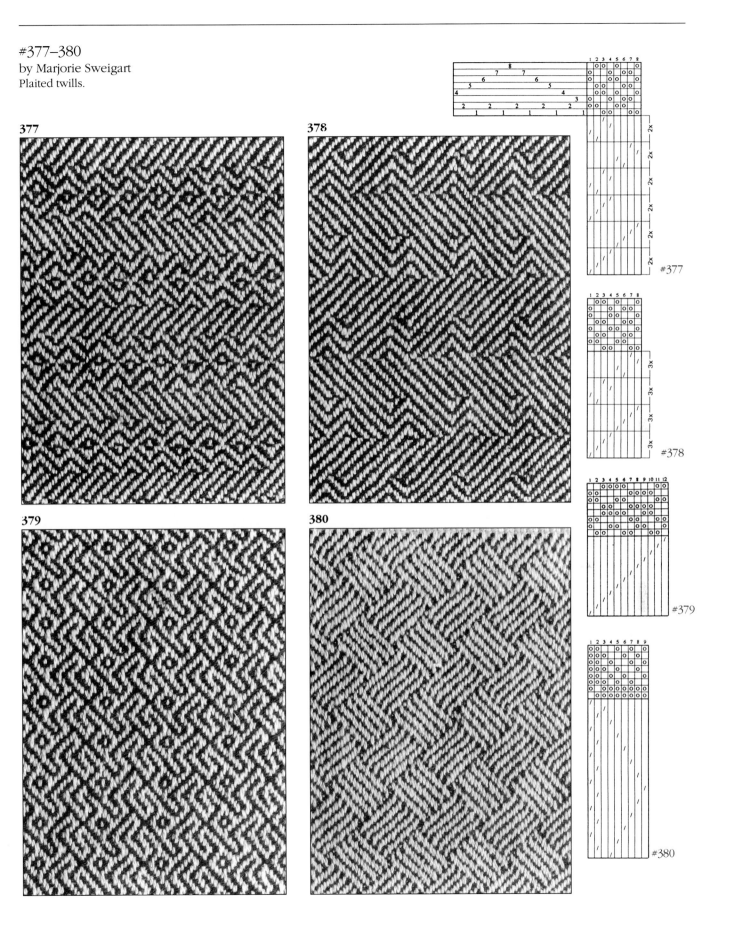

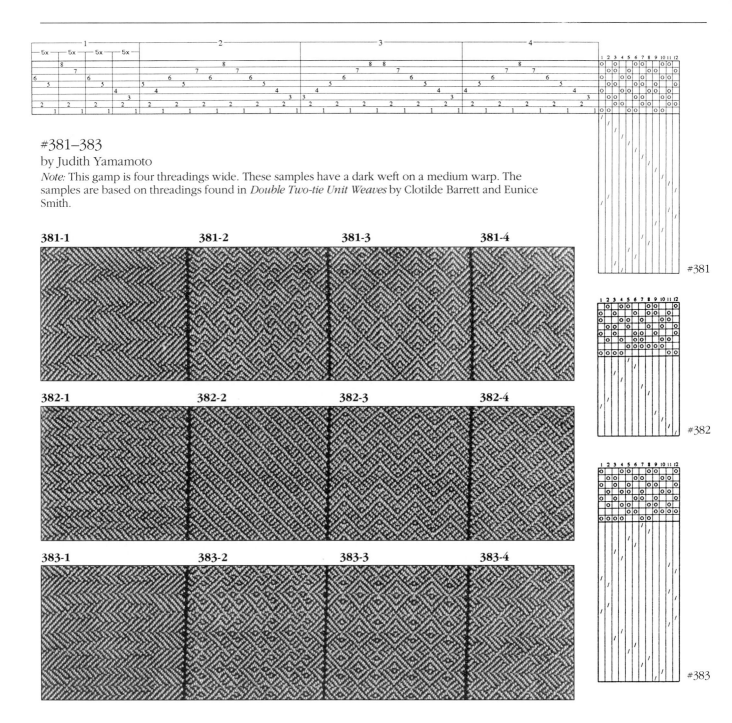

#381–383
by Judith Yamamoto

Note: This gamp is four threadings wide. These samples have a dark weft on a medium warp. The samples are based on threadings found in *Double Two-tie Unit Weaves* by Clotilde Barrett and Eunice Smith.

#384–387

by Judith Yamamoto (continued)

The threadings are the same as those in #381–383.

*These samples have light weft on medium warp.

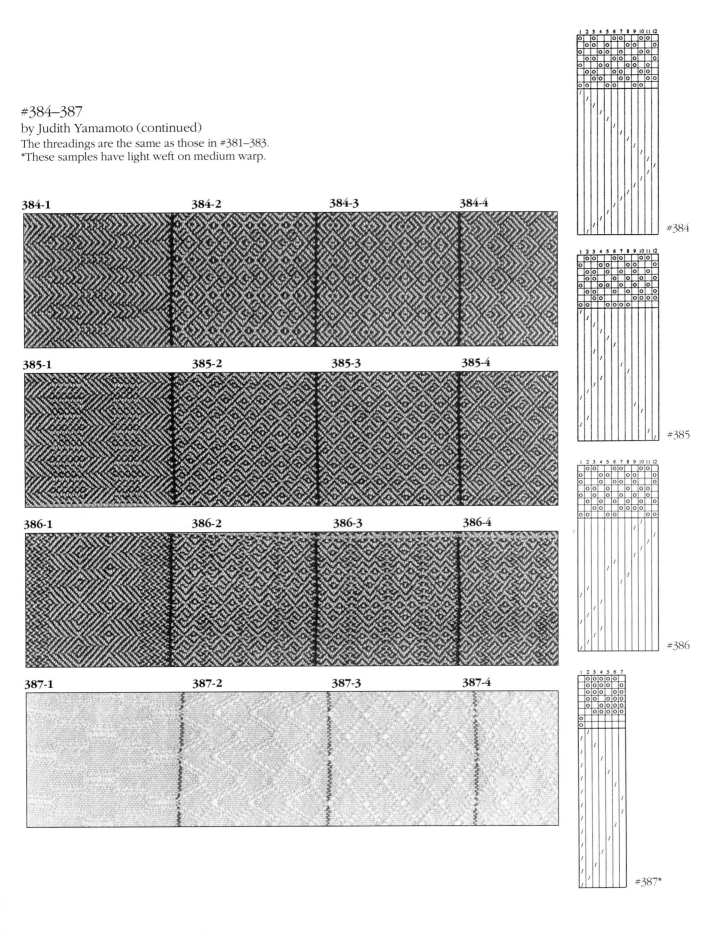

384-1 384-2 384-3 384-4

385-1 385-2 385-3 385-4

386-1 386-2 386-3 386-4

387-1 387-2 387-3 387-4

#384

#385

#386

#387*

Chapter 11
"AS IF'S"

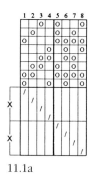

11.1a

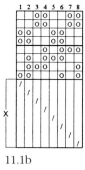

11.1b

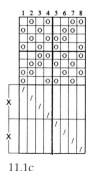

11.1c

"As if's" is a coined term for fabrics in which one threading is woven as if it were something else, with the conversion taking place in the tie-up and treadling. All of the samples in this chapter were woven on twill threadings—straight, point, and 2-block.

There are two different approaches represented in this chapter. One is to divide the tie-up in half (either vertically or horizontally) and tie and treadle each half as if it were a different weave. This is called "ganging" or "grouping" (see figure 11.1).

In figure 11.1a, half of the treadles treat whatever threading is being used as a 2/3/1/2 twill, and the other half treat the entire threading as a crepe. The two weaves alternate as horizontal bands in the fabric if treadled as shown.

In figure 11.1b, half of the shafts weave double-faced twill (alternately 1/3 and 3/1 twill), while the other half weave 2/2 basket weave. The two alternate as vertical stripes in the fabric if treadled as shown.

The tie-up can also be quartered and the quarters exchanged. In figure 11.1c, one set of four treadles weaves half of the shafts as 2/2 twill and the other half as plain weave. The other set of treadles reverses the relationship.

The pattern resulting from any of these tie-up/treadling combinations depends somewhat on which twill is threaded.

The other approach to "as if's" conversion is to treat the *threading* as if it were something else. In mathematics this is called "mapping". In a straight twill threading there are eight threads that can be used individually or in any combination. Therefore an 8-shaft straight twill threading can be tied up and treadled to weave as if it were any 4-shaft threading that has an 8-thread repeat. Examples are shown in figure 11.2.

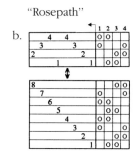

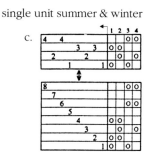

11.2

Likewise, an 8-shaft point twill threading can be woven as if it were any 4-shaft threading with a 14-end symmetrical pointed motif that reverses on the eighth thread. Examples are shown in figure 11.3.

extended point twill   a small overshot

11.3

#388–392

by Helen Bobisud

Note: Some of these patterns are strikingly different on the back.

*This sample has a light weft on a light warp. This tie-up and treadling weave the point twill twill threading as if it were 2-shaft plain weave framing 6-shaft waffle weave.

+This tie-up and treadling weave stripes of 2/2 and 1/3 twill on one set of four shafts and plain weave on the other set.

#This tie-up weaves 1/3 twill on one set of shafts while it weaves plain weave on the others. The sets shift.

~This tie-up combines huck on some shafts with plain weave on the others.

^This tie-up combines a 2/2 point twill on shafts 3-6 with huck on shafts 1-2 and 7-8.

388

389

390

391

392

#393–400
by Susan and Martin Hall

Note: These samples are tied up to weave a variety of dice, crepe, and basketweaves on a 2-block twill threading.

393

394

395

396

397

398

399

400

#401–410

by Judie Eatough; designed by Carol Strickler

Note: The left column has the two-block threading; the right column has the point threading.

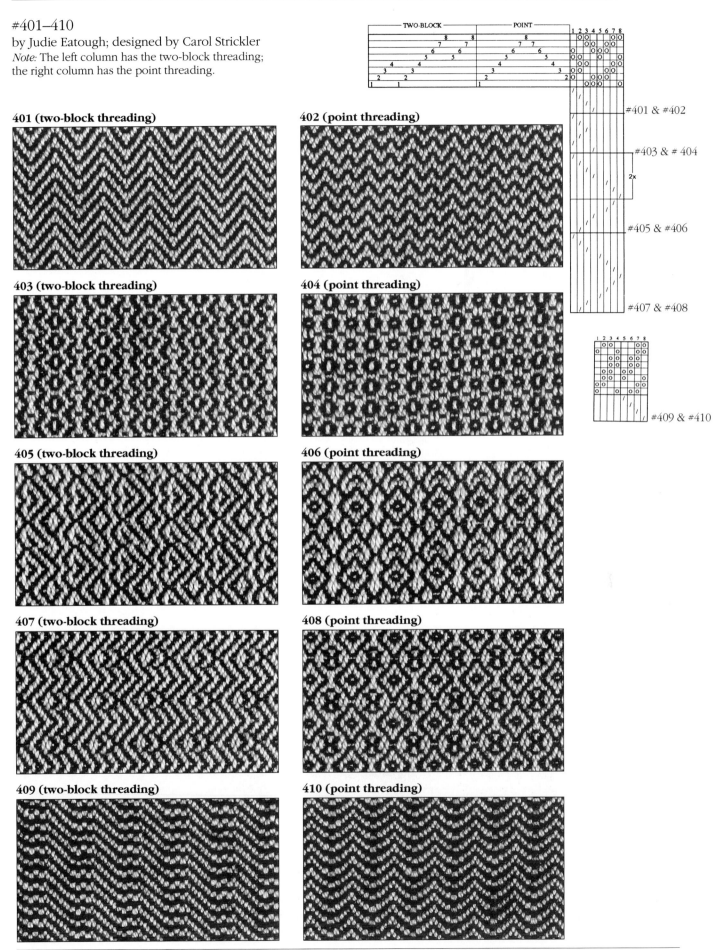

401 (two-block threading)

402 (point threading)

403 (two-block threading)

404 (point threading)

405 (two-block threading)

406 (point threading)

407 (two-block threading)

408 (point threading)

409 (two-block threading)

410 (point threading)

Chapter 12
REPEAT TWILL AND OVERSHOT

A *repeat twill* (also called "progressing twill") is one in which each pair of adjacent ends of an unbroken twill is repeated two or more times before progressing to the next shaft.

The *overshot* weave (also called "colonial overshot") is one of the weaves Tidball calls "Twill Derivatives". In its classic form it is a repeat twill with a plain-weave ground and supplementary-weft pattern. Each pair of shafts is repeated in alternation in the threading to make blocks of pattern-weft floats that vary in size. Whereas an ordinary small repeat twill threading is usually woven as a twill (with single weft and sequential treadling), overshot is threaded and treadled with some blocks larger than others and is traditionally woven with the pattern weft repeating in the same shed, each pick followed by a tabby. Some combinations of small repeat twill threading with sections of straight or point twill are what Tidball calls "Hybrid (Twill-Overshot) System".

Threading

In a typical small repeat twill, each pair is repeated only two or three times and all blocks are nearly alike in size. Each 2-shaft block is circled in the following draft (figure 12.1); this shows how each shares a thread with its neighbor on each side. When the twill is a point, there is an odd number of threads in the blocks at reversing points. In the point draft below, one pivotal block (1-2) has been increased to five ends and the other (8-1) has been reduced to three ends.

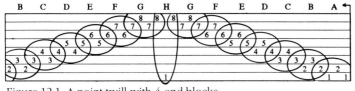

Figure 12.1. A point twill with 4-end blocks.

In its 4-shaft form, overshot has four blocks of pattern. The A block is threaded alternately on shafts 1 and 2, B on 2 and 3, C on 3 and 4, and D on 1 and 4. If the "standard" 2/2 twill tie-up is used with two tabby treadles and the blocks follow one another in unbroken order in the threading, each pattern block weaves as weft floats over and under a plain-weave ground and is flanked on both sides by "halftone" blocks in which the pattern weft weaves in one of the plain-weave sheds.

There are three major different ways a 4-shaft overshot pattern can be enlarged to 8 shafts (or a new 8-shaft pattern can be designed):*grouped, 4-block,* and *8-block* overshots.

There are two forms of 8-shaft *grouped* overshot. In one, an entire *repeat* of a 4-shaft pattern is threaded on shafts 1-4 and another *repeat* of the same pattern follows it on shafts 5-8 (possibly inverted to maintain the odd/even alternation). In the other form, a *motif* or *part of a repeat* is drafted on 1-4 and the other *part* after it on 5-8.

Both of these forms can be tied up to weave the pattern as though it were the original 4-shaft design, but there are many ways that the 8-shaft version can also be woven differently because the repeats or motifs are independent. For example, one group can be treadled rose-fashion at the same time the other group is weaving star-fashion. Or one group can use a 3/1 tie-up while the other uses 1/3 (just as in block twill). The samplers in this book include two in which the *repeats* are grouped (#439–442 and #449–452) and one in which the *motifs* are grouped (#443–448).

A second way of threading overshot on eight shafts is to use a *4-block* design, threading each block on an independent pair of shafts (A on 1,2; B on 3,4; C on 5,6; D on 7,8). These patterns, too, can be tied up to weave identically to a 4-shaft version but have far more potential than that. Different tie-ups can change the position of the halftone blocks, or produce halftones in all of the background blocks, or produce no halftones at all. Adjacent blocks can weave pattern simultaneously (making longer weft skips). "Opposite" blocks can weave pattern simultaneously, a variation impossible in the 4-shaft version.

In *8-block* overshot each block is threaded on a pair of adjacent shafts, with the blocks overlapping the way they do in 4-shaft overshot. Block A is 1,2; B is 2,3; C is 3,4; D is 4,5; E is 5,6; F is 6,7; G is 7,8; and H is 1,8. This means that 8-block 8-shaft overshot has some of the same characteristics and limitations as the 4-block 4-shaft weave. But even in this weave, some of the blocks can be combined. Halftones (in blocks other than those adjacent to the pattern block) can be controlled. "Opposite" blocks can be woven simultaneously.

The samplers in this book include two in which one traditional 4-shaft pattern has been expanded to both the 4-block and the 8-block forms of 8-shaft overshot (samples #479 & 480 and #481 & 482).

Tie-up

If the odd/even alternation has been maintained in the threading, tabbies are 1-3-5-7 vs 2-4-6-8.

The tie-up of an 8-shaft repeat twill or overshot depends on which form is threaded and what result is planned. For a *grouped* threading, divide the tie-up into the groups of shafts and tie each group to do what is desired (figure 12.2).

In figure 12.2a, one group will weave rose-fashion when the other is weaving star-fashion. In figure 12.2b, the group on the upper shafts will weave as warpwise columns regardless of the treadling used for the lower group.

For a *4-block* threading, tie to weave the four blocks as pattern and then tie the rest of the blocks to weave halftones (by raising one of the block's two shafts) or undershots (by lifting both of the block's shafts). See the examples in figure 12.3.

For an *8-block* threading, tie to weave the eight blocks as pattern and then tie the rest of the blocks to weave halftones or undershots (figure 12.4).

In any of the forms, raising or lowering three adjacent shafts will make two adjacent blocks weave together as longer floats.

Treadling Order

The two primary ways of treadling a repeat twill or overshot threading are as a twill (without tabby) and as an overshot (repeated pattern shots, with tabby). The twill treadling sequence can be straight, point, extended point, M & W, broken, undulating, or repeat twill. When an overshot (supplementary-weft) treadling is used, one shuttle carries the pattern weft and another the tabby weft. In this form, the blocks of threading on pairs of shafts are treated like blocks—pattern sheds that are repeated as desired in the treadling, with a tabby shot following each pattern pick.

Variations

To enlarge a repeat twill or an overshot, add pairs of threads on the two shafts of any block (recognizing that more threads in a block mean longer weft skips), or add blocks. If a large block seems to be getting too long, add threads on a different shaft at regular intervals to act as tie-downs.

To reduce an overshot, subtract pairs of threads from the desired blocks. To miniaturize an overshot, reduce all small blocks to two or three threads and all large blocks to four or five threads.

There are thousands of existing 4-shaft repeat twill and overshot patterns that can be expanded to 8-shaft designs in one of the three ways described. Or new patterns can be designed. There are hundreds of ways to vary the threading, tie-up, and treadling of any of them. Some possibilities are listed at right. Many of these produce structures that are different from the usual single warp and compound weft structure of classic overshot. Together with the changes that can be made in yarns and color effects there are many more possibilities than can be covered in such a book as this. For more detail about overshot variations, consult textbooks such as Black, Davison, Tidball, etc. or one of the books or monographs specifically about overshot.

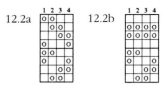

12.2 Example tie-ups for grouped overshot.

12.3 Example tie-ups for 4-block overshot.

12.4 Example tie-up for 8-block overshot.

Repeat twill and overshot variations
Threading changes:
—shortened or lengthened blocks
—miniaturizing or enlarging pattern
—drafting on opposite blocks
—rearranging blocks or multi-block motifs
—drafting parts upsidedown or alternating as star/rose

Tie-up changes:
—halftones shifted or eliminated
—two or more blocks woven together
—a twill formula tie-up used

Treadling variations:
—star-fashion (ADI)
—rose-fashion
—changed block order and height
—twill (with or without tabby)
—monk's belt or columns
—swapping pattern and tabby wefts
—lace-fashion
—honeycomb
—swivel
—weft-faced, such as flamepoint
—pattern and tabby woven with one shuttle

#411–414
by Andrea L.B. Anderson
Repeat twill.

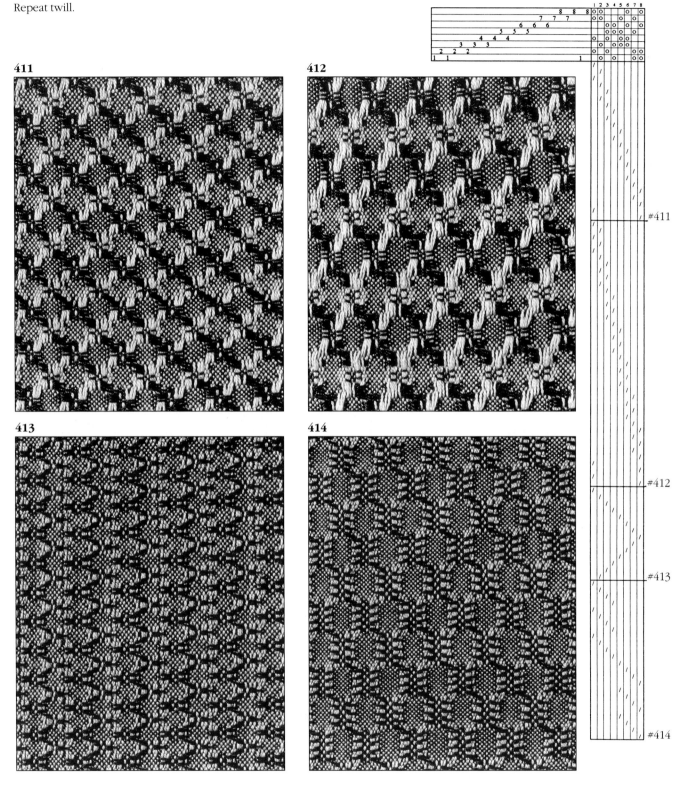

411

412

413

414

#415–422

by Ardis Dobrovolny

Eight-block point repeat twill, designed by Carol Strickler.

415

416

417

418

419

420

421

422

#423–425

by Ardis Dobrovolny

Undulating repeat twill, designed by Carol Strickler. *Note:* Because of the 2-thread block on shafts 4-5, there appears to be a break warpwise in the fabric.

423

424

425 face

425 back

#426–429
by Betty Hancock Smith
A combination twill.

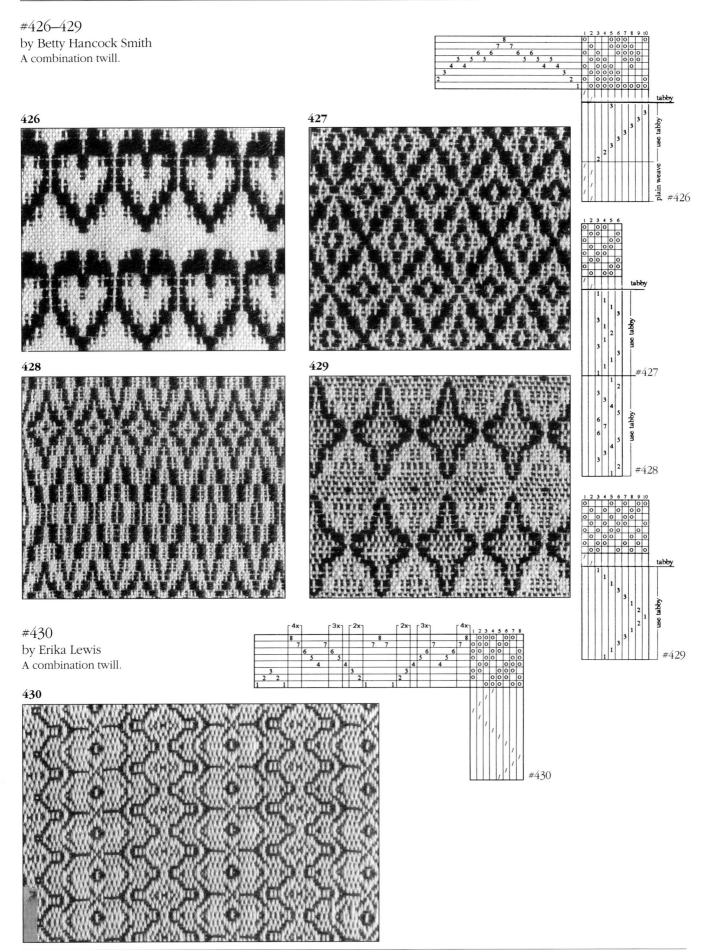

426

427

428

429

#430
by Erika Lewis
A combination twill.

430

#431–434

by Eileen Shannon
"Quilt Fun", a
combination twill.
Note: The designer
of these samples
suggests that
experimentation is easier with a skeleton tie-up that allows using the tie-downs independently. For more on
skeleton tie-ups, see the Introduction.

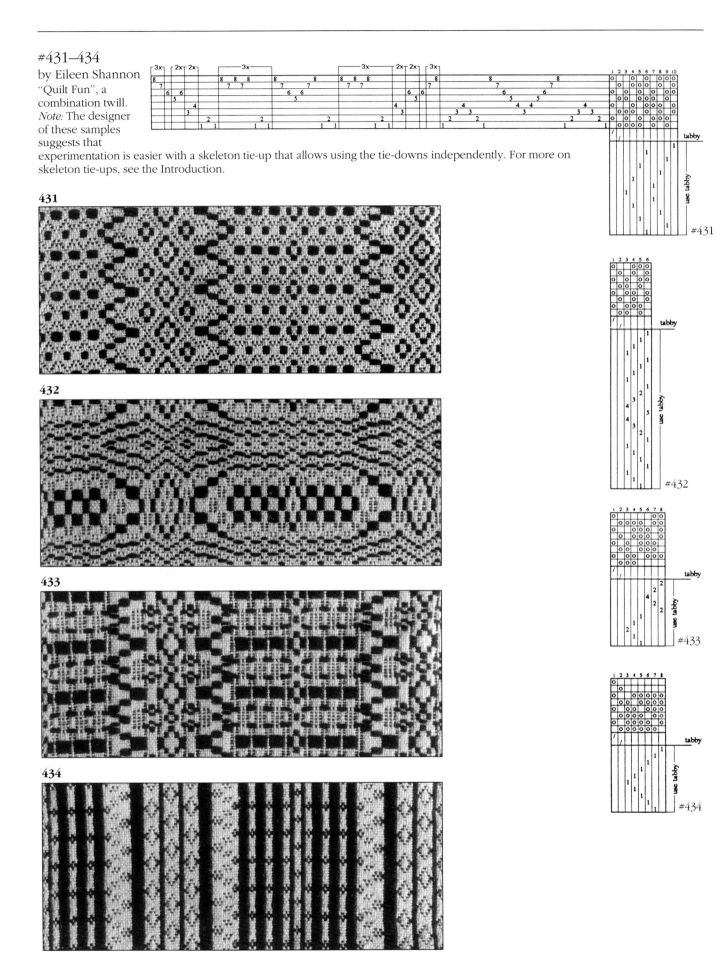

431

432

433

434

#435–438
by Eileen Shannon
"Radiating diamonds", a combination twill.

Note: Since weaving these fabrics face-up involves lifting more than half of the shafts, you may want to use the tie-up as a sinking shed tie-up and weave the fabric face down for easier lifting.

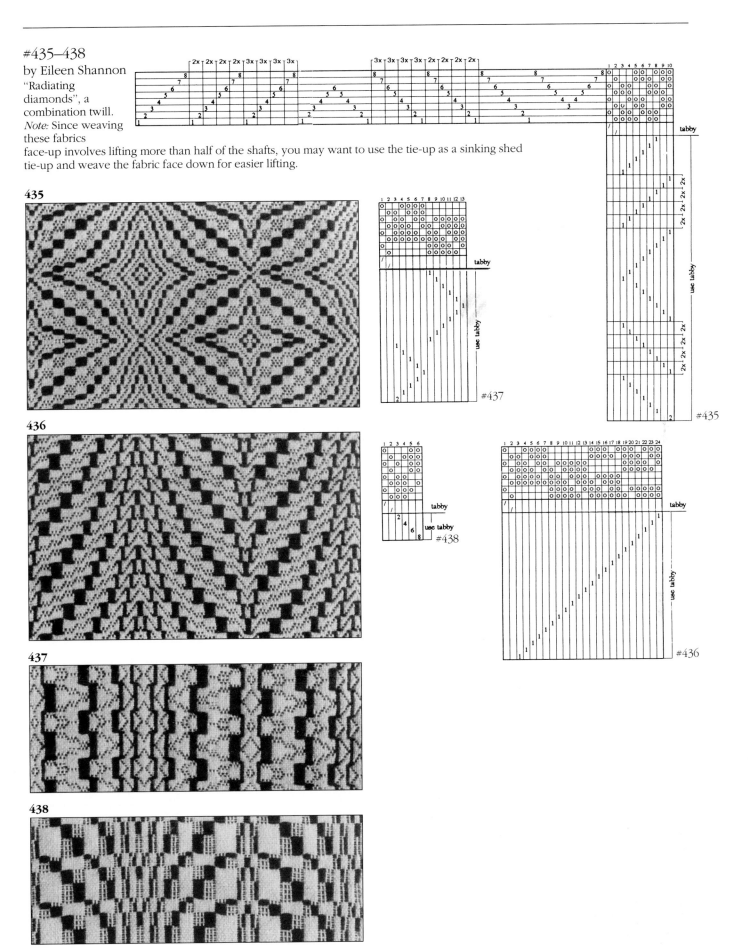

435

436

437

438

#439–442
by Dianne Ney Totten
"Star of Bethlehem",
grouped repeats
designed by Carol
Strickler.

439

440

441

442

same treadling
as #439

#443–448

by Jean Anstine

"Gallinger Gem", from *The Complete Book of Bertha Hayes' Patterns*, grouped motifs adapted for 8 shafts by Carol Strickler. *Note:* These samples use only two treadlings: one for a 4-treadle tie-up and one for an 8-treadle tie-up. Only the tie-ups change. The first sample is woven like the 4-shaft original.

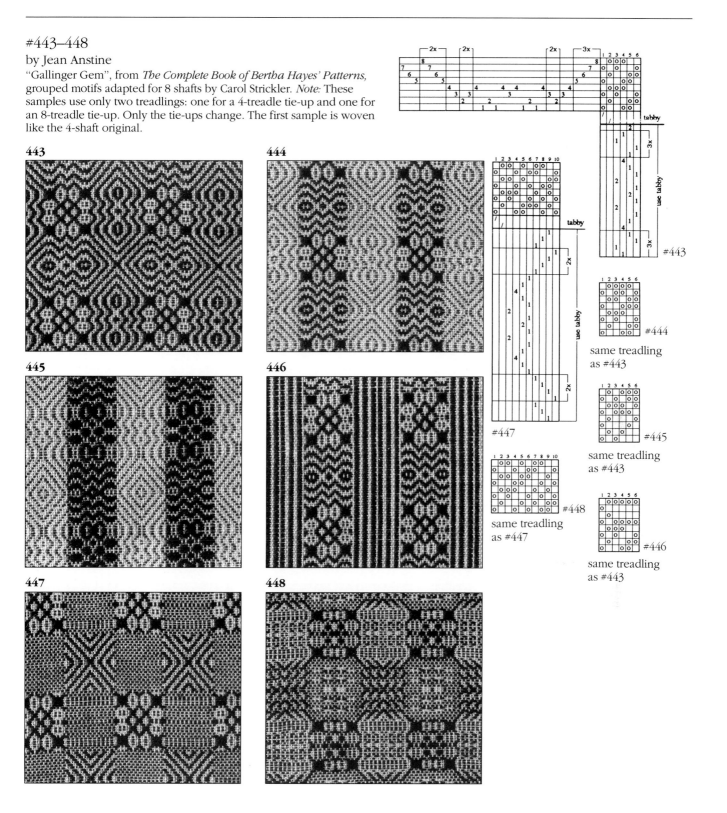

443

444

445

446

#447

same treadling as #443 #444

same treadling as #443 #445

same treadling as #447 #448

same treadling as #443 #446

same treadling as #443

447

448

#449–452

by Betty Hancock Smith

"Four-Leaf Clover", grouped repeats adapted for eight shafts by Carol Strickler. *Note:* There are broken twill lines in some of these samples where inverted or reversed motifs do not connect.

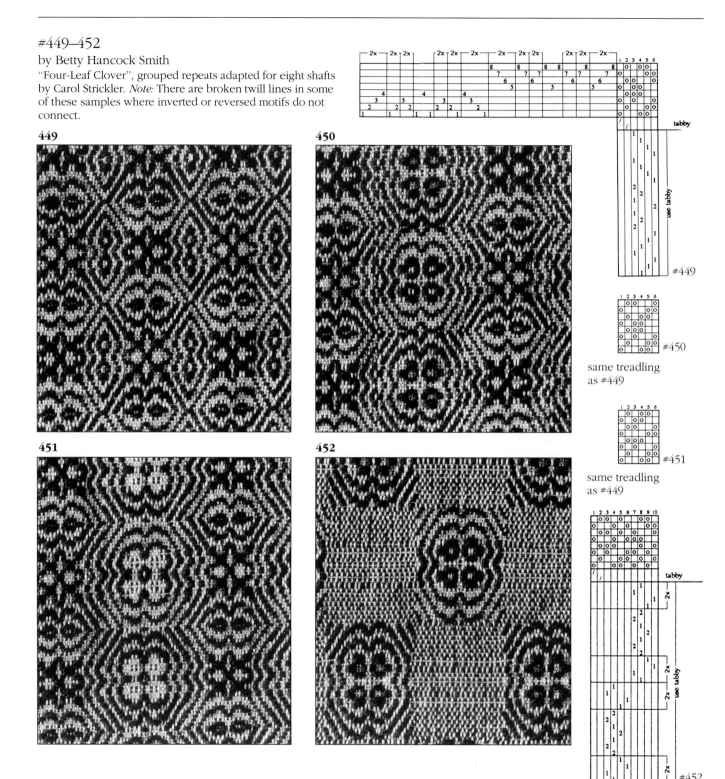

449

450

451

452

same treadling as #449

same treadling as #449

#449

#450

#451

#452

#453 & #454
by Betty Johannesen
This threading is from *Creative Monk's Belt* by Margaret Windeknecht.

453

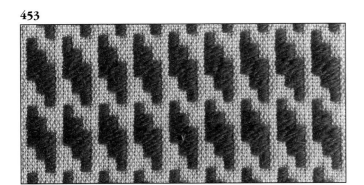

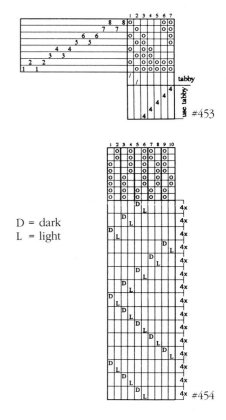

454

D = dark
L = light

#455 & # 456
by Betty Johannesen

Note: This is a 4-block monk's belt in which pairs of small blocks combine to make large blocks.

455

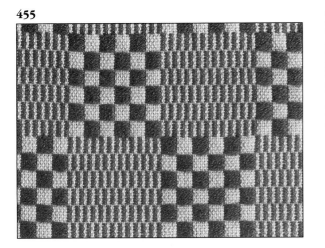

456

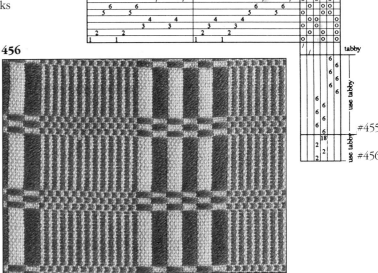

#457–461
by Sue Peters

Four-block asymmetric "monk's belt" borders with blocks combined in different ways.

457

458

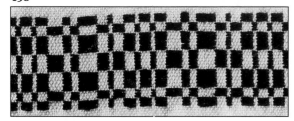

459

460

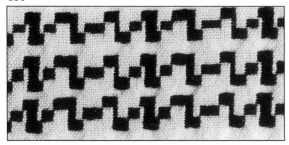

461

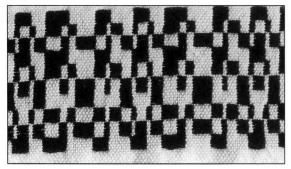

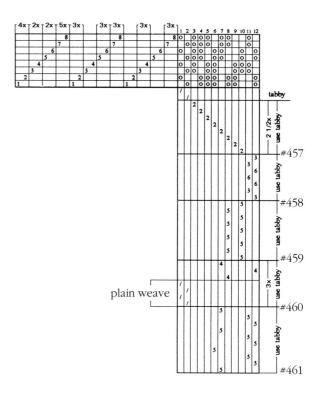

plain weave

#462–466

by Joyce Fisher Robards
This is a miniature
overshot, draft #239, from
*The Weaving Roses of
Rhode Island* by Isadora
Safner, corrected and
converted to 4-block
8-shaft overshot by Carol Strickler.
*A huck-fashion treadling using a single weft.
+A small point repeat twill treadling using a single weft.

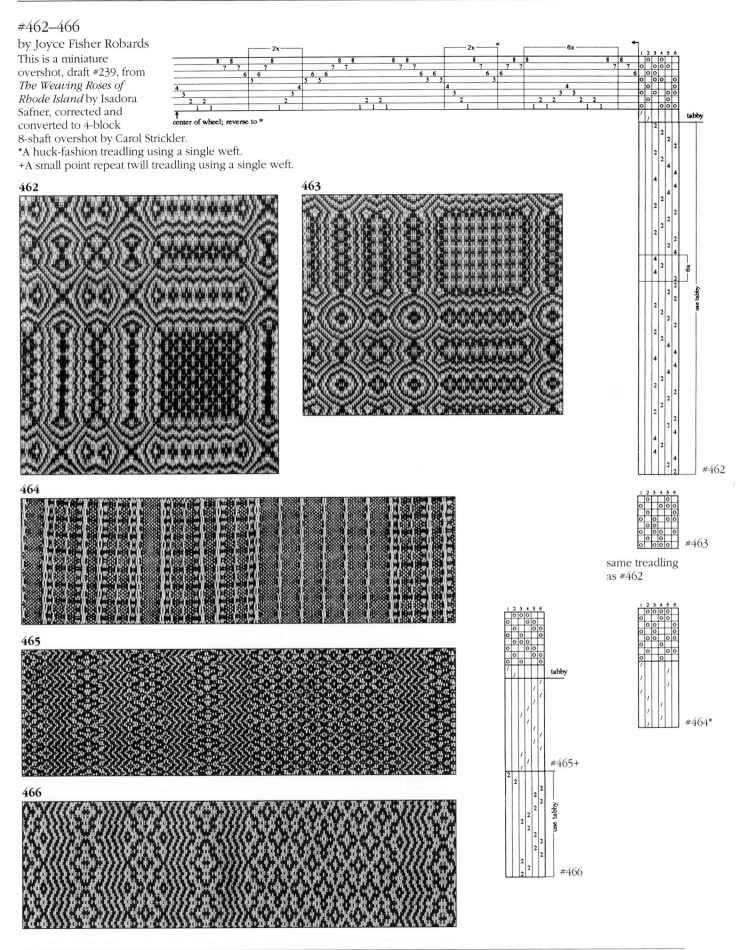

462

463

464

465

466

#462

#463

same treadling
as #462

#464*

#465+

#466

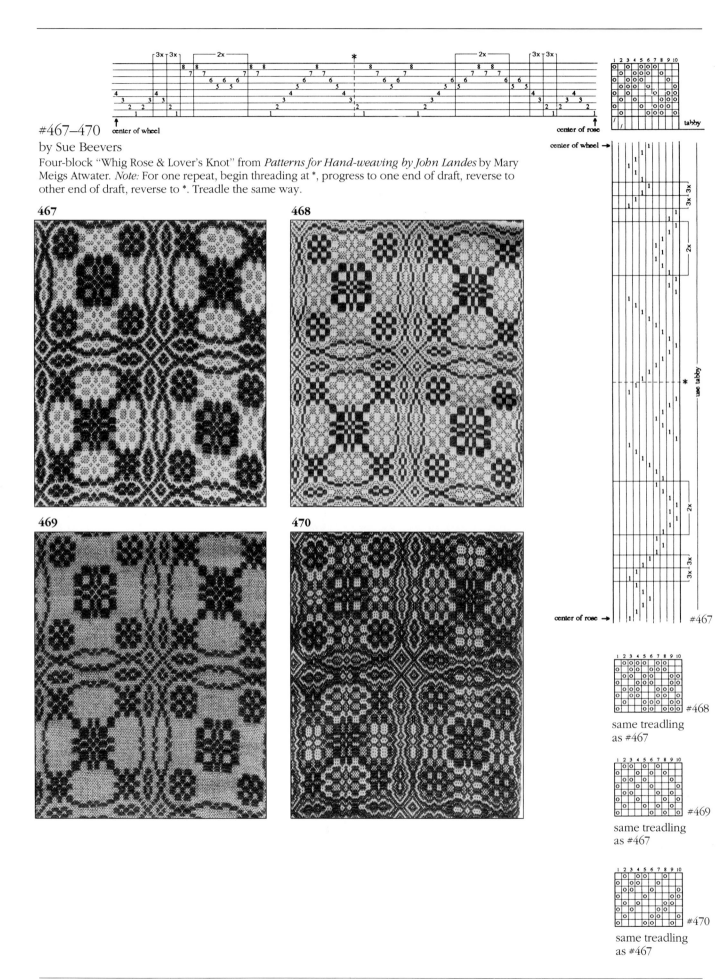

#467–470

by Sue Beevers

Four-block "Whig Rose & Lover's Knot" from *Patterns for Hand-weaving by John Landes* by Mary Meigs Atwater. *Note:* For one repeat, begin threading at *, progress to one end of draft, reverse to other end of draft, reverse to *. Treadle the same way.

467

468

469

470

same treadling as #467

same treadling as #467

same treadling as #467

#471–474

by Sue Beevers

Four-block adaptation of "Fish in the Pond" from *The Shuttle-Craft Book of American Hand-Weaving* by Mary Meigs Atwater. Pattern treadling is "literally as-drawn-in" using tabby.

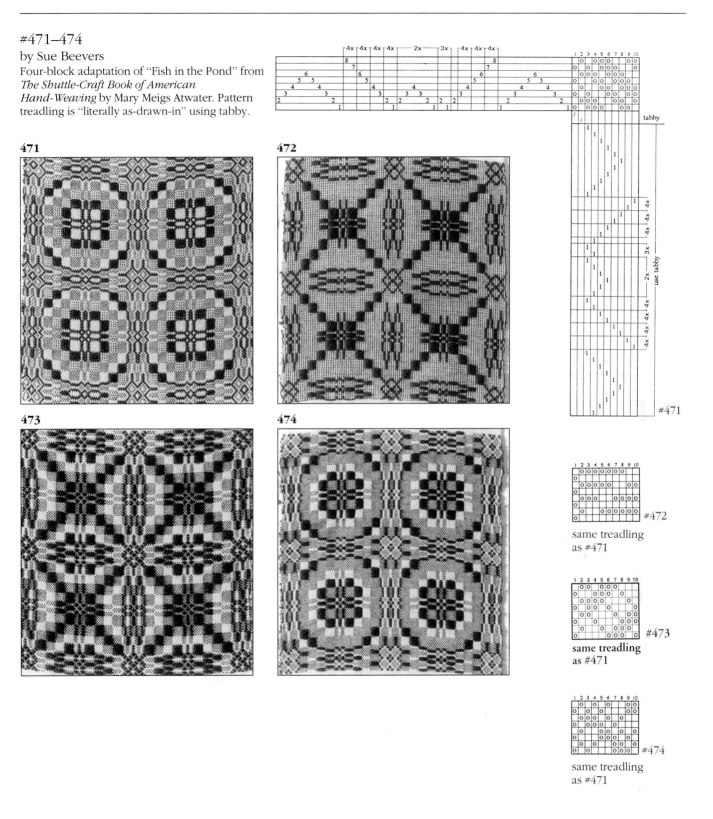

471

472

473

474

#471

#472

same treadling as #471

#473

same treadling as #471

#474

same treadling as #471

#475–478

by Leslie K. Alperin

Four-block "Primrose & Diamonds", adapted by Alberta Parkinson from *A Handweaver's Pattern Book* by Marguerite P. Davison.

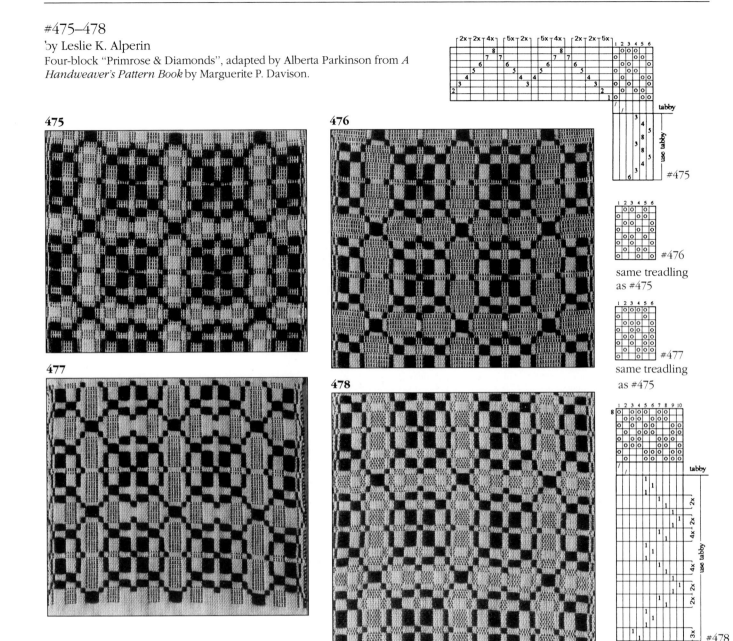

475

476

477

same treadling as #475

same treadling as #475

478

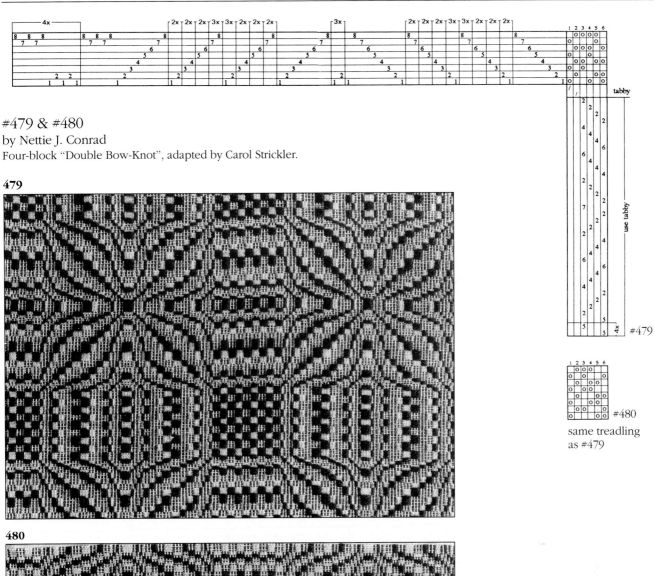

#479 & #480
by Nettie J. Conrad

Four-block "Double Bow-Knot", adapted by Carol Strickler.

479

480

tabby

use tabby

#479

#480

same treadling
as #479

#481 & #482

by Susan Ehrlich
Eight-block
"Double
Bow-Knot",
adapted by Carol
Strickler.

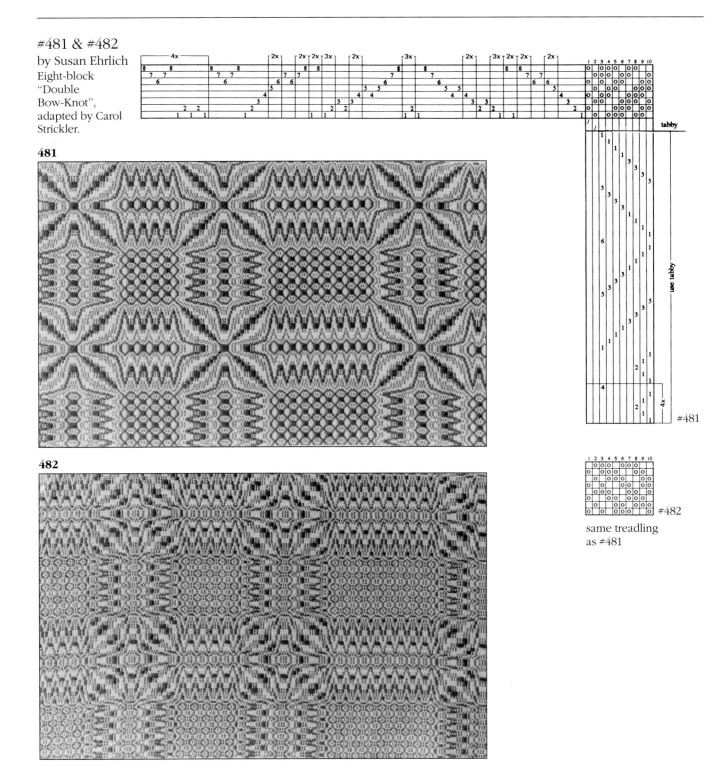

481

482

#482

same treadling
as #481

#483–487
by Ilse R. Sonner
Eight-block overshot.
*A honeycomb treadling.

D = dark
L = light

483

484

485

486

487

#487*

#483

#484

#485
same treadling
as #483

#486

#488 & #489

by Karen Wiley

Diamond in lace and overshot from *Manual of Swedish Handweaving* by Ulla Cyrus-Zetterström.

Note: This is a repeat twill treadling with no tabby. It is light weft and light warp.

488

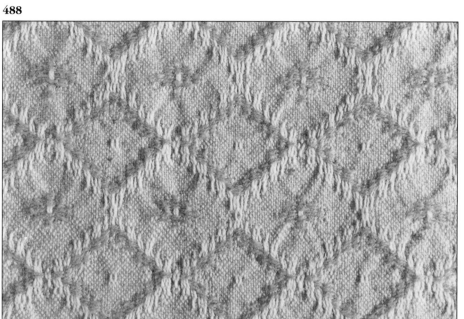

489

Chapter 13
CRACKLE

Because, to her, the weave looked like crackling or crazing on pottery, Mary Atwater gave the name *crackle* to the weave known in Sweden as "Jamtlandsväv" or "Jamtlandsdräll" ("weave from Jamtlands"). This is another threading that Tidball classifies as a "Twill Derivative".

Crackle threading is based on repeatable 4-end blocks of 3-shaft point twill, with transitional threads added to (or subtracted from) the ends of some blocks to keep the twill progression (figure 13.1). In 4-shaft crackle there are four blocks of pattern. Threadings do reverse like point twills when the block draft reverses direction. Tie-up of the classic 4-shaft form is standard 2/2 twill, and in the treadling pattern picks alternate with tabby picks. With this tie-up, any one block always weaves pattern together with one of its neighboring blocks because of the shared predominant shafts. If the rules for drafting crackle (see below) are followed, the resulting fabric has blocks that are columns of pattern weft interlacing 1/3 in the pattern and 3/1 in the background on a plain-weave ground. There are 2-thread pattern skips at the block junctions.

Threading

Eight-block crackle is threaded on eight shafts by following the same principle. (In this book, block A is predominantly shaft 1, B is mostly 2, etc. Some other authors label the blocks differently.) The threading in each block is reversed when the blocks are threaded in descending order. Figure 13.2 shows the key for 8-block 8-shaft crackle.

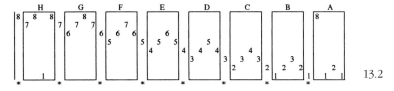

13.2

In *Designing and Drafting for Handweavers*, Berta Frey gives some rules to follow to maintain a consistent crackle structure. Briefly summarized, they are:

1—Maintain unbroken twill order, alternating odd-numbered and even-numbered shafts.

2—Keep the 3-shaft character of the point twills within each block.

3—Never draft more than three threads in a sequence on any two adjacent shafts.

4—Never draft more than four threads in a sequence without changing the direction of the twill.

Frey points out that the complexity of drafting crackle leads easily to errors, and if the design is symmetrical it is better to draft the first half very carefully and then copy it in reverse, thread by thread. Because of the complex nature of crackle and its overlapping blocks, the best block designs for this weave are relatively simple ones in which the *blocks* progress in straight or point twill order.

There are different types of crackle sampled in this chapter. In the first, each block is threaded once in twill progression and transition threads are added where needed. The appearance of this design is like a busy point twill. In the second form, block crackle, threading for each block is repeated following a profile draft, with transitional threads only at the end of the threading for each block of repeats. The rest of the samples are *parallel shadow weave* based on a crackle threading—patterns that produce a near-plain-

4-shaft crackle key:

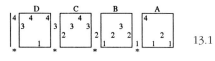

13.1

* = transitional threads

* = transitional threads

13.3

Tie-up for crackle.

or

13.4

Examples of tie-up for parallel shadow weave.

weave structure like that of shadow weave. (In crackle-based parallel shadow weave, each thread of a 4-shaft crackle draft is followed or preceded by a shadow thread on one of the upper four shafts. Usually the pattern and shadow threads are two different colors. For more detail, see the chapter on Shadow Weave in this book, as well as the monograph *Parallel Shadow Weave* by Elizabeth Lang and Erica Dakin Voolich.)

Tie-up

If the odd/even alternation of shafts has been maintained in the threading, tabbies are 1-3-5-7 vs 2-4-6-8. In the shadow form, tabbies are 1-2-3-4 vs 5-6-7-8.

For the twill and block forms of crackle the tie-up is usually a formula tie-up: $\dfrac{1}{2}\ \dfrac{1}{1}\ \dfrac{2}{1}$ (figure 13.3).

For the parallel shadow weave the tie-up is divided into quadrants with the upper half lifting the opposite of the lower half (figure 13.4).

Treadling Orders

For the *twill* form (single threading blocks) of crackle the pattern treadling is often "literal as-drawn-in", with or without tabby. The *block* form (repeated threading blocks) is usually woven with each pattern shed repeated several times, with a tabby pick after each pattern shot. *Parallel shadow* crackle is often treadled "literally as-drawn-in" with alternating dark and light weft in pattern and shadow sheds. It can also be treadled like a color-and-weave-effect spot Bronson, alternating one of the tabby treadles with the pattern treadles in dark/light order.

Variations

To stay within the rules and remain true crackle, the threading groups must be repeated intact. So a threading can be enlarged or reduced by repeating or removing 4-end groups. If a threading is changed, it is important to watch the transitional threads between blocks and to check the draft against the rules. For suggestions of possible tie-up and treadling variations, study the samples in this chapter (many of which are excerpted from long successful experimental samplers).

#490–492
by Maisie Harris
Single unit crackle.

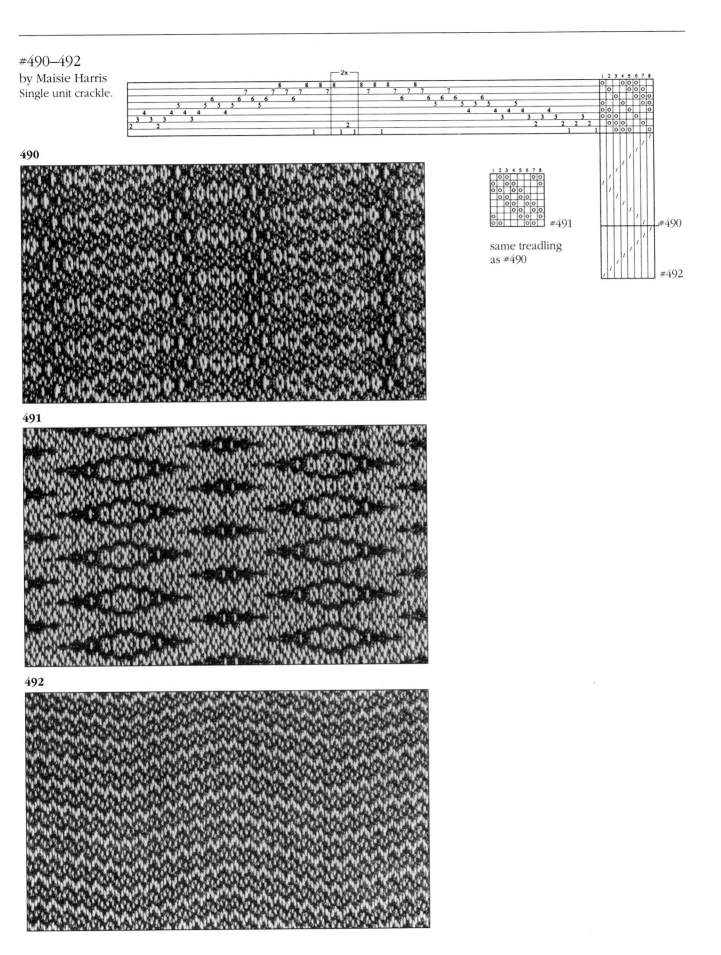

490

491

#491

same treadling
as #490

#490

#492

492

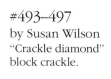

#493–497
by Susan Wilson
"Crackle diamond"
block crackle.

493

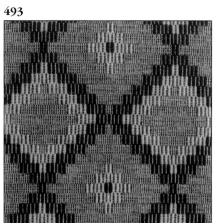

494

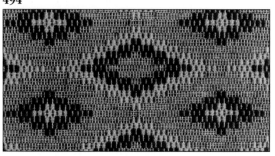

495

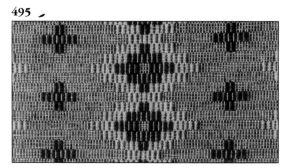

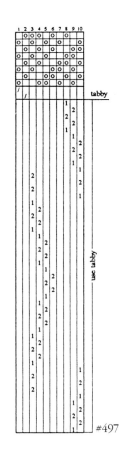

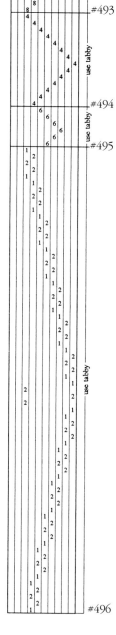

496

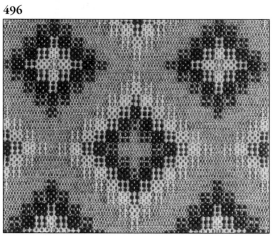

497

498

499

500

501

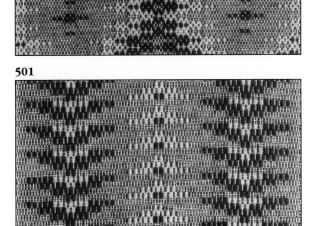

#498–501
Susan Wilson continued

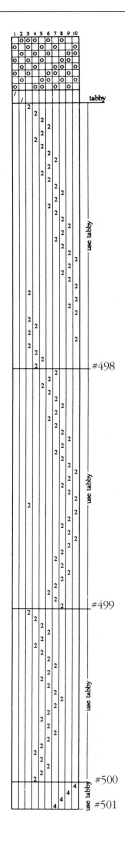

tabby

use tabby

#498

use tabby

#499

use tabby

#500

use tabby #501

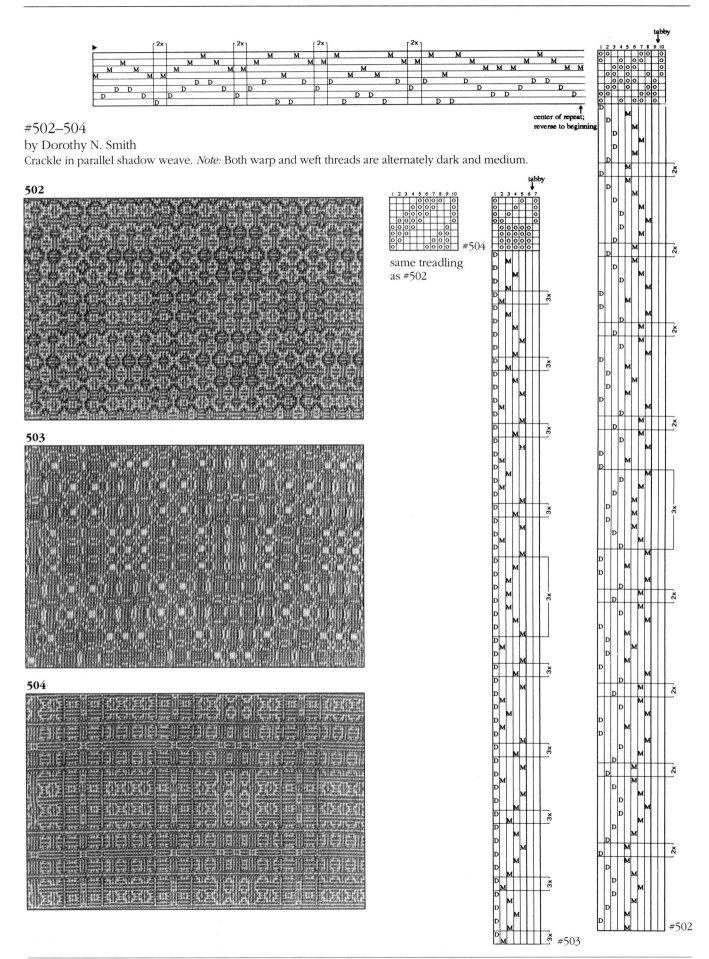

#502–504
by Dorothy N. Smith
Crackle in parallel shadow weave. *Note:* Both warp and weft threads are alternately dark and medium.

502

503

504

same treadling
as #502

#504

#503

#502

#505–510

by Beverly Kent

Parallel shadow weave from *Parallel Shadow Weave* by
Elizabeth Lang and Erica Dakin Voolich.

D = dark
L = light

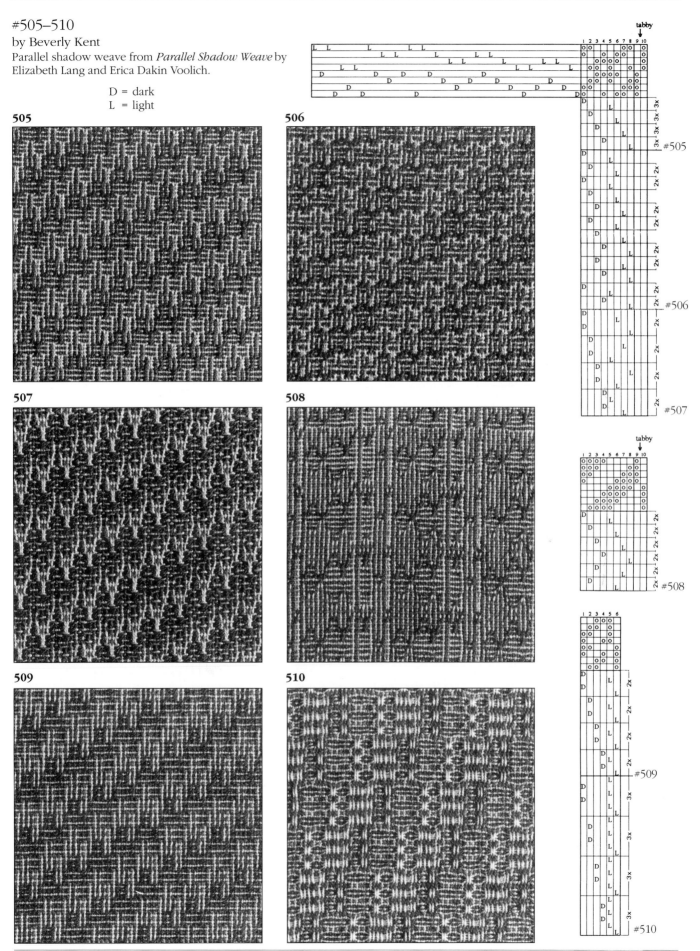

505

506

507

508

509

510

single plain diagonal

or

double plain diagonal

14.1

Chapter 14
WAFFLE WEAVE

Waffle weave is sometimes called "honeycomb" (although the name honeycomb is used in this book for a completely different weave). As the term waffle is used here, it means the weave with square or triangular cells formed by warp and weft skips of increasing length concentric around a plain center. The fabric resembles the square dents of quick-bread made in a waffle-iron (with this difference: in the fabric the dents on the face are the square outlines on the back and vice versa).

Threading

The threading draft for multiple-shaft waffle is usually a simple point twill of five or more shafts. Occasionally the threading is another twill (such as straight or extended point). The more shafts in the twill, the deeper the waffle cells can be. For firm waffles the weave requires a closer-than-usual sett because there are fewer interlacements of warp and weft than in an ordinary twill.

Tie-up

If the threading is an unbroken twill, plain weave will be odd shafts vs even shafts. (But plain weave is seldom treadled with waffle in the same fabric because of the extreme differences in take-up.)

The cells are formed by a tie-up which has one or more diagonals of plain weave (one shaft up, the next down). All of the shafts in the triangle beyond the "down" are raised and all of the shafts in the triangle beyond the "up" remain down. There is usually one more treadle than the total number of shafts, to make the waffle squares symmetrical. The greater the number of diagonals of plain weave and the smaller the solid triangles in the tie-up, the shallower the cells will be (figure 14.1).

Treadling Order

If the threading is point twill and the tie-up is an uncomplicated waffle tie-up such as the above examples, the treadling is usually a point using all the treadles. The beat must be emphatic enough to weave firm cloth in the plain-weave diagonals of squared cells.

Variations

The cells of waffle weave can be made smaller and/or shallower by reducing the number of shafts used in the threading and by increasing the number of diagonal "stitching" rows in the tie-up. The threading can also be a straight twill, an extended point twill, or even a point twill with repeat twill at the points.

The tie-up of waffle weave can have "stitching points" added or subtracted in the solid triangles to bind the long warp and weft floats and "decorate" the outlines of the cells.

The treadling can be straight (which weaves triangular half-cells on the usual threading and tie-up). Or it can be varied to make half-cells interlock like teeth of two combs.

Some warnings about waffle weave:

1—The deeper and less interlaced the cells, the more the shrinkage and collapse of the finished fabric. The usual point draft with one "stitching" diagonal in the tie-up might have as much as 50% take-up and shrinkage!

2—The appearance of a waffle fabric changes drastically with washing. Yarns differ, but most relax and twist and curl in the long floats when washed; the severe rectilinear design of waffle cells in unwashed waffle weave fabric will soften dramatically.

3—The three-dimensional depth of waffle weave can be destroyed by heavy pressing or ironing of the cloth (which makes the cells shallower but usually does *not* straighten out the curl of long floats).

Some of the samples in this chapter are woven on the same threading, tie-up, or treadling draft. They illustrate such aspects of the weave as color, cell-depth, and yarn types. One weaver uses a 2-block point twill threading to weave areas of 4-shaft waffle alternating with areas of plain weave.

#511
by Janet Johnston
A 7-shaft waffle with "stitched" corner. Every fourth repeat of the threading and treadling uses dark threads; the remaining threads are light.

511

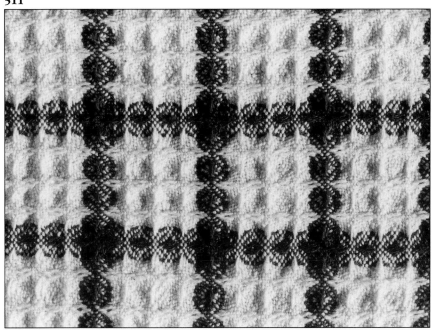

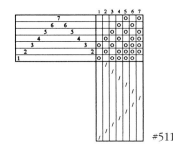

#511

#512
by Diane Ayers
An 8-shaft waffle. *Note:* Both edges of the waffle cells are decorated with tie-downs. This sample has a dark weft and a light warp.

512

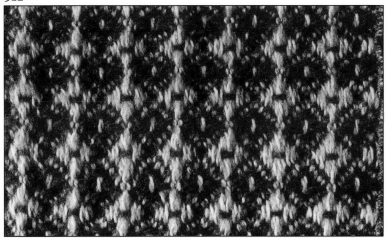

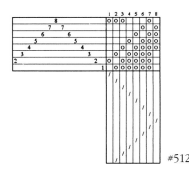

#512

#513 & #514
by Lyndsay Topham
These samples have a dark weft on a light warp.

513

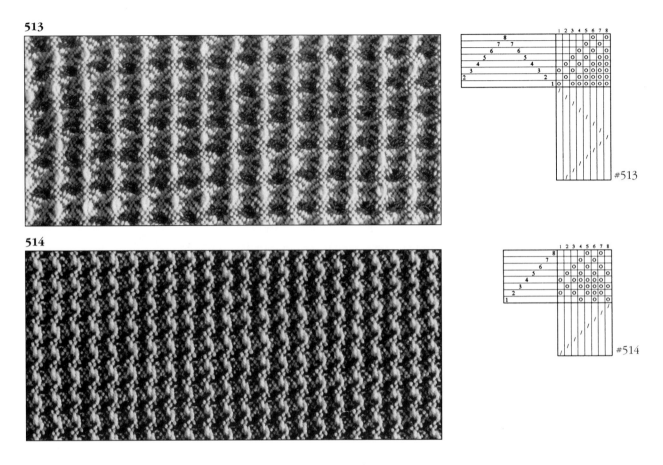

#513

514

#514

#515
by Carolyn Pavlovic
Note: This 16-treadle tie-up and threading produce interlocking cells.
This sample has a light weft on a light warp.

515

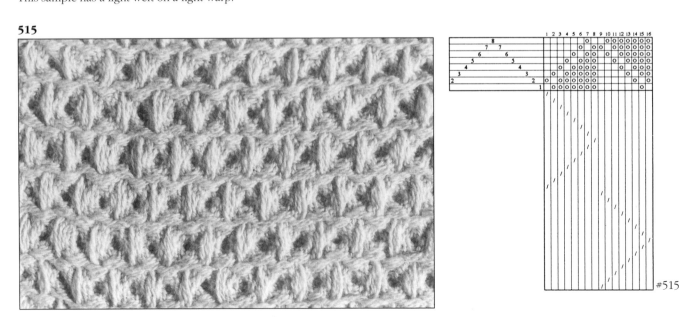

#515

#516 & #517
by Marguerite Stoiber
This half-waffle variant from *The Weaving Book* by Helene Bress has a doubled thread on shaft 1 in the threading. A medium weft on light warp is used.

516

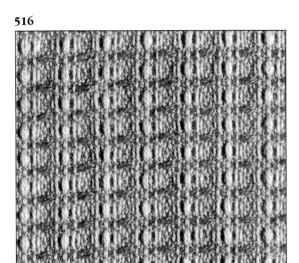

517

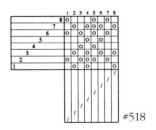

#518
by Wanda H. Leonard
This Brighton honeycomb is from *The Structure of Weaving* by Ann Sutton. This sample has a medium warp and weft.

518

#519–521

by Susan E.J. White

Note: Tabby is 1-3-6-8- vs 2-4-5-7 for this block point twill, to weave blocks of plain weave and waffle weave. This first sample has a light warp and weft; the second sample has a dark weft on a light warp, and the third sample has dark and light wefts as indicated.

*A honeycomb-like treadling.

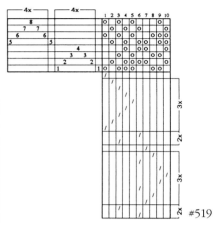

519

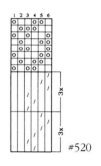

520

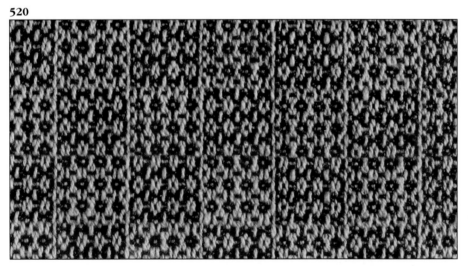

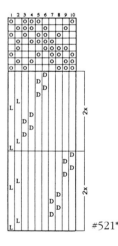

521

144

Chapter 15
SUMMER & WINTER

A unit weave is a pattern weave in which every group of warp ends and weft picks (the unit) interlaces identically to form either pattern or background. In a *tied unit* weave, certain warp ends in the threading unit function to tie supplementary-weft pattern floats to a ground cloth.

A tied unit threading is sometimes identified by the number of shafts required to carry one pattern block and the number of shafts used for tie-down ends. Thus a "single 2-tie unit weave" uses two tie-downs shafts plus one (a single) shaft per pattern block. A "double 2-tie unit weave" uses two tie-down shafts plus two shafts per pattern block. A "single 3-tie unit weave" uses three tie-down shafts plus one shaft per block, and so forth.

Summer & winter is the simplest and best-known of the single 2-tie unit weaves. The origin of the weave is uncertain, but its name probably comes from the fact that in its classic form (dark pattern weft on light ground) the fabric is predominantly dark on one face and light on the other. In that classic form (a 4-block design on 6 shafts, with the blocks used alone, uncombined) the supplementary pattern wefts float over 3/under 1 in the pattern blocks and under 3/over 1 in the background blocks, with some 2-end skips at pattern/background junctions. Each pattern pick is followed by a tabby pick, with alternating tabbies forming a plain-weave ground for the pattern and background textures.

Threading

Summer & winter is extended to 8 shafts with no alteration of the units except addition of pattern shafts. The threading sequence for each unit is four warp ends: first tie-down, pattern, second tie-down, same pattern. The threading units always follow the same internal sequence and do *not* reverse when the block direction reverses (true of units in general). In this key, shafts 1 and 2 are the tie-downs; 3 through 8 are the pattern shafts (figure 15.1):

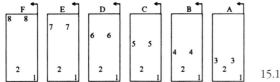

15.1

Because all units in summer & winter weave use the same tie-downs in the same order, units can be repeated as few or as many times in succession as desired without changing the structure of the cloth (also true of units in general).

Tie-up

If the threading units are repeated unaltered, tabbies are 1-2 vs 3-4-5-6-7-8.

Blocks in summer & winter can be woven independently or together in any combination (including "all pattern" or "no blocks/all background"). To weave pattern in a block, two treadles are used for the pattern weft; one lifts shaft 1 plus all of the background-block pattern shafts, and the other lifts shaft 2 plus the same patterns. (Pattern picks alternate with tabby picks.)

With six blocks of summer & winter there are 64 different possible block combinations so 130 treadles would be needed for a full tie-up to weave tabby and all combinations with both tie-downs! The usual solution is to use a skeleton tie-up, one in which the

Example of a full tie-up for a pattern.

A skeleton tie-up of the above.

Tabbies in this skeleton are the left two treadles vs the right two treadles.

15.2

various combinations needed for the particular design are divided among available treadles in such a way that different pairs of adjacent treadles share the job and two or more treadles are pushed at a time. The necessities for summer & winter are: two adjacent treadles lifting shaft 1 and shaft 2, plus one treadle (or two adjacent treadles) lifting shafts 3-4-5-6-7-8. The remaining treadles can be tied to pattern-only shafts in a way that one or two of them together will lift each of the needed combinations (figure 15.2).

If the whole summer & winter design is very unbalanced and the pattern blocks are consistently outnumbered by background blocks, it is more efficient (with lighter lifting) to weave the fabric face down. To do that, lift 1 and 2 with the *pattern-block* pattern shafts, not the *background-block* pattern shafts.

Treadling Orders

The usual way to weave summer & winter is to use a fine smooth warp and tabby and a softer pattern weft about twice the diameter. The sett is usually such as will allow the pattern wefts to form solid areas of pattern over a balanced plain-weave ground.

If the threads are properly balanced, one unit of summer & winter treadling is a particular 8-pick sequence of four pattern shots (each followed by a tabby shot, with the tabbies used alternately). There are several different standard sequences, including these (shown here on a tie-up that weaves A-B pattern, C-D-E-F background). See figure 15.3 below.

15.3

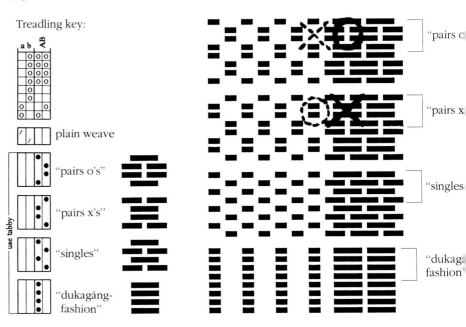

Treadling key:

The "pairs" treadling that lifts the tie-downs in 1,2,2,1 sequence weaves the pattern blocks in small o's (and the background forms small x's). The "pairs" treadling that lifts the tie-downs in 2,1,1,2 sequence weaves the pattern blocks in small x's (and the background in small o's). The allover texture of either "pairs" treadling is one of double floats that overlap by half like bricks in a traditional wall. One additional subtle variation is often worked on these two treadlings: reversal of the tabby alternation, which makes a slight difference in the way the pairs of weft floats fall together or are held apart.

Lifting the tie-downs alternately ("singles") results in pattern blocks that are not exactly symmetrical. The allover texture is that of fine slender bricks (the same width but half as thick as those produced by the pairs treadlings).

In the "dukagång-fashion" treadling only one of the tie-downs is lifted for all pattern picks; the other always remains down. If shaft 1 is the one lifted, the pattern wefts form vertical columns of 3-end pattern floats in the blocks on the face of the fabric, just as in the Scandinavian inlay weave called "Dukagång". The background has corresponding 3/1 columns, with 2-thread columns at the block edges.

Variations

To enlarge or reduce a summer & winter pattern, repeat the threading and treadling units more or fewer times, *always using complete units*.

Any 4-block profile design can be woven in summer & winter on six shafts. Since up to six blocks are possible on an 8-shaft loom, any such design could be adapted or expanded to the capacity of the loom.

"Polychrome" summer & winter is a technique in which two or more pattern wefts are thrown before each tabby. One color is used for one block combination, another color is used for another block combination (using the same tie-down), and then the tabby is thrown. The effect is to make certain motifs stand out on the face in different colors. This technique requires either wider sett or finer pattern wefts than normal to keep a balanced design. (See samples #556, #557, and #560 of polychrome summer & winter.)

The drafts given in this chapter are profile drafts, with notations of the standard treadling units that were used.

#522–526
by Noreen Rustad
Note: This is a sampler of treadling variations, all on the same profile (see text above).

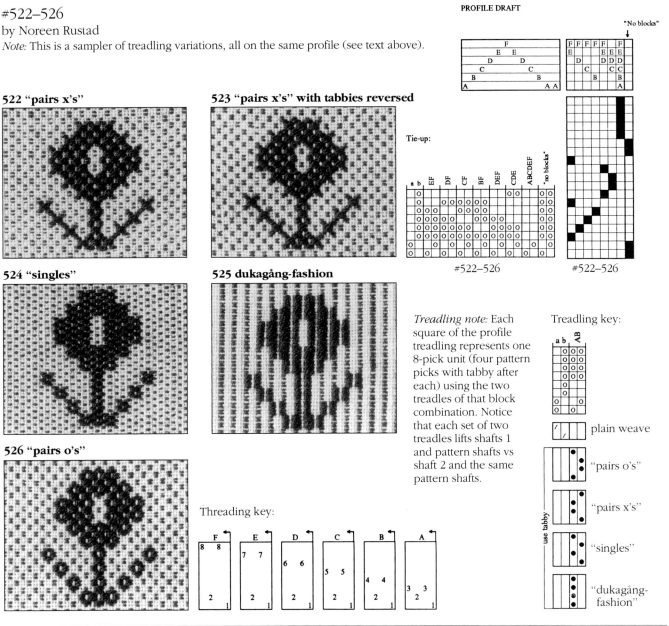

PROFILE DRAFT

522 "pairs x's"

523 "pairs x's" with tabbies reversed

524 "singles"

525 dukagång-fashion

Tie-up:

#522–526

#522–526

Treadling note: Each square of the profile treadling represents one 8-pick unit (four pattern picks with tabby after each) using the two treadles of that block combination. Notice that each set of two treadles lifts shafts 1 and pattern shafts vs shaft 2 and the same pattern shafts.

Treadling key:

plain weave

"pairs o's"

"pairs x's"

"singles"

"dukagång-fashion"

526 "pairs o's"

Threading key:

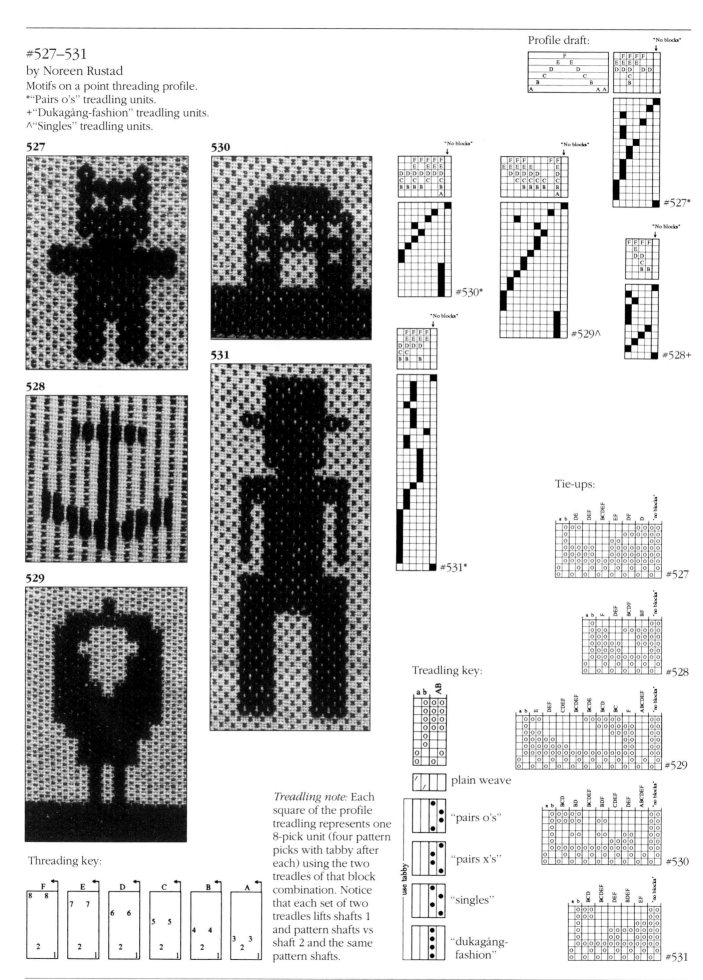

#527–531

by Noreen Rustad

Motifs on a point threading profile.
*"Pairs o's" treadling units.
+"Dukagång-fashion" treadling units.
^"Singles" treadling units.

527

528

529

530

531

Profile draft:

#527*

#530*

#529^

#531*

#528+

Tie-ups:

#527

#528

#529

#530

#531

Treadling key:

plain weave

"pairs o's"

"pairs x's"

"singles"

"dukagång-fashion"

use tabby

Treadling note: Each square of the profile treadling represents one 8-pick unit (four pattern picks with tabby after each) using the two treadles of that block combination. Notice that each set of two treadles lifts shafts 1 and pattern shafts vs shaft 2 and the same pattern shafts.

Threading key:

#532–534
by Marguerite Gingras and Yolande Bolduc
*"Singles" treadling units.
+"Dukagång-fashion" treadling units.

Profile draft:

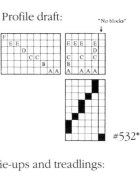

#532*

532

533

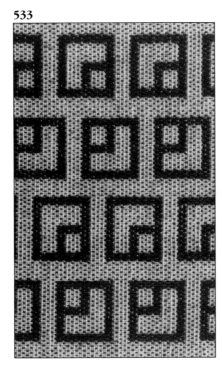

Profile tie-ups and treadlings:

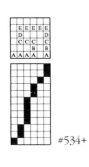

#534+

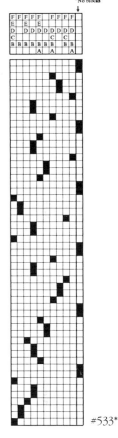

#533*

534

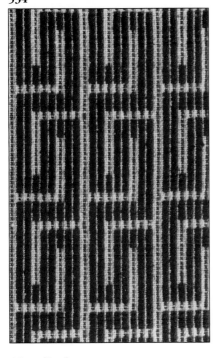

Tie-ups:

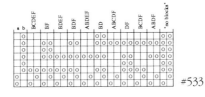

#532

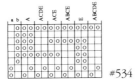

#533

#534

Treadling key:

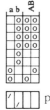

 plain weave

 "pairs o's"

 "pairs x's"

use tabby

 "singles"

 "dukagång-fashion"

Threading key:

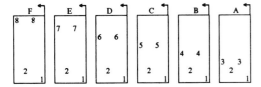

Treadling note: Each square of the profile treadling represents one 8-pick unit (four pattern picks with tabby after each) using the two treadles of that block combination. Notice that each set of two treadles lifts shafts 1 and pattern shafts vs shaft 2 and the same pattern shafts.

#535–538
Marguerite Gingras and Yolande Bolduc continued.
*"Pairs o's" treadling units.
+"Singles" treadling units.
#"Dukagång-fashion" treadling units.
Note: Profile threading and threading and treadling keys are on page 149.

535

536

537

538

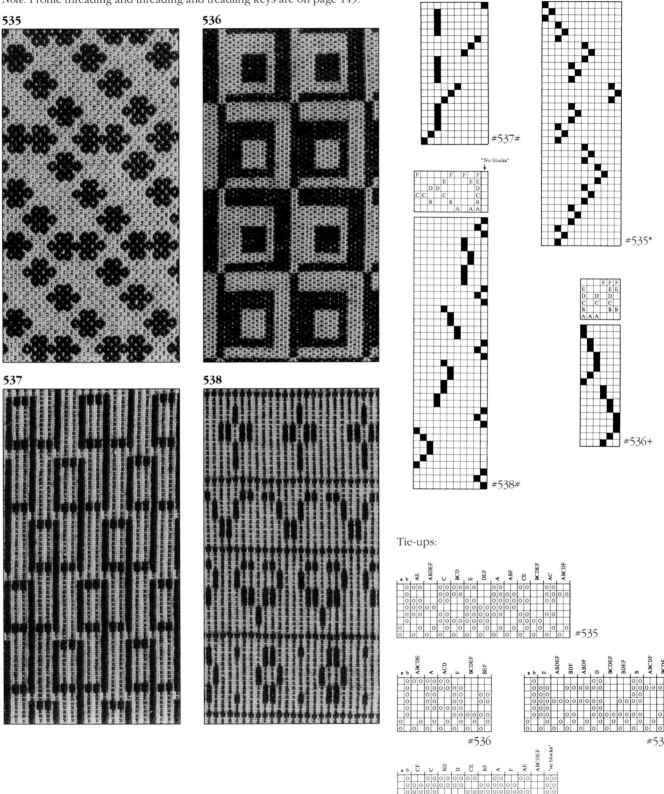

Tie-ups:

#535

#536

#537

#538

#537#

#535*

#536+

#538#

#539–542

by Marguerite Gingras and Yolande Bolduc

*"Pairs o's" treadling units.
+"Singles" treadling units.
#"Pairs x's" treadling units.

539

540

541

542

Profile tie-ups and treadlings:

#541*

#542#

Profile draft:

#539*

#540+

Tie-ups:

#539

#540

#541

#542

Treadling note: Each square of the profile treadling represents one 8-pick unit (four pattern picks with tabby after each) using the two treadles of that block combination. Notice that each set of two treadles lifts shafts 1 and pattern shafts vs shaft 2 and the same pattern shafts.

Treadling key:

plain weave

"pairs o's"

"pairs x's"

"singles"

"dukagång-fashion"

use tabby

Threading key:

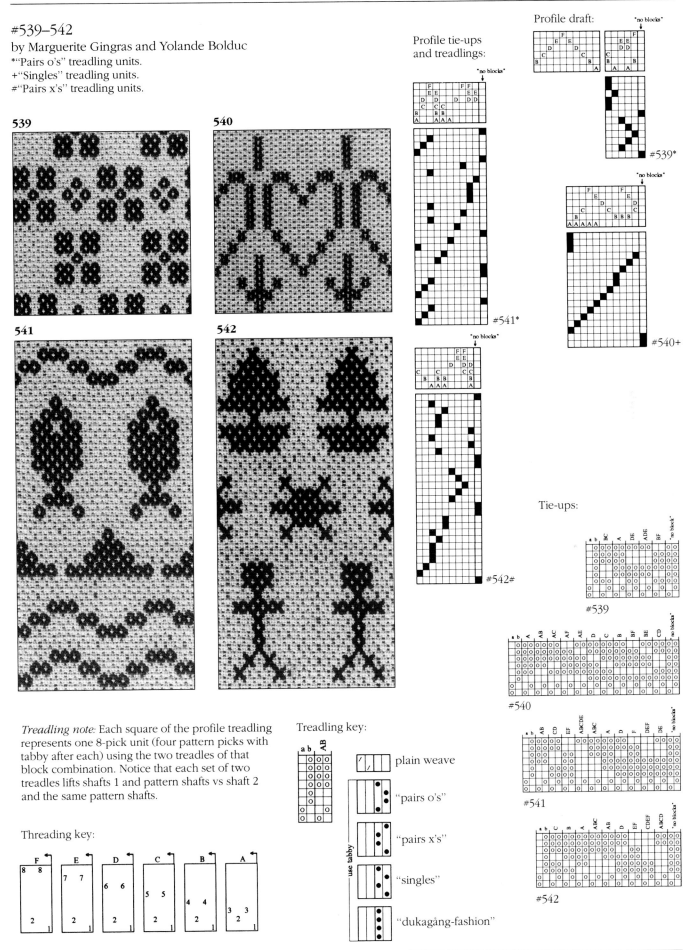

#543–545

by Marguerite Gingras and Yolande Bolduc continued.
+"Singles" treadling units.   *"Pairs o's" treadling units.
Note: Profile draft and threading and treadling keys are on page 151.

Tie-ups:

543

544

545

#543

#544

#545

#543+

#544*

#545+

#546
by Jean Anstine
This is block draft #244 from *The Shuttle-Craft Book of American Hand-Weaving* by Mary Meigs Atwater. "Pairs x's" treadling units.

546

#547
by Carol Strickler
"Ringed Stars" with "pairs o's" treadling units.

547

Profile draft:

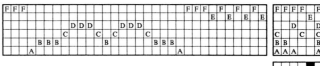

Tie-up:

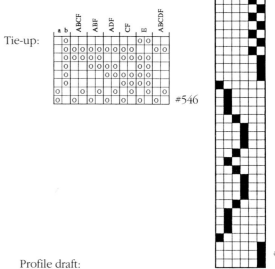

#546

#546

Profile draft:

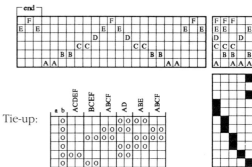

Tie-up:

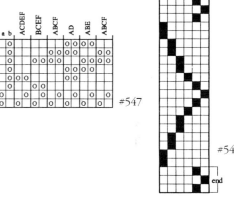

#547

#547

Treadling key:

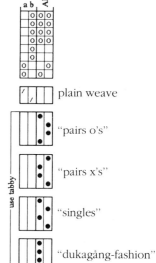

	plain weave
	"pairs o's"
	"pairs x's"
	"singles"
	"dukagång-fashion"

Threading key:

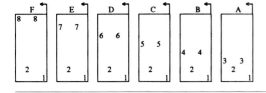

Treadling note: Each square of the profile treadling represents one 8-pick unit (four pattern picks with tabby after each) using the two treadles of that block combination. Notice that each set of two treadles lifts shafts 1 and pattern shafts vs shaft 2 and the same pattern shafts.

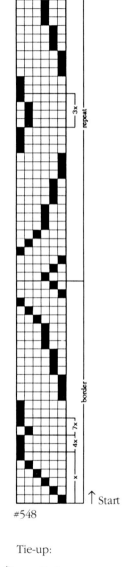

#548

by Carol Strickler (with Ardis Dobrovolny, Jean Anstine, and Janet Johnston)

Note: Samples #548–551 have been made into six-block designs. All begin with the pine tree border with the same 21 blocks. All are treadled in "pairs o's", dark side up. This sample is adapted from "Snowball in Ring", an unpublished 5-block double-weave coverlet.

548

#548

Threading key:

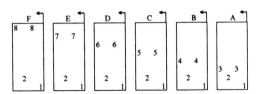

Treadling key:

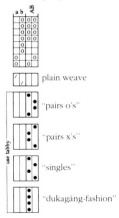

Tie-up:

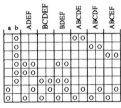

#548

Treadling note: Each square of the profile treadling represents one 8-pick unit (four pattern picks with tabby after each) using the two treadles of that block combination. Notice that each set of two treadles lifts shafts 1 and pattern shafts vs shaft 2 and the same pattern shafts.

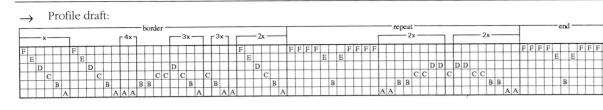

#549

Carol Strickler continued,

This sample is adapted from "Virginia Beauty", a 5-block double-weave coverlet from *Country Cloth to Coverlets* by Sandra Rambo Walker. Use threading and treadling keys on the opposite page.

549

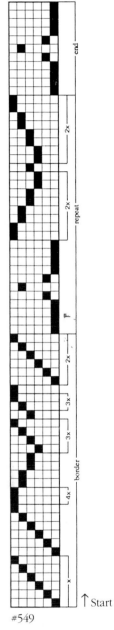

#549

Tie-up:

#549

#550
Carol Strickler continued.

Profile draft:

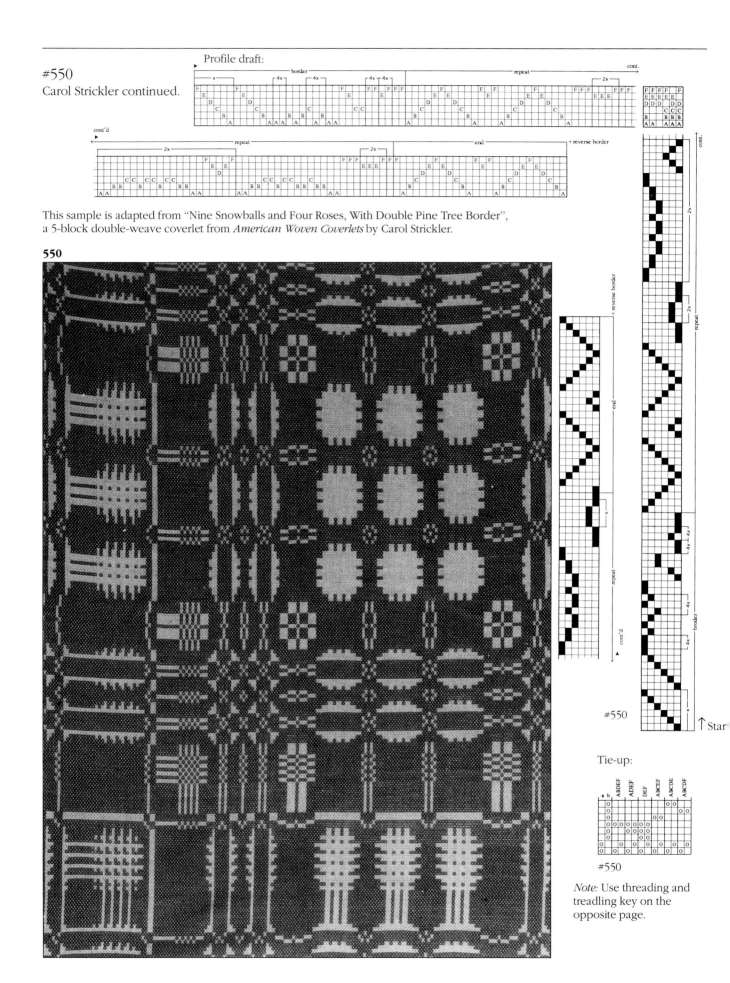

This sample is adapted from "Nine Snowballs and Four Roses, With Double Pine Tree Border",
a 5-block double-weave coverlet from *American Woven Coverlets* by Carol Strickler.

550

#550

Tie-up:

#550

Note: Use threading and
treadling key on the
opposite page.

#551
Carol Strickler
continued.

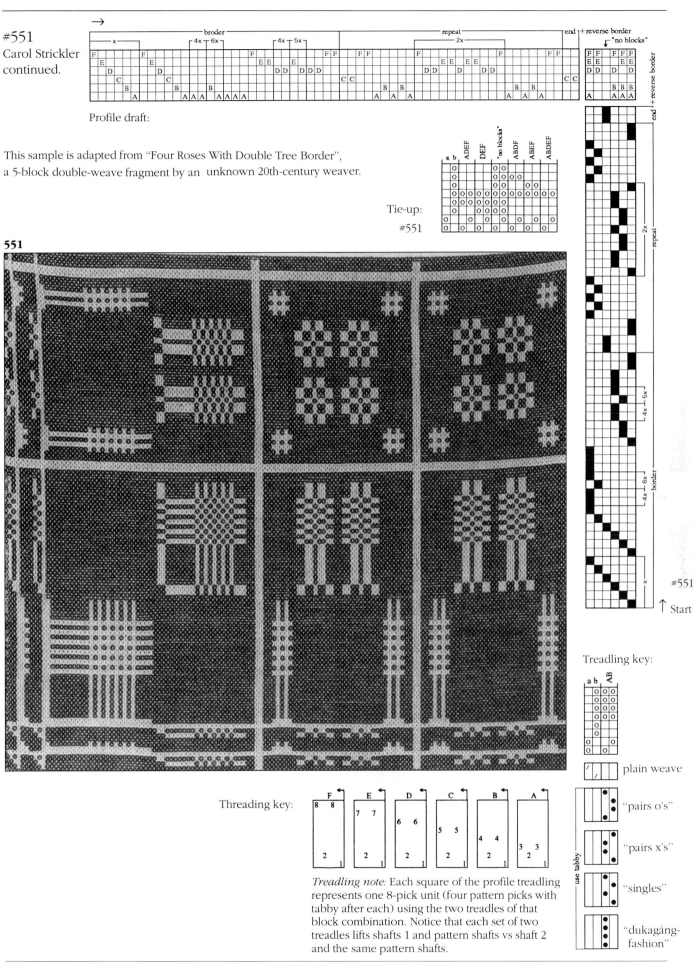

Profile draft:

This sample is adapted from "Four Roses With Double Tree Border",
a 5-block double-weave fragment by an unknown 20th-century weaver.

Tie-up:
#551

551

#551

↑ Start

Treadling key:

plain weave

"pairs o's"

"pairs x's"

"singles"

"dukagång-fashion"

use tabby

Threading key:

Treadling note: Each square of the profile treadling
represents one 8-pick unit (four pattern picks with
tabby after each) using the two treadles of that
block combination. Notice that each set of two
treadles lifts shafts 1 and pattern shafts vs shaft 2
and the same pattern shafts.

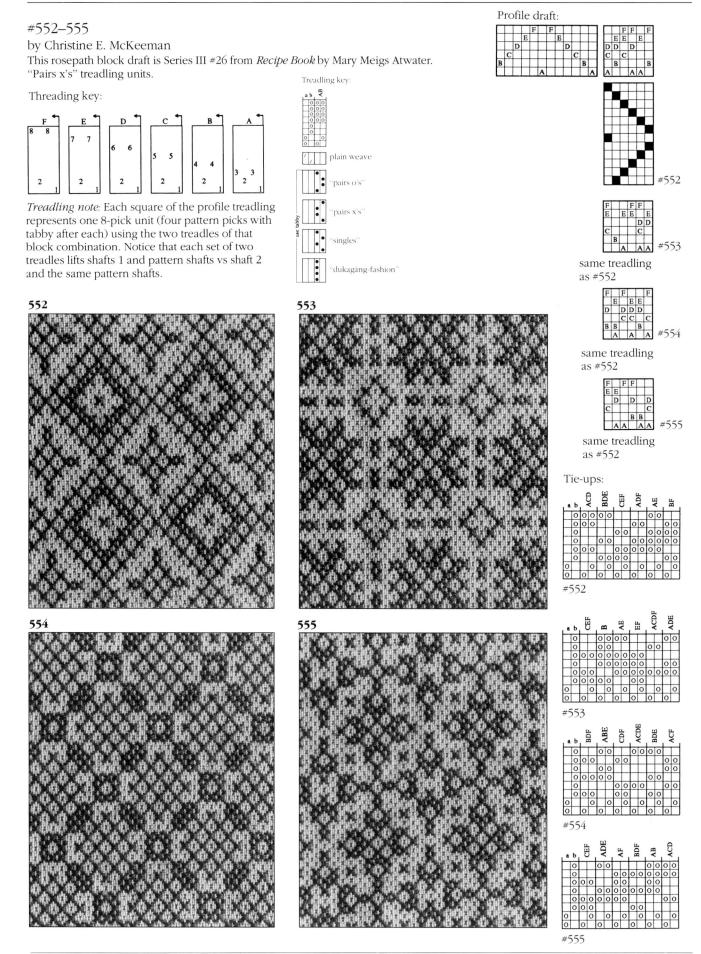

#552–555

by Christine E. McKeeman

This rosepath block draft is Series III #26 from *Recipe Book* by Mary Meigs Atwater.
"Pairs x's" treadling units.

Threading key:

Treadling key:

Treadling note: Each square of the profile treadling represents one 8-pick unit (four pattern picks with tabby after each) using the two treadles of that block combination. Notice that each set of two treadles lifts shafts 1 and pattern shafts vs shaft 2 and the same pattern shafts.

plain weave

"pairs o's"

"pairs x's"

"singles"

"dukagång-fashion"

Profile draft:

#552

#553
same treadling
as #552

#554
same treadling
as #552

#555
same treadling
as #552

Tie-ups:

#552

#553

#554

#555

552

553

554

555

158

#556 & #557
by Judy Steinkoenig

These 6-shaft polychrome "Ribbons" samples were designed by Carol Strickler. Both use "pairs x's" treadling units of 12 picks (tabby after each two pattern picks).

556

557

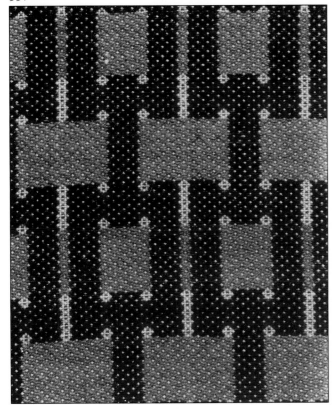

Profile draft:

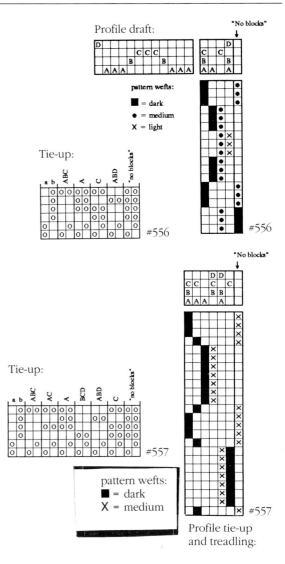

pattern wefts:

■ = dark

● = medium

X = light

Tie-up:

#556

#556

#557

Tie-up:

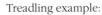

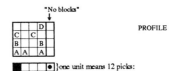

pattern wefts:

■ = dark

X = medium

#557

Profile tie-up and treadling:

Treadling example:

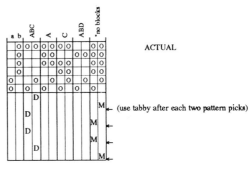

PROFILE

}one unit means 12 picks:

ACTUAL

← (use tabby after each two pattern picks)

Threading key:

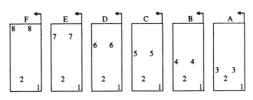

#558
by Sarah Saulson

+"Dukagång-fashion" treadling units. This sample has a medium warp and a dark weft.

Profile draft:

#558+

558

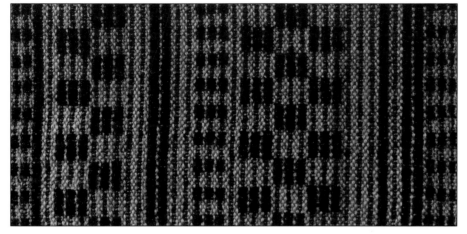

Tie-up:

#558

#559
by Sarah Saulson

*This sample is woven with "dukagång-fashion" treadling units. It has a medium striped warp and a dark weft.

Profile draft:

two extra tabby shots{

#55

559

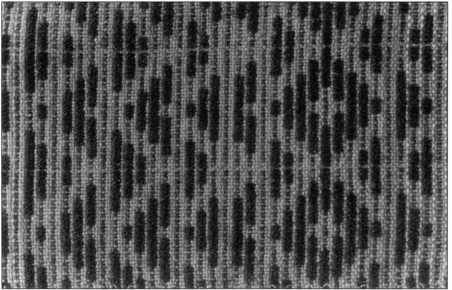

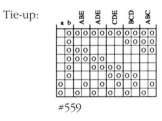

Tie-up:

#559

Threading key:

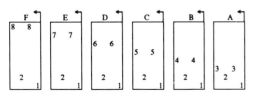

Treadling note: Each square of the profile treadling represents one 8-pick unit (four pattern picks with tabby after each) using the two treadles of that block combination. Notice that each set of two treadles lifts shafts 1 and pattern shafts vs shaft 2 and the same pattern shafts.

Treadling key:

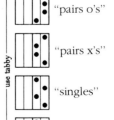

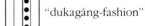

plain weave

"pairs o's"

"pairs x's"

"singles"

"dukagång-fashion"

#560
by Barbara Meier

Block draft #247 from *The Shuttle-Craft Book of American Hand-Weaving* by Mary Meigs Atwater. "Pairs x's" polychrome treadling units. This pattern also can be woven as "ribbons" on an unadorned ground, without the roses.

560

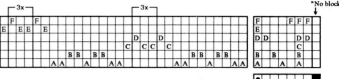

pattern wefts:
■ = dark
● = medium

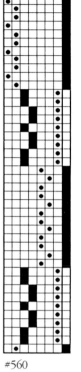

#560

Tie-up:

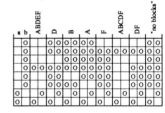

#560

Treadling example:

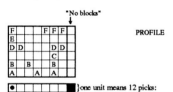

PROFILE

}one unit means 12 picks:

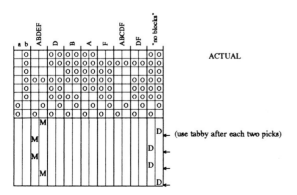

ACTUAL

(use tabby after each two picks)

Threading key:

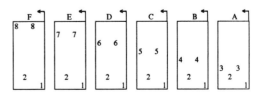

Chapter 16
TIED OVERSHOT

Tied overshot weaves (some called "even-tied overshot", "uneven-tied overshot", or sometimes just "overshot") are also single 2-tie weaves; the units use two tie-down shafts, and one pattern shaft is required for each block. Most of the patterns seem to have been derived from early 19th-century woven coverlets of professional weavers in the Pennsylvania region.

For technical detail about threadings, tie-ups, and treadling orders see the samples in this chapter and consult articles and coverlet books that discuss these weave structures.

#561
by Ena Marston
This tied overshot is adapted from a 10-shaft pattern in *Patterns for Hand-Weaving by John Landes* by Mary Meigs Atwater.

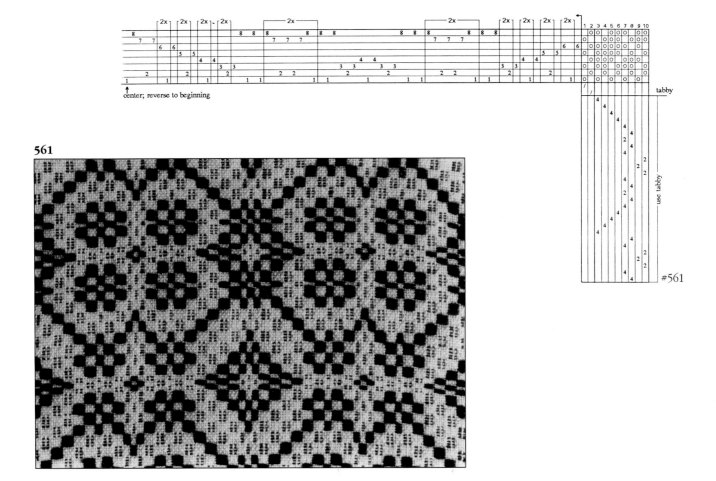

561

#562–565

by Julia Benson

Carol Strickler adapted this pattern from "La Belle Creole" in Mary Meigs Atwater's *Recipe Book*.

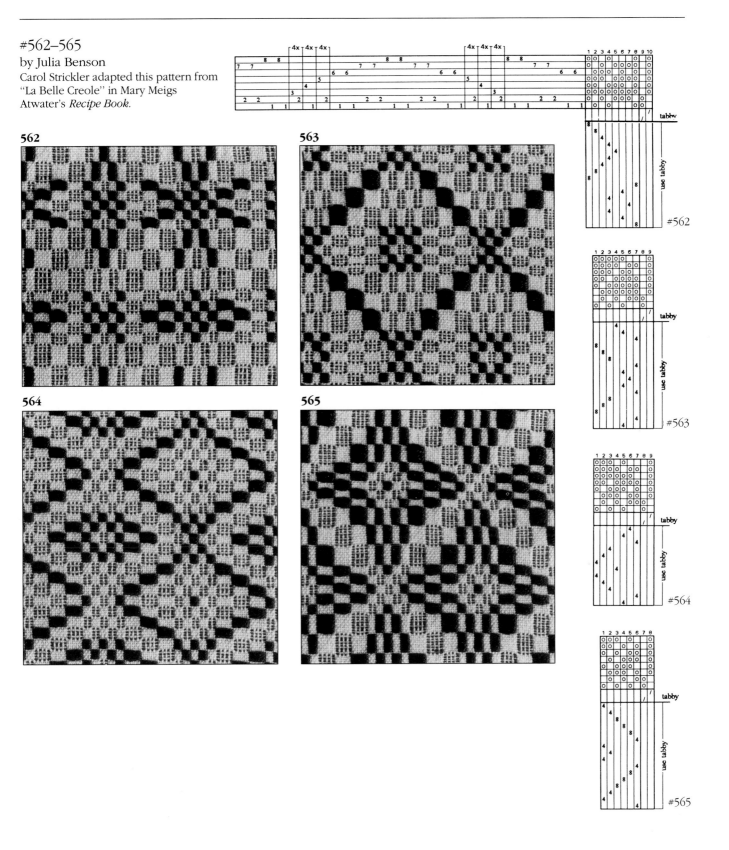

562

563

564

565

#566 & #567

by Beverly Fitzgerald

This sampler was adapted by Carol Strickler and Beverly Fitzgerald from *200 Patterns for Multiple-Harness Looms* by Russell Groff and *Keep Me Warm One Night* by Dorothy and Harold Burnham.

Threading key:

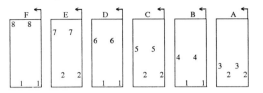

Profile draft:

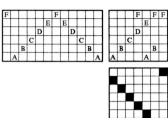

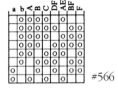

#566

566

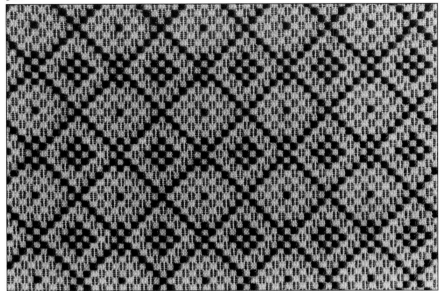

Tie-up:

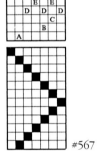

#566

Profile tie-up and treadling:

567

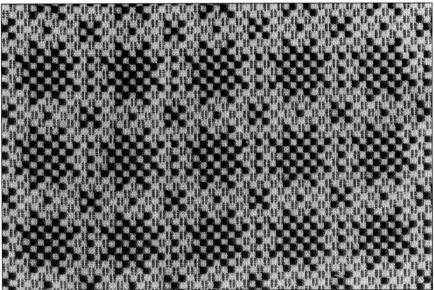

#567

Tie-up:

#567

Treadling note: Each square of the profile treadling represents one 8-pick unit (4 repeats of the pattern treadle, with a tabby pick after each).

#568 & #569
Beverly Fitzgerald continued
(Profile threading and threading key are on the previous page.)

Profile tie-up and treadling:

#568

Tie-up:

#568

Profile tie-up and treadling:

#569

Tie-up:

#569

Threading profiles:

straight

point

rosepath

17.2

Base tie-up:

17.3

Chapter 17
DIVERSIFIED PLAIN WEAVE

As presented to handweavers by Klara Cherepov in her monograph on the weave, *diversified plain weave* is a structure in which *heavy* warps of one color and wefts of another make single skips over and under each other to form the apparent pattern; *fine* warps and wefts also interweave in a plain weave that ties down every heavy skip in both directions. Where one color shows on the face of the fabric, the other color shows on the back.

Threading

In diversified plain weave, threading and treadling units each contain six threads. The threading is: fine ground (shaft 2), heavy pattern (odd pattern shaft), fine ground (shaft 2), fine ground (shaft 1), heavy pattern (even pattern shaft), fine ground (shaft 1). The pattern shafts each form a block of pattern, so 6-block patterns can be woven on eight shafts (figure 17.1).

H = heavy
f = fine

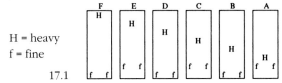
17.1

Threads on odd and even pattern shafts must always alternate to form the units in the threading; a large solid area must therefore use two blocks (for example, ABABABA).

Successful profile threading orders for diversified plain weave are 6-block twill orders. The samples in this book are woven on the threading profiles shown in figure 17.2.

Tie-up

The greatest opportunities for variation of any diversified plain weave pattern come in the tie-up. The fundamental tie-up is two tabby treadles, with the remaining treadles tied to use 1 and 2 alternately along with selected pattern shafts (figure 17.3).

Any 6-high by 6-wide "pattern" can be inserted into the blank area of the base tie-up to determine the lifting order of the heavy pattern threads. Some examples are shown in figure 17.4. On any pattern treadle, the pattern shafts (3 through 8) that are raised weave spots of the heavy warp while the ones that are not raised weave spots of the heavy weft. (Notice that the drafts in this chapter are *profile* drafts, which indicate heavy *weft* blocks; convert the block tie-up to its negative to insert in the rising-shed base tie-up.)

17.4

Treadling Order

The treadling units have six picks: fine ground (odd tabby), heavy pattern (2 and pattern), fine ground (odd tabby), fine ground (even tabby), heavy pattern (1 and pattern), fine ground (even tabby). Successful treadling orders are derived from 6-block twills. The samples in this book use primarily straight and point treadling orders (figure 17.5).

Other Factors

Color, relative size of the yarns used, and sett are important factors in the appearance of diversified plain-weave fabrics.

Color is a major element. The pattern appears best if two contrasting colors are used, with the *fine warp and the heavy weft* one color and the *heavy warp and fine weft* the other color. In this case, the fine threads visually blend with the heavy floats they cross, and the pattern emerges as solid areas of the two colors. If, on the other hand, both warps are one color and both wefts are another (as in many of the samples in this book) the pattern appears more dotted and shadowy (because light fine threads weave with dark heavy ones and vice versa).

Relative yarn size is another factor that is crucial to the fabric's appearance. Traditionally, the fine ground warps and wefts have been the same smooth, firm thread. The heavy warps and wefts are usually alike in size and at least five or six times the diameter of the fine ones. The heavy threads, too, should be smooth and straight for clearest pattern results, but they can be softer than the ground threads.

The sett is whatever would weave balanced (squared) plain weave if the heavy threads were used alone; each fine/heavy/fine half-unit should be sleyed together in the same dent of the reed as though it were the single heavy thread.

Variations

The structural threading and treadling units cannot be enlarged. Variations to *those* elements include altering the profile—the order in which the blocks are used.

The *tie-up* allows seemingly infinite variation; any 6-block design can be converted to rising-shed tie-up and inserted into the pattern section of the base tie-up.

Yarns can be varied somewhat. Fine and heavy elements closer to each other in size make the pattern more shadowy. Textured yarns obscure the crisp geometric nature of the structure.

The greatest virtue of this weave is that there are no floats so it is very practical for utilitarian fabrics such as upholstery. Theoretically the structure can be woven in spider-fine threads for delicate light-weight clothing fabric, or in strong linen and coarse rug wool for a dense firm rug, with equal success. In the past this weave has been relatively little-known, leaving lots of room for experimentation.

Note: Many of the samples in this chapter are based on drafts from two sources: the monograph *Diversified Plain Weave* by Klara Cherepov, and the magazine article, "Weaver's Challenge: Diversified Plain Weave" by Kathryn Wertenberger in the November/December 1987 HANDWOVEN. The concept of base tie-up was developed by Sandra Url.

Treadlings:

straight treadling

f = fine

H = heavy

17.5

point treadling

#570 & #571
by Jennifer Trepal
Warp—heavy dark, fine light
Weft—heavy light, fine dark
Use treadling key below.

Threading key:

Profile draft:

#570

Tie-up:

#570

**Profile tie-up
and treadling:**

#571

Tie-up:

#571

570

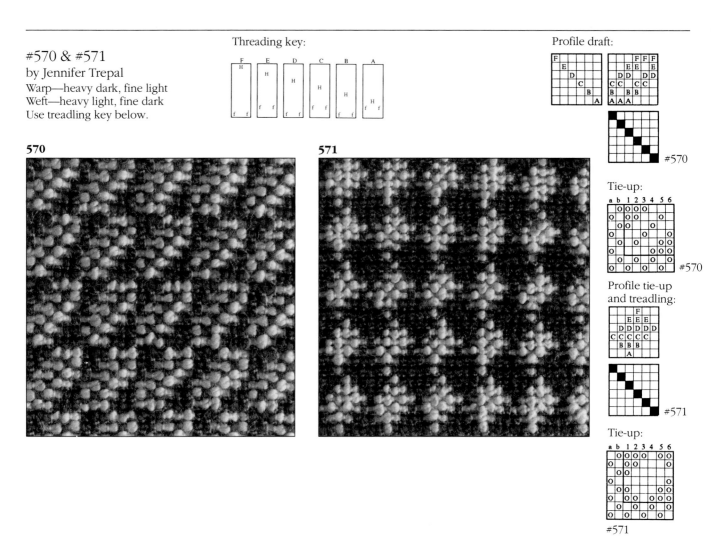

571

#572
Jennifer Trepal continued.
Use threading key above.

Profile draft:

#572

Tie-up:

#572

572

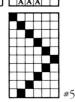

Treadling key

Treadling note:
Each square of the
profile treadling
represents one
fine-heavy-fine
sequence.

#573 & #574
by June Hillyer
Warp—heavy light, fine light
Weft—heavy dark, fine light

573

574

Threading key:

Treadling key:

Treadling note:
Each square of the profile treadling represents one fine-heavy-fine sequence.

Profile draft:

#573

Tie-up:

#573

Profile tie-up and treadling:

#574

Tie-up:

#574

#575 & #576
by Jennifer Trepal
Warp—heavy light, fine dark
Weft—heavy dark, fine light
See keys above.

575

576

Profile draft:

#575

Tie-up:

#575

Profile tie-up and treadling:

#576

Tie-up:

#576

#577–580
by Sandra Url
Warp—heavy dark, fine dark
Weft—heavy light, fine light

Profile draft:

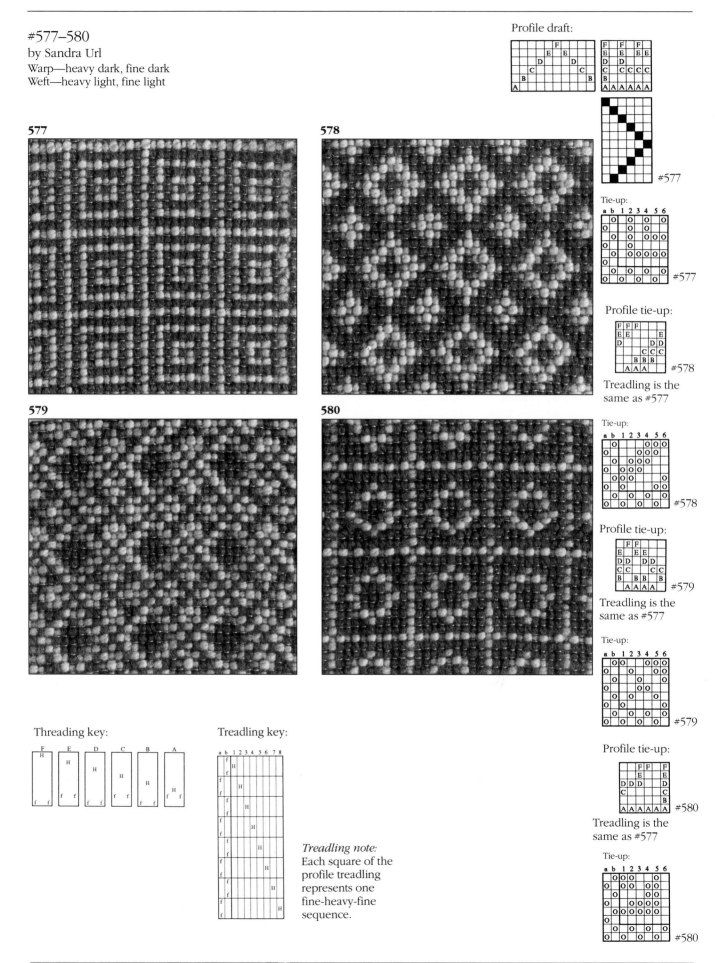

577

578

579

580

Threading key:

Treadling key:

Treadling note:
Each square of the profile treadling represents one fine-heavy-fine sequence.

#577

Tie-up:
#577

Profile tie-up:
#578

Treadling is the same as #577

Tie-up:
#578

Profile tie-up:
#579

Treadling is the same as #577

Tie-up:
#579

Profile tie-up:
#580

Treadling is the same as #577

Tie-up:
#580

#581–586
Sandra Url continued.

Note: Use the threading and treadling keys on the previous page.

Note: Use the threading and treadling keys on the previous page.

581

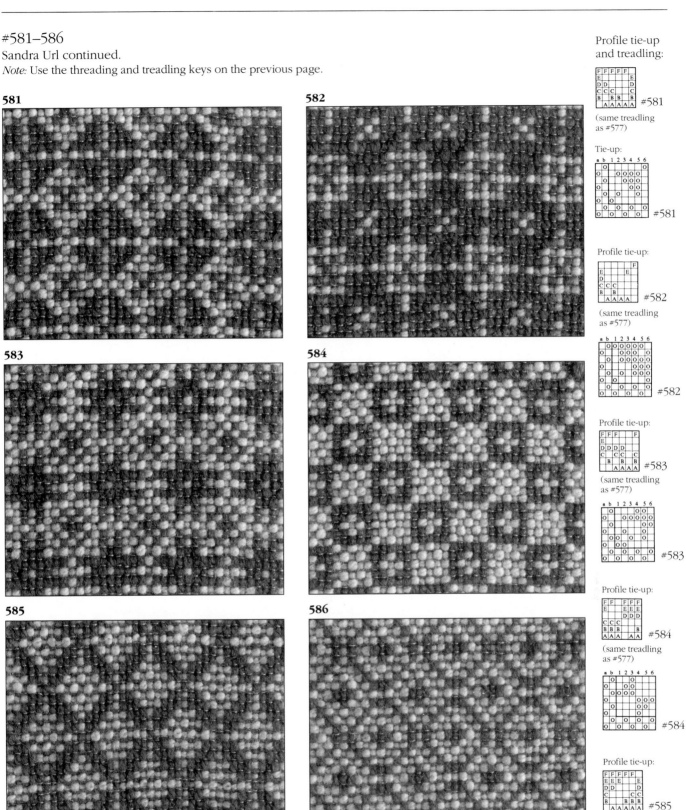

582

583

584

585

586

Profile tie-up and treadling:

#581

(same treadling as #577)

Tie-up:

#581

Profile tie-up:

#582

(same treadling as #577)

#582

Profile tie-up:

#583

(same treadling as #577)

#583

Profile tie-up:

#584

(same treadling as #577)

#584

Profile tie-up:

#585

(same treadling as #577)

#585

Profile tie-up:

#586

(same treadling as #577)

Tie-up:

#586

#587

by Nadine Janke

Warp—heavy dark, fine light
Weft—heavy light, fine dark

#588

by Marie Wynne

Warp—heavy light, fine dark
Weft—heavy dark, fine light

#589 & #590

by Mary Jane Thorne

Warp—heavy dark, fine light
Weft—heavy light, fine light

Threading key:

Treadling key:

Treadling note:
Each square of the
profile treadling
represents one
fine-heavy-fine
sequence.

Profile draft:

#587

Tie-up:

#587

Profile tie-up
and treadling:

#588

Tie-up:

#588

Profile tie-up
and treadling:

#589

Tie-up:

#589

Profile tie-up
and treadling:

#590

Tie-up:

#590

Note: All these samples use the same profile threading, and threading and treadling keys.

587

588

589

590

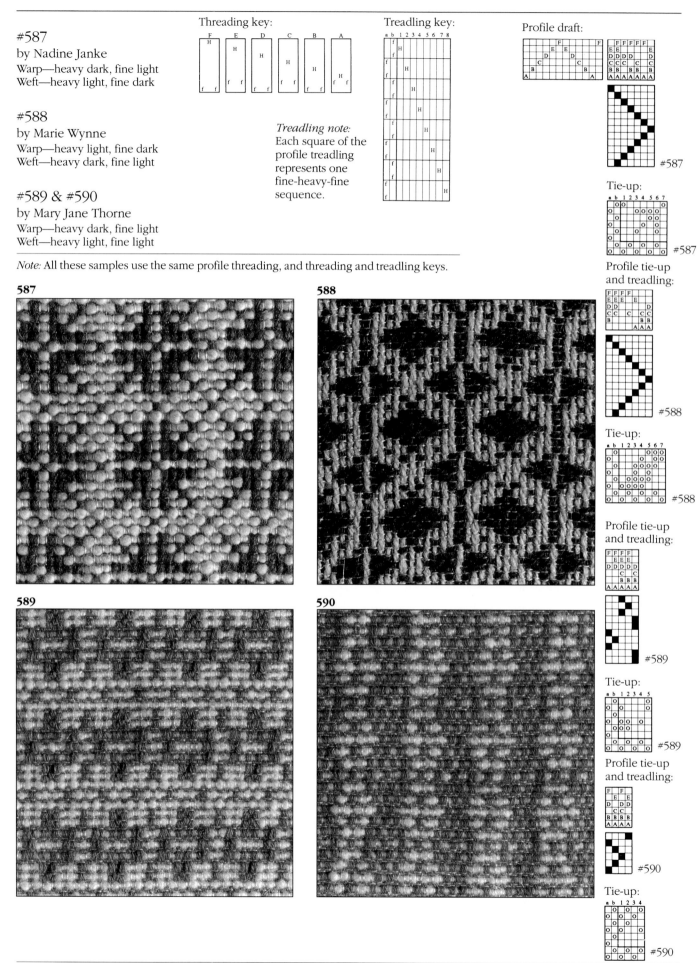

Chapter 18
OTHER TIE WEAVES AND SIMILAR THREADINGS

There are many variations possible using the concept of tie-down threads. In fact, some of these threadings fall into a "gray area" and cannot be classified as unit or tied weaves at all.

The weaves touched on here include *double 2-tie unit weave*, which Tidball calls "double summer & winter" because its threading units look just like summer & winter units but use two pattern shafts per block instead of one. (See Barrett and Smith's *Double Two-Tie Unit Weaves* monograph for more information on the weave.) The only double 2-tie sampler in this chapter (swatches #592 and #593) is a variant of the weave that Barrett and Smith call "double two-tie twill".

The weave sometimes called *tied beiderwand* (pronounced "by-der-vahndt") is also an extension of summer & winter; two pattern shafts are used for each unit. A weave with a similar threading is *Beiderwand* (German for "both walls"), which is really a double weave. Different forms of either weave are sometimes identified by the ratio of pattern or main ends to tie-down or secondary ends in the threading units. For details about these weaves, see the samples and other resources.

The "single 3-tie" threadings in this chapter are samples of so-called *half-satin* and *Bergman*. Some other threadings included here are Dr. William G. Bateman's tied weave variations (*boulevard* and *chevron*) and some weaves common in eastern Europe and Baltic countries but unknown to American handweavers until recently.

For more information about these weaves, see the samples in this chapter, Harriet Tidball's monograph *The Handloom Weaves*, Virginia I. Harvey's "Shuttle Craft Guild Monographs" on Dr. Bateman's weaves, and other resources about complex weaves.

591

#591
by Judith Gordon
4:1 tied beiderwand, "Expanded Zigzag". *Note:* In tied beiderwand, both faces of the cloth show spots of pattern weft in the background.

Threading key:

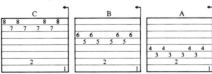

Treadling note: Each square of the profile treadling represents one 24-pick unit (the two pattern treadles of a block combination alternated 6X, with a tabby pick after each pattern pick).

Profile draft:

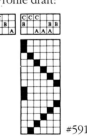

#591

Tie-up:

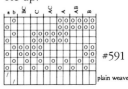

#591

plain weave

#592 & #593

by Aletha Hay

Double 2-tie unit weave, single units in reversing point threading.

+On the back, the pattern is sharply defined dark lines on a light ground.

*This is a point twill treadling. No tabby is used.

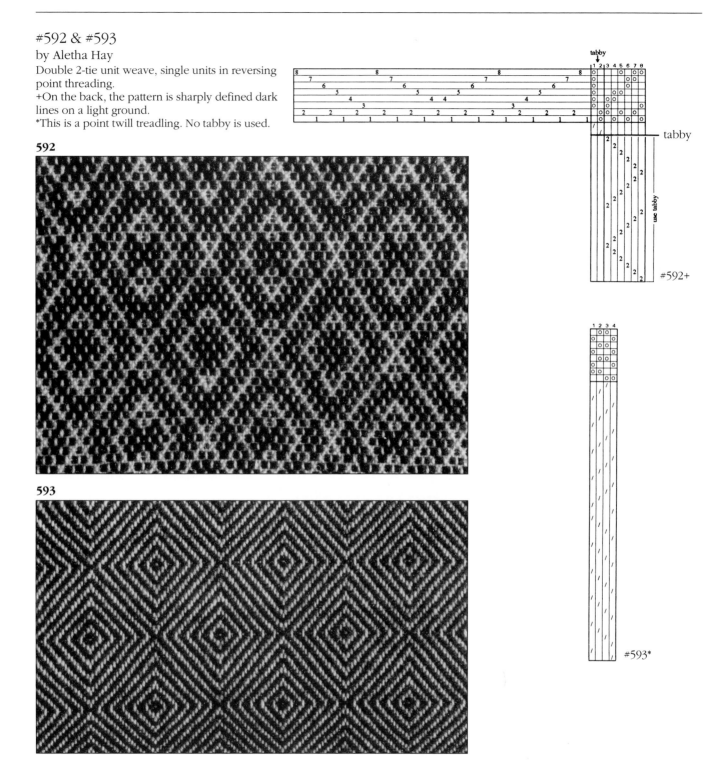

592

593

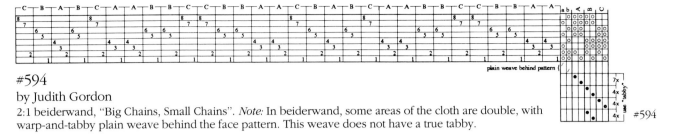

#594

by Judith Gordon

2:1 beiderwand, "Big Chains, Small Chains". *Note:* In beiderwand, some areas of the cloth are double, with warp-and-tabby plain weave behind the face pattern. This weave does not have a true tabby.

plain weave behind pattern

use "tabby" 7x 4x 4x 4x

#594

594

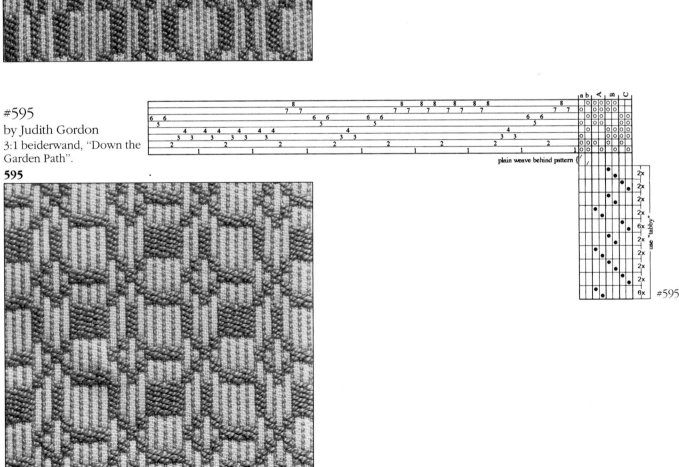

#595

by Judith Gordon

3:1 beiderwand, "Down the Garden Path".

plain weave behind pattern

use "tabby" 2x 2x 2x 2x 6x 2x 2x 2x 2x 6x

#595

595

#596–598

by Louise Giddings

4:1 tied beiderwand. *Note:* In this threading and treadling, one square represents 1/2 unit; two squares represent a whole unit. Tie-downs (1 and 2) alternate in the threading. The colors used in this sampler are: light pattern warps, dark tie-down warps, dark pattern weft, and light tabby weft.

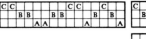

596

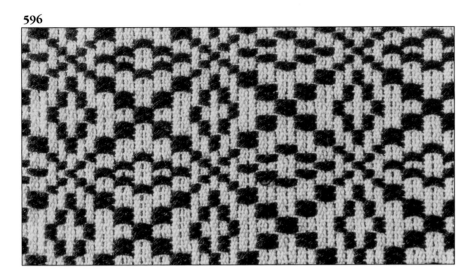

597

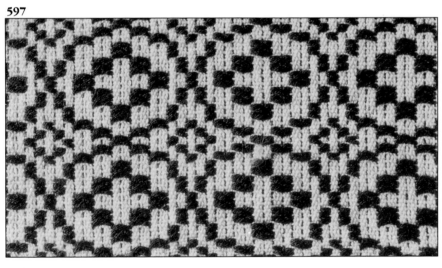

598

Threading key:

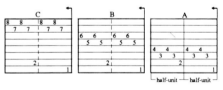

Tie-up and treadling key:

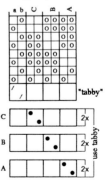

#599

by Noreen Rustad

3:1 beiderwand. *Note:* In this profile threading and treadling, one square represents a 1/2 unit. Tie-downs (1 and 2) alternate in the threading. This sampler uses a dark tie-down warp, light pattern warp, dark pattern weft, and light tabby weft.

599

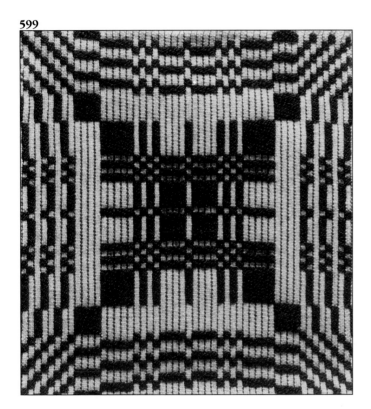

Profile draft:

#599

Threading key:

C B A

half-unit — half-unit

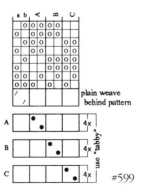

Tie-up and treadling key:

plain weave
behind pattern

A   4x
B   4x   use "tabby"
C   4x

#599

#600–602

by Gisela Evitt

Half satin weave, point twill profile draft.
Treadling note: Each two squares in these profile treadlings represent the number of pattern and tabby shots needed to "square" the two threading repeats (12 ends) of a block. Using these yarns, in patterns #600 and #602 that is 16 picks (eight each of pattern and tabby). In #601, it is 18 picks (9 each of pattern and tabby). At block changes, the pattern shafts change, but the rotation of the tie-down shafts (1, 2, and 3) remains the same. In #600, that rotation is 1, 1, 2, 2, 3, 3. In #601, they are used in 1, 2, 3, 1, 3, 2 order. In #602, only the shaft-1 tie-down is raised for each pattern shot.

Threading key:

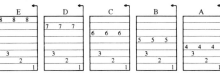

Profile draft:

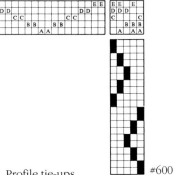

Tie-ups:

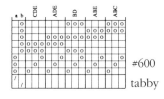

#600 tabby

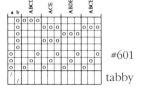

#601 tabby

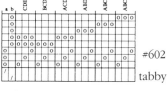

#602 tabby

Profile tie-ups and treadlings:

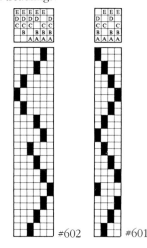

#600

#602   #601

600

601

602

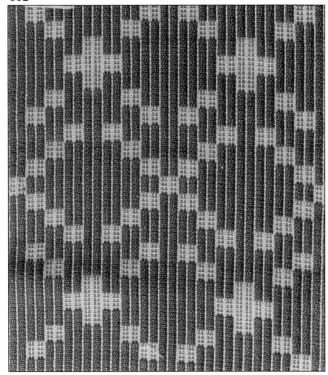

#603–605
by Ulla Bruhns
Bergman weave.

Threading key:

Profile draft and profile tie-ups and treadlings:

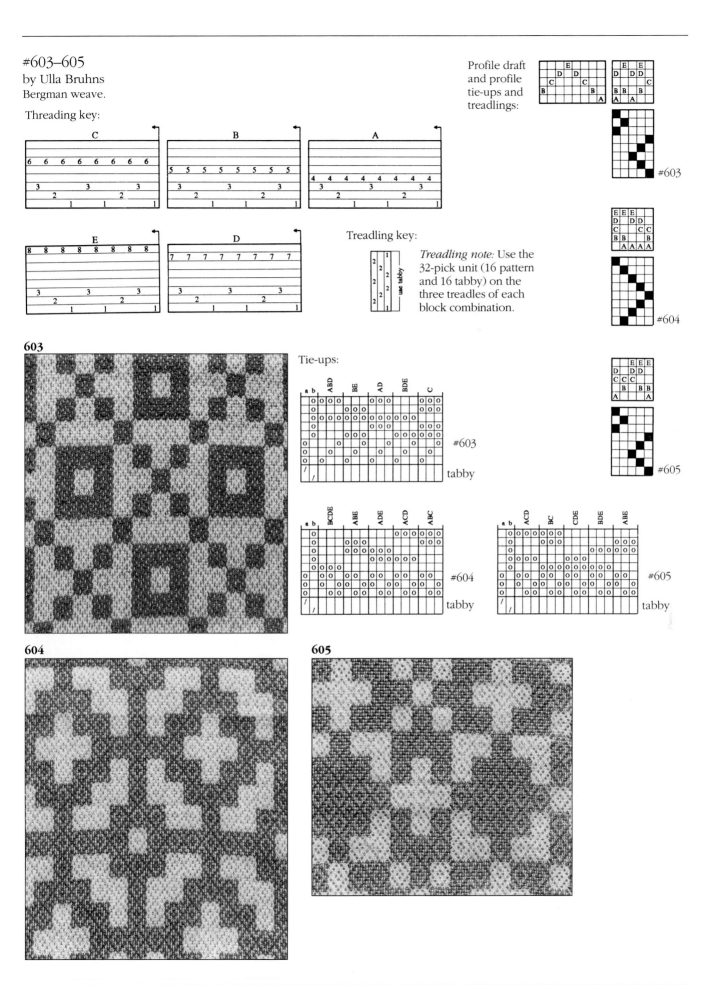

#603

#604

#605

Treadling key:

Treadling note: Use the 32-pick unit (16 pattern and 16 tabby) on the three treadles of each block combination.

Tie-ups:

#603 tabby

#604 tabby

#605 tabby

603

604

605

#606 & #607

by More Than 4 Study Group, Edmonton
Weavers' Guild
Boulevard weave.
*The back of the fabric has a dark grid with
light squares.

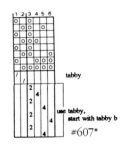

606

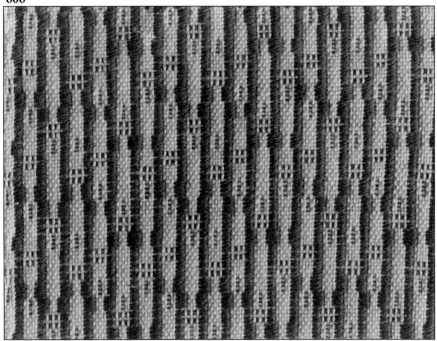

607

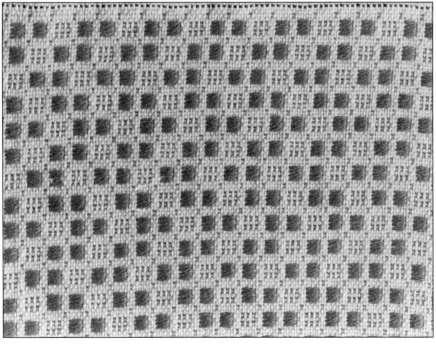

#608 & #609

by Mary Oehler

Chevron, draft #102 from *Boulevard, Chevron, and Combination Weaves,* edited by Virginia I. Harvey, Shuttle Craft Guild Monograph.
Note: This threading uses two of the 48 possible chevron blocks. See Shuttle Craft Guild Monograph #38, pages 67–68 for a complete listing of the blocks.

608

609

Chapter 19
ATWATER-BRONSON LACE

In the late 1920s, Mary M. Atwater rediscovered a spot weave used in early America for "diaper" table linens. She named that weave Bronson I, since she had found it in a book published in 1817 by J. and R. Bronson. As she worked with the weave she added a warp thread to stop the weft float at the end of each spot so that spots could be repeated in the threading. This newly-invented weave she called Bronson II (even though it had nothing to do with the Bronsons). The resulting confusion caused her to rename the weaves Bronson Spot and Bronson Lace, respectively. It was Harriet Tidball who, in her 1957 monograph *The Handloom Weaves*, suggested "Atwater Lace or at least Atwater-Bronson Lace" as a "more appropriate and definitive" name for the latter weave.

Tidball classifies the weave as a System in the Unit Class because it meets the definition of a weave having "rigidly set draft units to which there are no exceptions". Atwater-Bronson lace is usually woven with one weft which forms blocks of "spots" or "lace" in some areas and plain weave in others.

Threading

In Atwater-Bronson lace, shaft 1 carries alternate warp ends, shaft 2 is used to catch the float at the end of each unit, and each additional shaft carries the pattern warp for one block. Thus this lace weave can have six blocks on eight shafts.

The threading unit is six ends, always in the order: shaft 1, pattern shaft, shaft 1, same pattern, shaft 1, shaft 2. The threading key is shown in figure 19.1.

19.1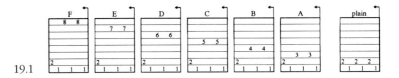

As shown in figure 19.1, blocks can also be threaded that will always weave plain weave regardless of which other blocks are weaving as pattern or plain weave. As with all unit weaves, units can be repeated at will in the threading but are not reversed.

If units are used singly they form spots of 5-end weft floats on the face of the fabric (with corresponding warp floats on the back). If they are repeated in the threading and treadling, they form lacy openwork between the floats within the pattern blocks. Each open space is divided by a + formed of a single warp end (on shaft 2) and weft pick (the sixth). Whether threaded for tied spots or for lace, the blocks not weaving as pattern automatically weave as plain weave.

Tie-up and Treadling Order

Plain weave is formed by lifting shaft 1 vs shafts 2-3-4-5-6-7-8.

Blocks can be woven independently or combined. It is also possible to weave "all blocks" (spots or lace all across, except where *threaded* for plain weave) or "no blocks" (plain weave). Each pattern block or block combination requires one treadle in addition to the tabbies. That treadle lifts shaft 2 plus the pattern shafts of the background (plain) blocks. A treadling unit is six picks: shaft 1, pattern, shaft 1, same pattern, shaft 1, tabby with shaft 2. (As mentioned above, using these units singly weaves spots; it takes two or more adjacent units in both threading and treadling to make lace.) Any blocks that are *threaded* plain weave (1, 2, 1, 2, 1, 2) always weave plain weave (see example in figure 19.2).

In the lace fabric, where there are pairs of weft floats on the face there are pairs of warp floats on the back. In the traditional form of the weave, the pattern is formed by blocks of weft floats (spots or lace) in the plain-weave ground. It is usually woven in fine, smooth threads with solid color warp and the same (or very similar) weft. But every block *can* be woven as weft skips *or* warp skips *or* plain weave on the face. It is possible to combine these and weave "turned lace" in which some blocks are warp floats, some are weft floats, and some are plain. The effect will show more clearly if the warp and the weft are contrasting solid colors. For such warp/weft lace, each block requires *two* treadles plus the tabbies. The six-pick treadling sequence for turned lace is:

1—shaft 1 plus warp-float shafts
2—shaft 2 plus warp-float plus plain-block shafts
3—same as first shed
4—same as second shed
5—shaft 1 alone
6—other tabby with shaft 2
(See figure 19.3 for an example.)

One extensive sampler in this book (#613–628) explores some of the possibilities of such turned lace. Because of the number of different lifts required for some of the patterns, a dobby or table loom may be needed for it.

Atwater-Bronson lace is traditionally woven of fine smooth threads at a sett that is slightly closer than that required for balanced plain weave (to allow for the collapse of the lace fabric.) The lace often doesn't show up very well when the fabric is still on the loom under tension; it takes the relaxation of the threads in washing or brisk manipulation to open up the lacy spaces.

Variations

Patterns in Atwater-Bronson lace can be enlarged or reduced by adding or subtracting 6-end units of threading or treadling. Blocks can be combined in the tie-up and treadling. Tie-up and treadling can be modified to make a pattern "turned lace". Color can be added to the traditional form by threading and/or treadling the shaft-1 threads one color, and the pattern and shaft-2 threads another color, in 1/1 alternation. The threading can also be used as a basis for a parallel shadow weave threading.

Atwater-Bronson lace can be treadled as a spot weave by using a heavy, contrasting pattern weft for each pattern pick in the treadling while the tabbies are kept fine. The treadling is altered to a 4-pick sequence: shaft 1, pattern, other tabby, same pattern. The "other tabby" thread forms a weftwise cord with the pair of pattern picks in the background blocks and it weaves plain weave behind the spots of pattern floats. This spot form of the weave is especially effective if the threading is single (unrepeated) units of lace. Samples #629–638 in this chapter were woven this way.

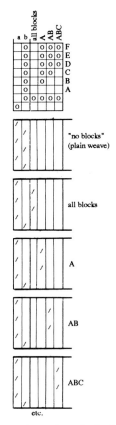

19.2

This is the traditional method of Atwater-Bronson lace tie-up and treadling.

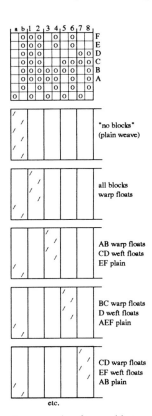

19.3

An example of turned lace.

#610

by Addie Lienau

"Concentric squares" from *Versatile Bronson* by Dorothy S. Burton. Use keys below.

610

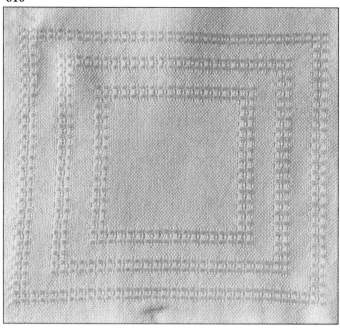

Profile draft:

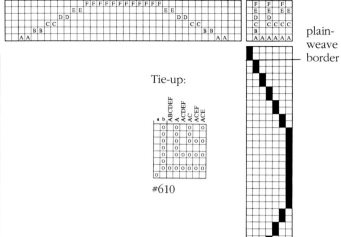

Tie-up:

#610

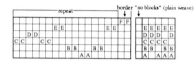
plain-weave border

#610

#611 & #612

by Margaret Gaynes

Note: Block F is used for borders, which, in these two samples, weaves plain weave. Because it *is* a block threading and not a plain-weave threading, it *can* weave as pattern.

*"Dogwood flowers" in Atwater-Bronson lace.

Profile draft:

#611*

611

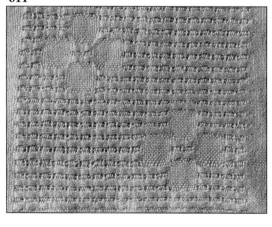

612

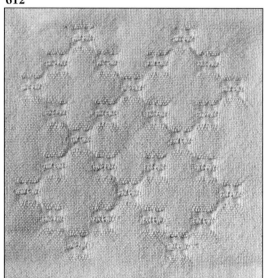

Profile tie-ups and treadlings:

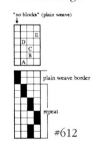

#612

Treadling note: For traditional Atwater-Bronson lace, each square of the profile treadling represents one 6-pick sequence: shaft 1, pattern treadle, shaft 1, same pattern, shaft 1, other tabby (2-3-4-5-6-7-8). A square in the profile column marked "no blocks" represents six picks of plain weave.

Tie-ups:

#611

#612

Example treadling unit:

Threading key:

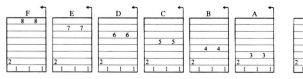

#613–616

by Mary Smith

Turned Atwater-Bronson lace. *Note:* All samples are woven with a dark weft on a light warp. *Treadling note:* For "turned lace" on an Atwater-Bronson lace threading, a profile diagram is given in place of the usual lettered profile tie-up. Each column of the diagram indicates which units are warp floats ⊞ , weft floats ⊟ , and plain weave ▢ . In the profile treadling, each square represents one 6-pick sequence using the two pattern treadles for that warp-weft-plain combination. The sequence is: pattern/1, pattern/2, pattern/1, pattern/2, shaft 1, other tabby (2-3-4-5-6-7-8); see this chapter's text for more detail.

A square in the profile column marked "no blocks" represents six picks of plain weave.

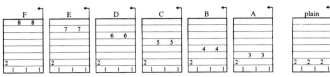

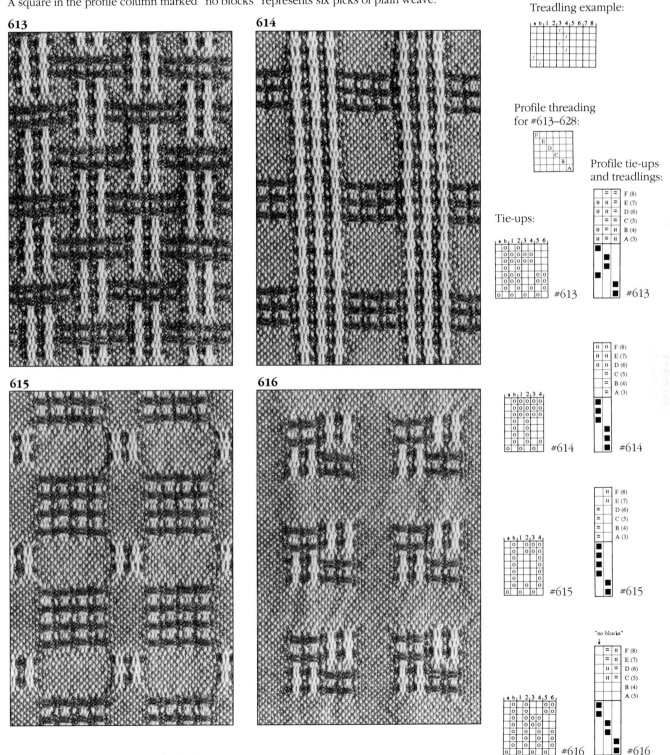

185

#617–622

Mary Smith continued.

Note: Use treadling and threading keys on the previous page.

Profile threading:

617

618

619

620

621

622

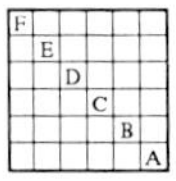

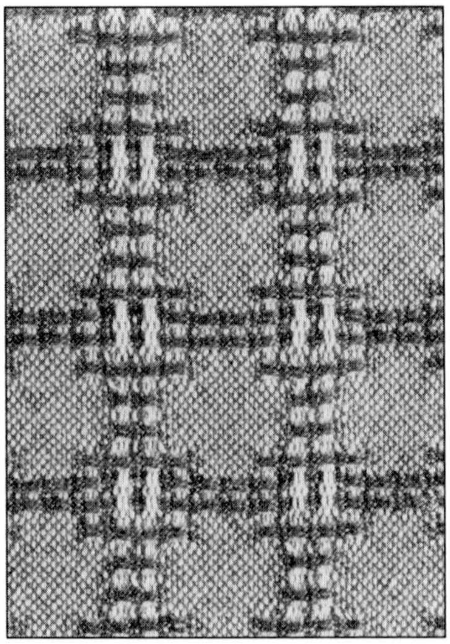

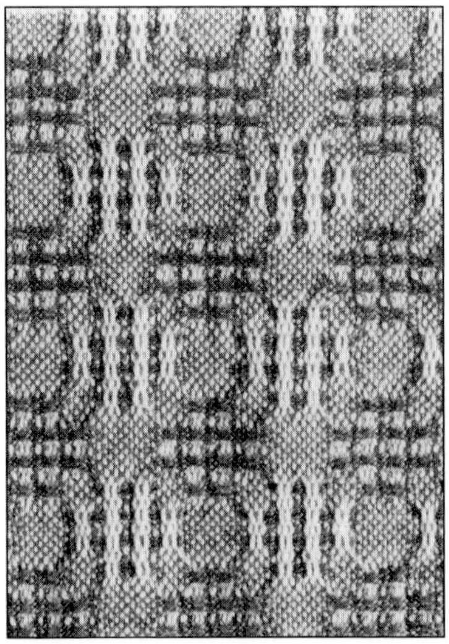

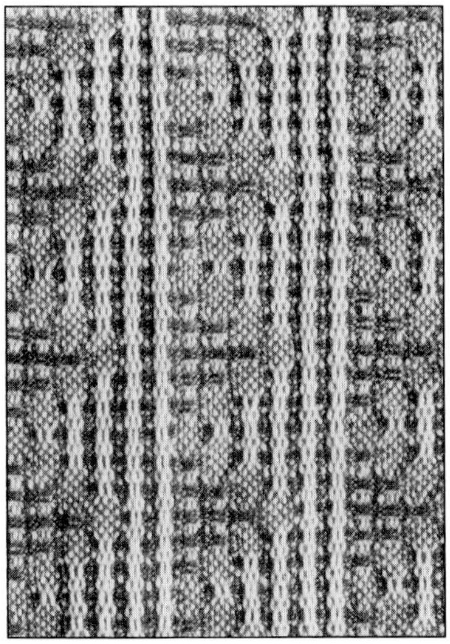

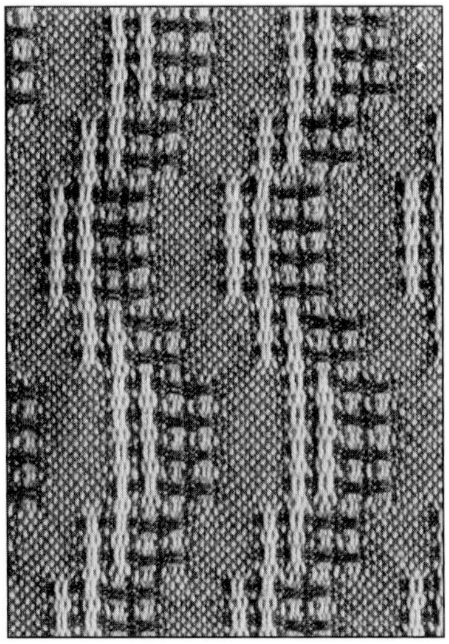

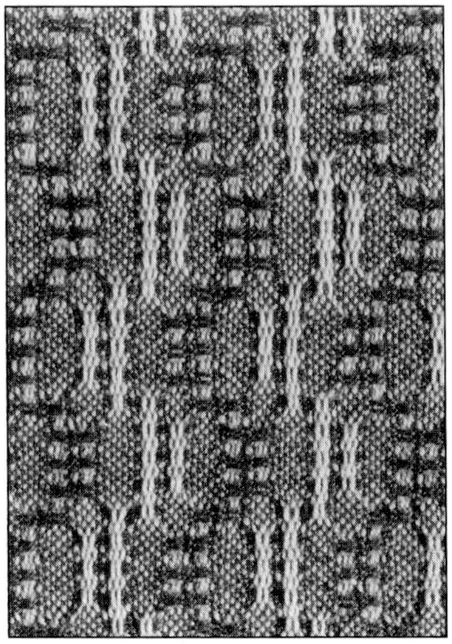

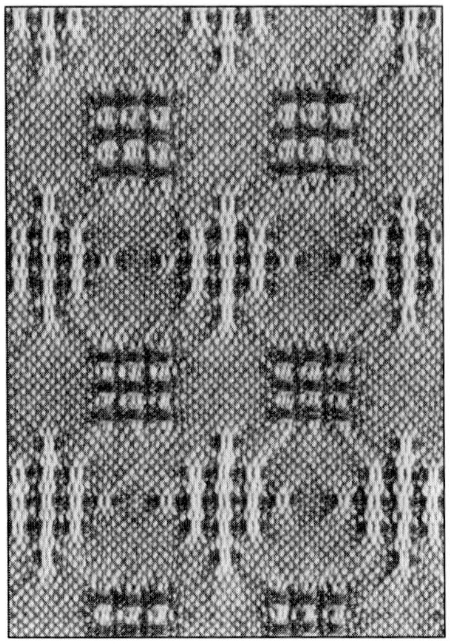

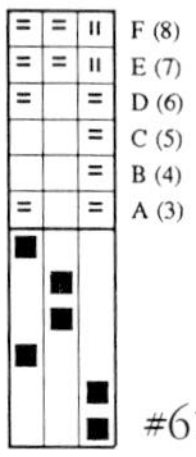

Tie-ups:

#617

#618

#619

#620

#621

#622

Profile tie-ups and treadlings:

#617

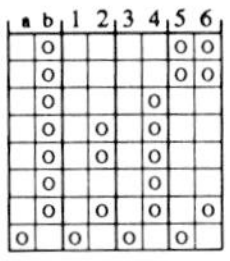

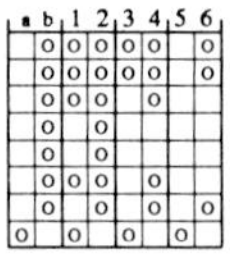

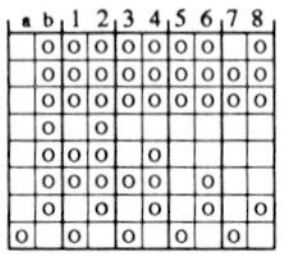

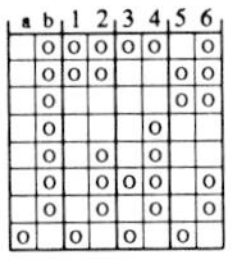

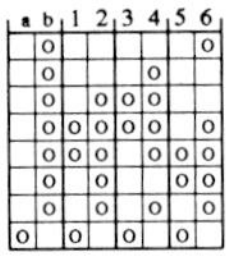

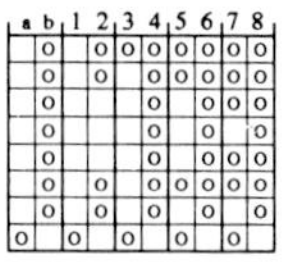

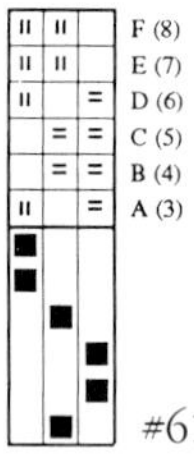

#618

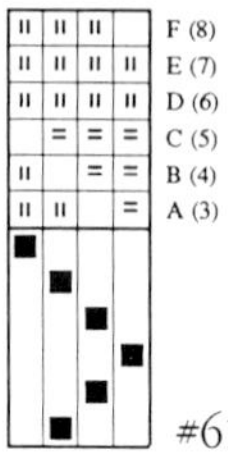

#619

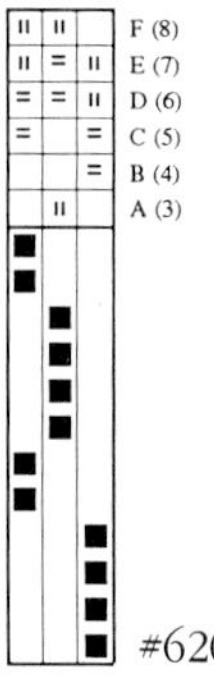

#620

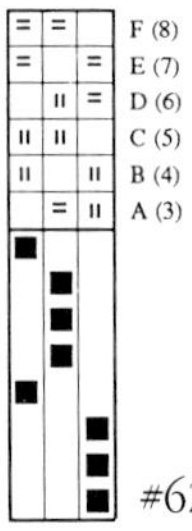

#621

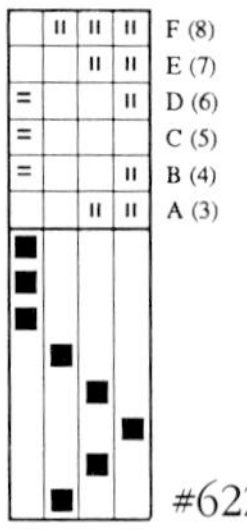

#622

Mary Smith continued.

Note: Use profile threading and threading and treadling keys shown on page 185.

Profile threading:

Profile tie-ups
and treadlings:

Tie-ups:

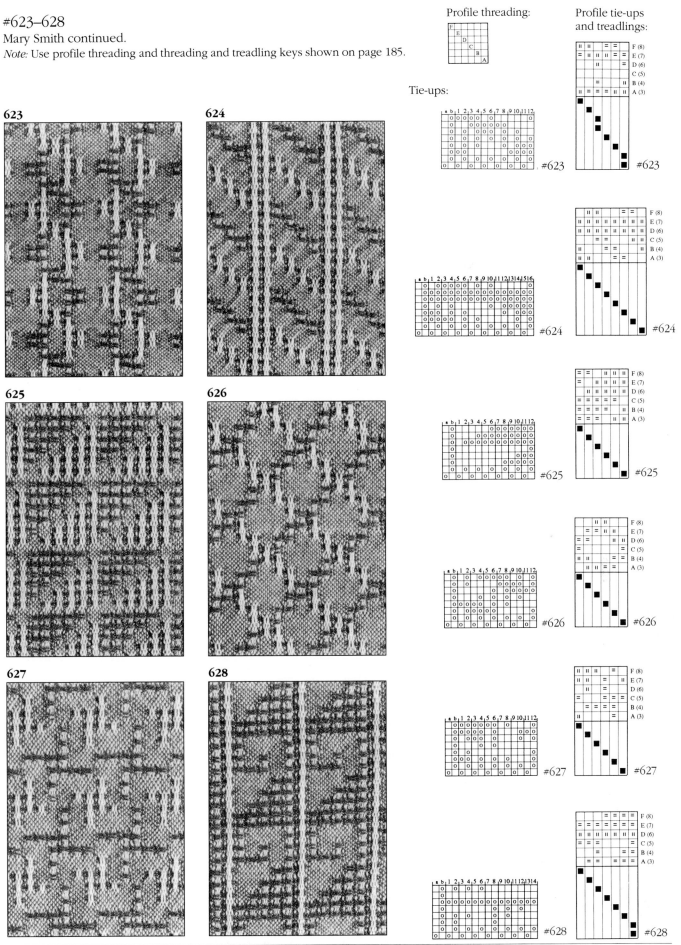

623

624

625

626

627

628

#629 & #630
by Jean E. Sucher

Atwater-Bronson lace woven as spot "Criss-cross Diamonds" adapted from *Recipe Book* by Mary Meigs Atwater.

629

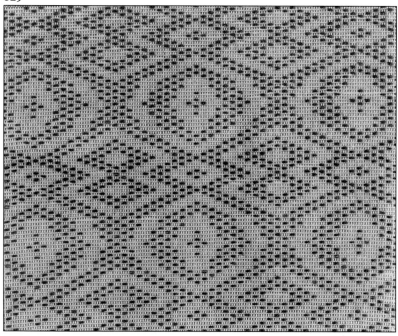

630

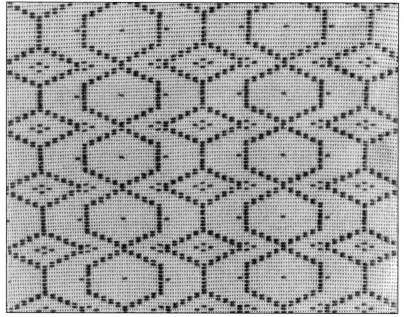

Profile draft:

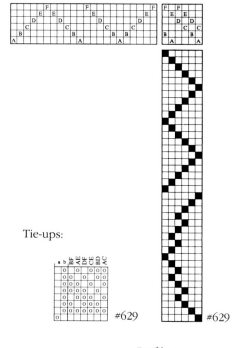

Tie-ups:

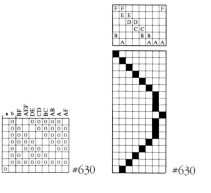

#629   #629

Profile tie-up
and treadling:

#630   #630

Treadling note: For this "heavy spot" treadling on an Atwater-Bronson lace threading, each square of the profile treadling represents a 4-pick sequence: shaft 1 (tabby weft), pattern (pattern weft), other tabby (tabby weft), same pattern (pattern weft).

A square in the profile column marked "no blocks" represents a 4-pick tabby-pattern-tabby-pattern sequence: a, b, b, b on the tabby treadles.

Threading key:

Example
treadling unit.

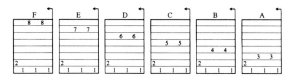

#631–638

by Jeanne Young Kudlicki

Lace woven as spot borders. *Note:* Some of these borders can be woven as repeating patterns with or without a "no-blocks" line between them. Use threading key and treadling note on previous page.

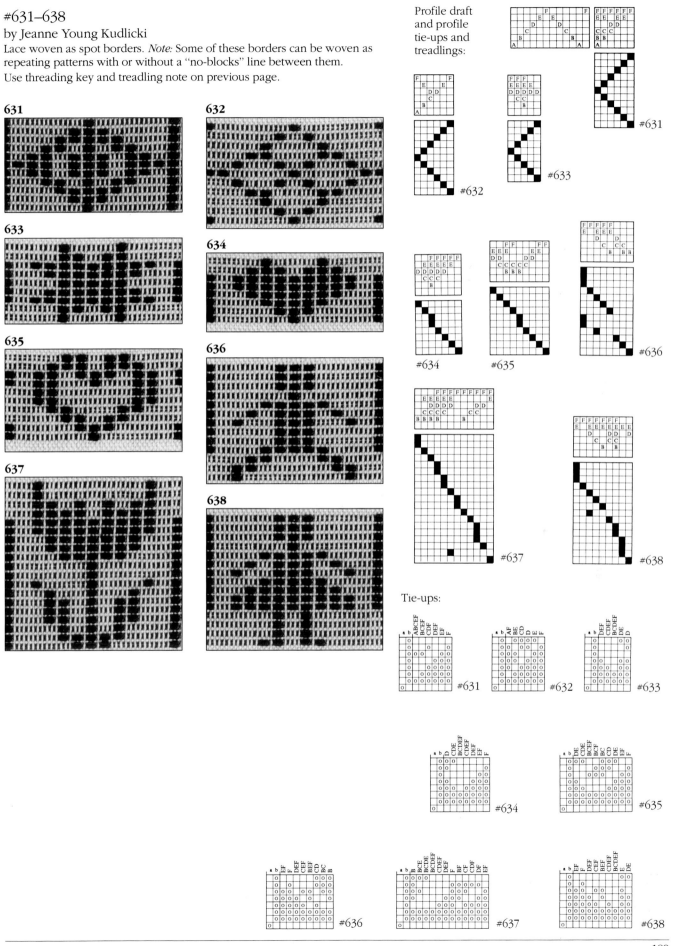

631

632

633

634

635

636

637

638

Profile draft and profile tie-ups and treadlings:

#631

#632

#633

#634

#635

#636

#637

#638

Tie-ups:

#631

#632

#633

#634

#635

#636

#637

#638

Chapter 20
SPOT BRONSON

Spot Bronson is a traditional linen weave which Mary Atwater discovered in the Bronsons' 1817 book and reintroduced to American handweavers. It is the weave she first called "Bronson I"—the structure which, modified with ends that anchor the floats, became Atwater-Bronson lace (see chapter 19). Spot Bronson has been a widely-known weave for a long time. According to Berta Frey it has been called "diaper" (in the Bronson book), "droppdräll" or "sjusprangdräll" (in Scandinavian countries), "Gerstenkornbindung" (German for "barleycorn"), and "spot weave" or "speck weave" (in colonial America). As traditionally woven, it is a one-shuttle weave with pattern formed by pairs of 5-end weft floats in some areas and plain weave in others. Weft floats on the face have comparable warp floats on the back.

Threading

In spot Bronson one shaft carries alternate threads (usually shaft 1 because it is closest to the weaver, and on a jack-type floor loom it requires less effort to lift). The remaining shafts carry the pattern threads, one shaft per block. Each block is formed by four threads and is not repeated (because repeating a group lengthens the floats). The key is shown in figure 20.1.

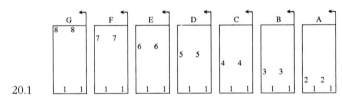

20.1

Blocks are usually threaded in straight or point or repeat twill order. Large areas of pattern can be woven by threading two blocks alternately—for example BCBCBCB. It is possible to thread areas of plain weave by sacrificing one of the seven blocks; repeat the threading for that block (such as 1, 2, 1, 2, 1, 2, 1, 2) as wide as the plain-weave area is to be, then tie and treadle it so that it always weaves plain weave, never pattern.

Tie-up and Treadling Order

Plain weave is formed by lifting 1 vs 2-3-4-5-6-7-8. A pattern treadling group is four picks of the same yarn: shaft 1, pattern shafts, shaft 1, same pattern. Each "pattern" treadle lifts the pattern shafts of whatever blocks are to weave plain weave. Float blocks must always alternate with plain blocks; that is, D can weave pattern at the same time as B or F but *not* with C or E (an example is shown in figure 20.2). If one block is reserved for plain weave in the threading, that block's pattern shaft must always be lifted on all pattern treadles.

Like Atwater-Bronson lace, Spot Bronson can be woven as turned spots (some weft and some warp spots). Sample #645 is an example of this. (In the tie-up, lift shaft 1 plus the warp-float pattern shafts vs all pattern shafts except the weft-float ones.)

Spot Bronson is traditionally woven of fine smooth yarns at a sett that is slightly closer than balanced plain weave (to allow for the collapse of the spots). The warp and weft are usually the same (or are closely related solid colors). If, instead, the warp is a solid color but the weft is two colors used alternately, with the pattern shots a contrasting color, the weft floats stand out as overshot spots on a pin-dotted background (see samples #646–648).

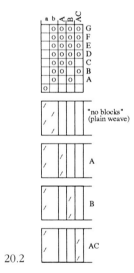

20.2

Variations

Spots can be shortened to two ends or lengthened to six ends in the threading, although the smaller spots tend to differ little from the plain weave. Spots of different sizes are seldom combined in one threading.

Another spot Bronson idea: The threading can also be used for a supplementary-weft structure by using a contrasting heavier weft for pattern, and by following each pattern pick with *two* (alternating) tabby picks.

#639–642

by Louetta Heindl Kambic

Spot Bronson—point profile from *The Shuttle-craft Book of American Hand-Weaving* by Mary Meigs Atwater.

Profile draft and profile tie-ups and treadlings:

639

640

641

642

Tie-ups:

#639

#640

#641

#642

#639

#640

#641

#642

Threading key:

Treadling note: For traditional spot Bronson, each square in the profile treadling represents one 4-pick unit: shaft 1, pattern treadle, shaft 1, same pattern treadle (using the same yarn unless otherwise noted). Example treadling unit:

#643 & # 644

by Nancy Mitchell

"Bethlehem Star", designed by Carol Strickler.
Note: Medium weft on light warp. See threading key
below and treadling note on page 191.

Profile draft:

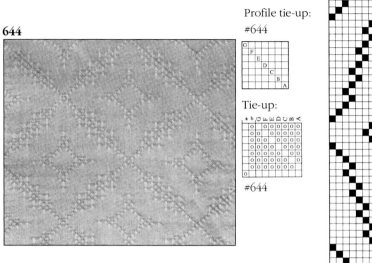

Profile tie-up:
#644

Tie-up:
#644

#643
&
#644

643

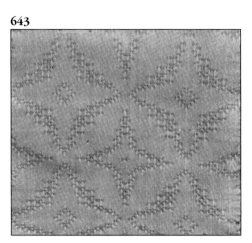

644

Tie-up:

#643

#645

by Kathryn Wertenberger

Turned spots. *Note:* Dark weft on medium warp.

645

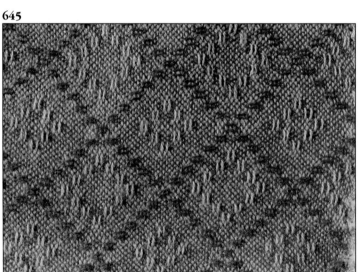

Profile draft:

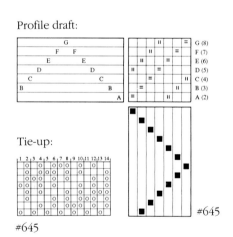

			G (8)
			F (7)
			E (6)
			D (5)
			C (4)
			B (3)
			A (2)

Tie-up:

#645

#645

Threading key:

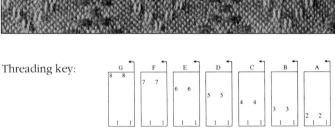

Treadling note: For "turned spot" on a spot Bronson threading, a profile diagram is
given in place of the usual lettered profile tie-up. Each column of the diagram indicates
which units are warp floats ⊞, weft floats ⊟, and plain weave ☐. In the profile
treadling, each square represents one 4-pick sequence using the two treadles for that
warp-weft-plain combination. The sequence is: 1/warp floats, 2/all except weft floats,
same as first, same as second. Example treadling unit:

a b 1 2 etc.

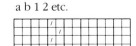

#646–648

by Priscilla Lynch

"Table & Diamonds", designed by Carol Strickler. *Note:* These samplers are woven with a dark pattern weft on a light warp with light tabby; 4-pick sequence is therefore: shaft 1 (tabby weft), pattern treadle (pattern weft), same as first, same as second.

Profile draft:

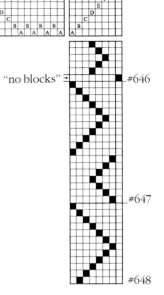

646

647

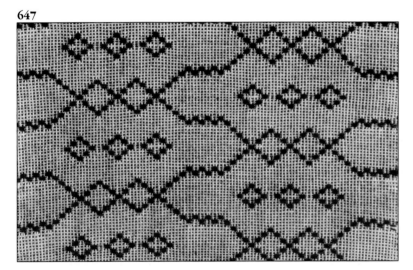

"no blocks"   #646

#647

#648

Tie-up:

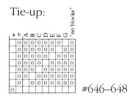

#646–648

648

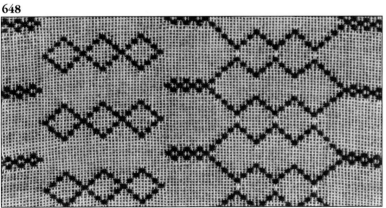

Treadling note: For traditional spot Bronson, each square in the profile treadling represents one 4-pick unit: shaft 1, pattern treadle, shaft 1, same pattern treadle (using the same yarn unless otherwise noted). Example treadling unit:

Threading key:

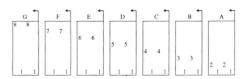

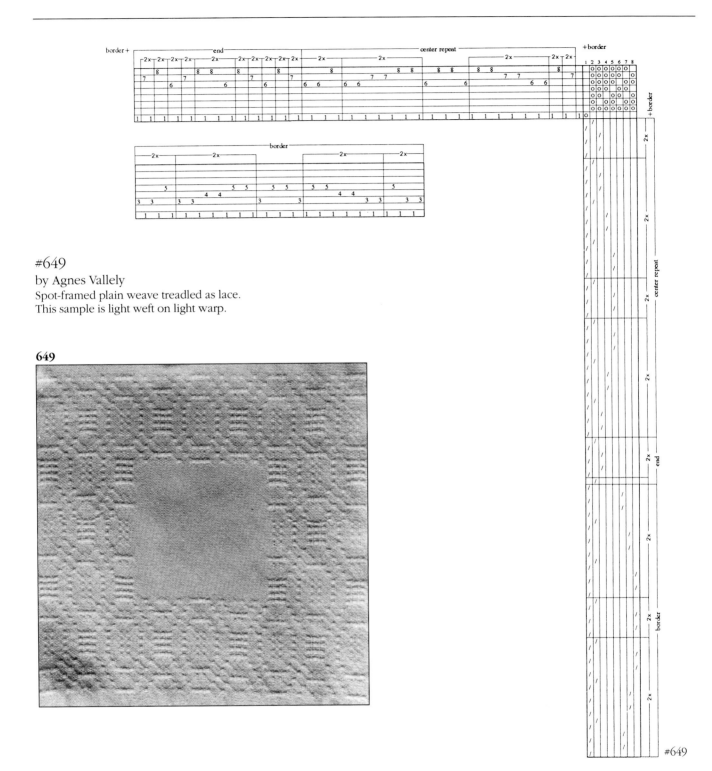

#649

by Agnes Vallely
Spot-framed plain weave treadled as lace.
This sample is light weft on light warp.

649

Chapter 21
HUCK AND HUCK LACE

Traditionally used for toweling, the weave known as *huck* (or "huckaback") is a one-shuttle structure with a pattern of weft-float spots and plain weave. In its original 4-shaft form the threading is 5-end half-units alternating on separate pairs of shafts. See figure 21.1. This is tied up and treadled so that when one half-unit weaves spots—pairs of weft floats (with corresponding warp floats on the back)—the alternate half-unit weaves plain weave.

Expansion of the threading to eight shafts makes possible spots of weft floats on plain, spots of warp floats on plain, and alternating warp and weft floats that form openwork (huck lace)—all in one fabric.

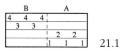

21.1

Full unit—two blocks

Threading

In 6-block 8-shaft huck two shafts are used throughout to form plain-weave sheds—shaft 1 in one half-unit and shaft 2 in the other. Each additional shaft provides a block of pattern. There must be an odd number of ends in each half-unit (usually five). Threading key for half-units is shown in figure 21.2.

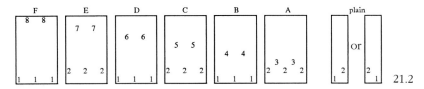

21.2

Odd-plus-2 and even-plus-1 half-units must alternate. So to thread a large area of pattern, two blocks must be alternated—ABABABA, for example. The most effective huck designs are threaded with the blocks in straight or point profile order. Areas threaded "plain" always weave as plain weave.

Half-units can be shortened to three ends or lengthened to seven, but are usually the same size throughout one piece (although one sampler in this chapter does effectively use a draft of mixed half-unit lengths).

Tie-up and Treadling Orders

Plain weave is woven by lifting "odds" vs "evens", 1-3-5-7 vs 2-4-6-8.

Warp-float blocks and weft-float blocks can alternate with plain blocks or with each other in the fabric. The profile tie-up can be written to indicate float direction of each block, as shown in figure 21.3.

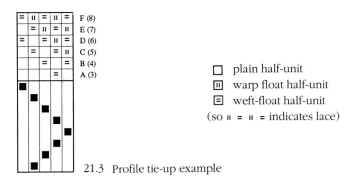

□ plain half-unit

Ⅲ warp float half-unit

🗏 weft-float half-unit

(so ‖ = ‖ = indicates lace)

21.3 Profile tie-up example

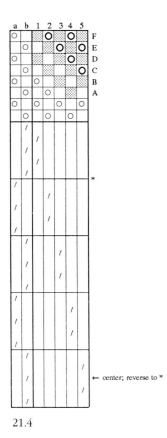

← center; reverse to *

21.4

When the threading is 5-end half-units, each treadling half-unit is five picks. One half-unit is:

       1—odd tabby (1-3-5-7)
       2—pattern (2-4-6-8 plus odd warp-float shafts minus even weft-float shafts)
       3—odd tabby
       4—same pattern
       5—odd tabby

The other half-unit is:

       1—even tabby (2-4-6-8)
       2—pattern (1-3-5-7 plus even warp-float shafts minus odd weft-float shafts)
       3—even tabby
       4—same pattern
       5—even tabby

Treadling sequences must be in full units (alternating half-units). For example, the full tie-up and treadling for the above profile example is shown in figure 21.4. (In this example, figure 21.4, the subtracted shafts have been shaded to accentuate their absence, and the added shafts are bold-faced to accentuate their addition.)

If the threading half-units have been altered in size, the treadling units can be correspondingly reduced to three picks or increased to seven, but are usually consistent throughout and not mixed in size. Three-end/three-pick half-units produce a delicately-textured cloth of single short floats. Seven-end/seven-pick half-units produce a bolder texture of longer triple warp floats and weft floats.

Variations

Huck is usually woven with a single weft the same as (or very similar to) the warp, but many variations are possible. A huck threading can be woven as a supplementary-weft weave, with a contrasting pattern weft that repeats pattern shots, each pick followed by a tabby pick. (The tabbies can repeat as in a huck unit, or they can alternate as they do in normal overshot and other supplementary-weft/plain-ground treadlings.) A few such variations are shown in this chapter. Color effects can be introduced or a huck threading can be used as the basis for a "parallel shadow weave".

It is also possible to thread *4-block* huck on eight shafts by using two separate shafts for each block, just as in the 4-shaft original form (see pp. 204–205).

#650

by Verna Gabourie
This sample is light
warp on light weft.

Threading key:

**Profile threading
for #650 & #651:**

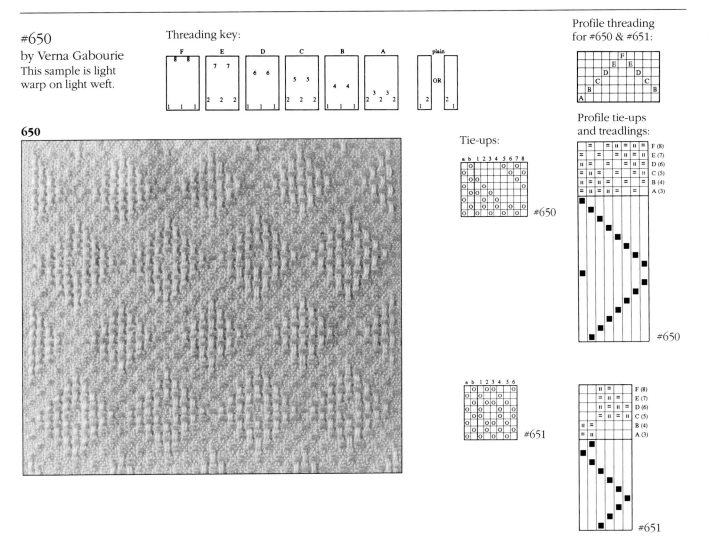

650

Tie-ups:

#650

**Profile tie-ups
and treadlings:**

=		=		=	‖	=	‖	=	F (8)
=			=		=		‖	=	E (7)
‖	=			=		=	‖	=	D (6)
=	‖	=			=		=	‖	C (5)
‖	=	‖	=			=		=	B (4)
=	‖	=	‖	=			=	A (3)

#650

#651

		‖	=				F (8)
	=	‖	=				E (7)
			‖	=	‖	=	D (6)
		=	‖	=	‖	C (5)
‖	=					B (4)
=	‖					A (3)

#651

#651

by Nonah Weavers

This sample is medium weft on light warp. It uses the same profile threading and keys as sample #650.

651

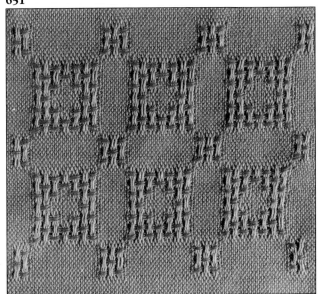

Treadling note: Each column of the profile tie-up diagram indicates which blocks weave as warp floats ▣ , weft floats ▣ , and plain weave ☐ . Each square in the profile treadling represents one 5-pick half-unit. One half-unit is: odd tabby, pattern-treadle-with-2, odd tabby, same pattern treadle, odd tabby. The other half-unit is: even tabby, pattern-treadle-with-1, even tabby, same pattern treadle, even tabby. The two types of half-units must alternate (or be separated by plain weave). Example of two half-units in treadling:

A column designated "no blocks" in the profile represents five picks of plain weave (*a, b, a, b, a* or *b, a, b, a, b*) unless otherwise noted.

Treadling example:

#652 & #653

by Joyce R. Schatz

Huck point from Marian Powell Carpenter.
This sample is light weft on light warp.

Profile threading:

652

Profile tie-ups
and treadlings:

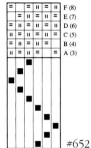

#652

Tie-ups:

#652

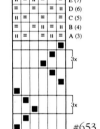

#653

653

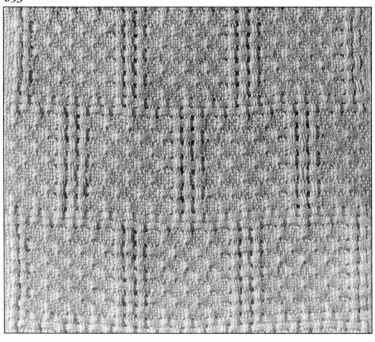

#653

Treadling note: Each column of the profile tie-up diagram indicates which blocks weave as warp floats ⊞ , weft floats ⊟ , and plain weave ☐ . Each square in the profile treadling represents one 5-pick half-unit. One half-unit is: odd tabby, pattern-treadle-with-2, odd tabby, same pattern treadle, odd tabby. The other half-unit is: even tabby, pattern-treadle-with-1, even tabby, same pattern treadle, even tabby. The two types of half-units must alternate (or be separated by plain weave). Example of two half-units in treadling:

A column designated "no blocks" in the profile represents five picks of plain weave (*a, b, a, b, a* or *b, a, b, a, b*) unless otherwise noted.

Treadling example:

#654
by Sue McKenzie
This sample is light weft on light warp.

654

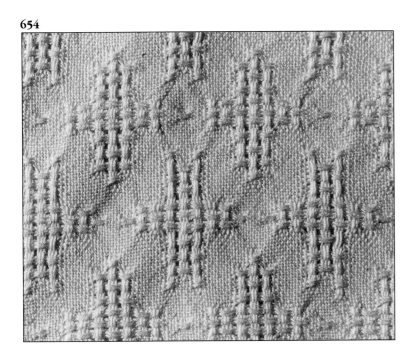

Note: Use the profile threading
and threading key, and
treadling note on the opposite
page.

Profile threading:

Tie-ups:

#654

#655

#656

Profile tie-ups
and treadlings:

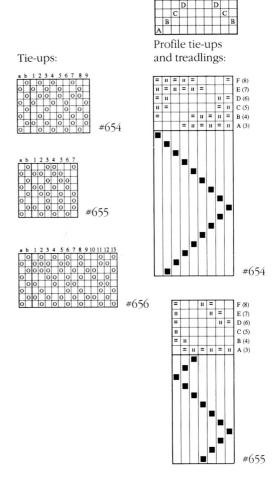

#654

#655

#655 & #656
by Frances Schultz, Lethbridge Handicraft Guild
These samples are light weft on light warp.

655

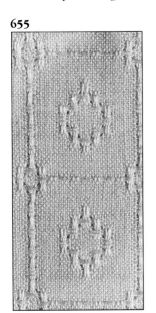

656

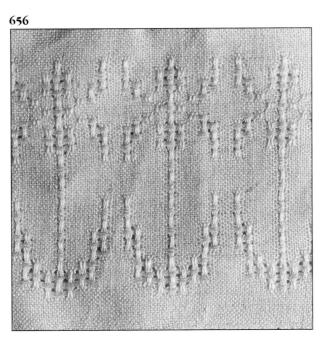

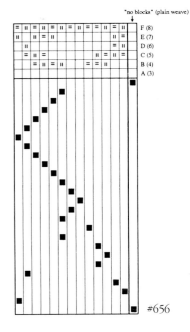

"no blocks" (plain weave)

#656

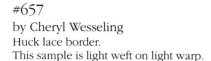

#657

by Cheryl Wesseling
Huck lace border.
This sample is light weft on light warp.

Threading key:

Profile threading:

657

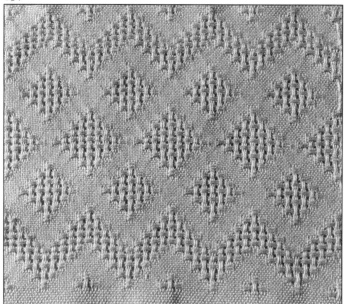

Profile tie-up
and treadling:

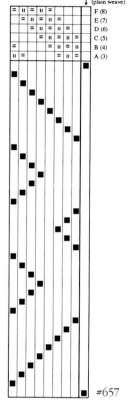

Tie-up:

#657

Treadling example:

Treadling note: Each column of the profile tie-up diagram indicates which blocks weave as warp floats ⊞ , weft floats ⊟ , and plain weave ☐ . Each square in the profile treadling represents one 5-pick half-unit. One half-unit is: odd tabby, pattern-treadle-with-2, odd tabby, same pattern treadle, odd tabby. The other half-unit is: even tabby, pattern-treadle-with-1, even tabby, same pattern treadle, even tabby. The two types of half-units must alternate (or be separated by plain weave). Example of two half-units in treadling:

A column designated "no blocks" in the profile represents five picks of plain weave (*a, b, a, b, a* or *b, a, b, a, b*) unless otherwise noted.

#658 & #659

by Joyce R. Schatz

Huck borders and huck diamond patterns from Marian Powell Carpenter. These samples are light weft on light warp.

Threading key:

Profile threading for #658:

658

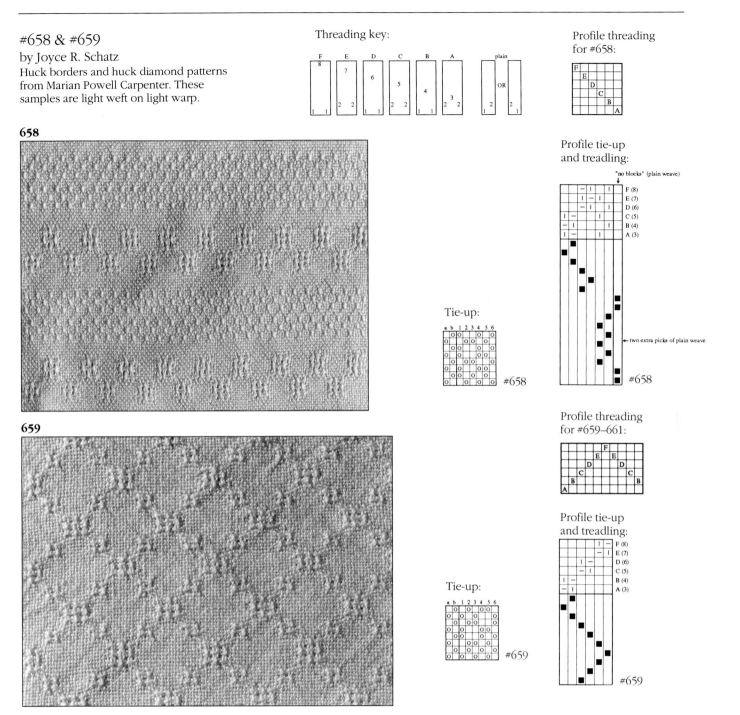

659

Tie-up:

#658

Profile tie-up and treadling:

"no blocks" (plain weave)

F (8)
E (7)
D (6)
C (5)
B (4)
A (3)

← two extra picks of plain weave

#658

Profile threading for #659–661:

Profile tie-up and treadling:

F (8)
E (7)
D (6)
C (5)
B (4)
A (3)

Tie-up:

#659

#659

Treadling note: Each column of the profile tie-up diagram indicates which blocks weave as warp float ▯ , weft float ▱ , and plain weave ☐ . Each square in the profile treadling represents one 3-pick half-unit. One half-unit is: odd tabby, pattern-treadle-with-2, odd tabby. The other half-unit is: even tabby, pattern-treadle-with-1, even tabby. The two types of half-units must alternate (or be separated by plain weave). Example of two half-units in treadling:

Treadling example:

#660 & #661
Joyce R. Schatz continued.

Threading key:

F 8	E 7	D 6	C 5	B 4	A 3	plain

2 2 | 1 1 ... (OR)

Profile threading:

660

661

Profile tie-ups and treadlings:

F (8) | E (7) | D (6) | C (5) | B (4) | A (3)

#660

#661

Tie-ups:

a b 1 2 3 4 5

#660

a b 1 2 3 4 5 6

#661

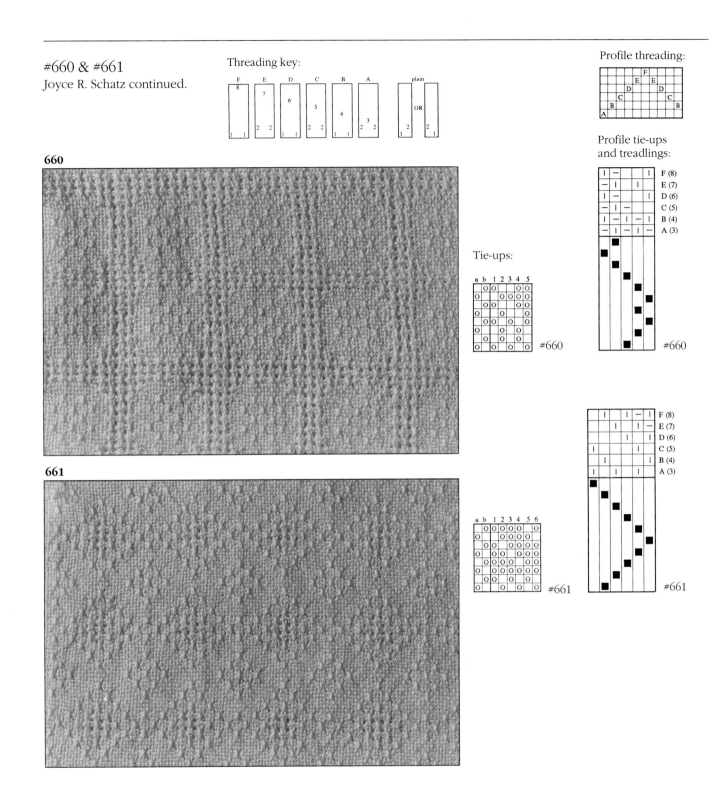

Treadling note: Each column of the profile tie-up diagram indicates which blocks weave as warp float ▣, weft float ⊟, and plain weave ☐. Each square in the profile treadling represents one 3-pick half-unit. One half-unit is: odd tabby, pattern-treadle-with-2, odd tabby. The other half-unit is: even tabby, pattern-treadle-with-1, even tabby. The two types of half-units must alternate (or be separated by plain weave). Example of two half-units in treadling:

Treadling example:

a b 1 2 3 4 5 6

#662–665

by Andrea Anderson

Samples #662–664 are light weft on light warp; #665 is dark weft on light warp. Use threading key and treadling note on the opposite page.

662

663

Tie-ups:

#662

664

#663

665

#664

#665

Profile tie-ups and treadlings:

#662

#663

#664

#665

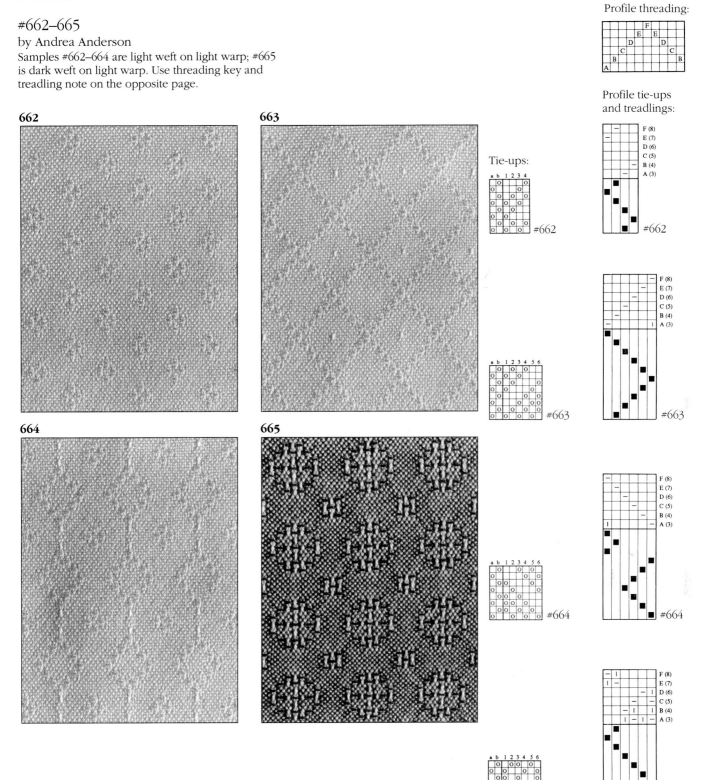

#666 & #667

Andrea Anderson continued.

These samples are dark weft on light warp. Use profile threading and keys on page 202.

Profile tie-ups and treadlings:

666

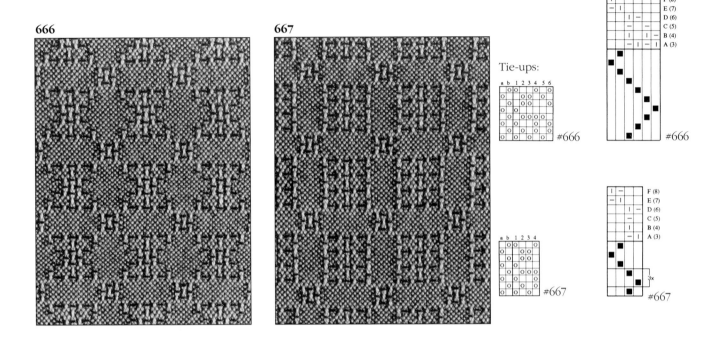

667

Tie-ups:

#666

#667

#666

#667

#668 & #669

#668 is woven by Trudy Fratschko; #669 is woven by Helen Budd, both from the London District Weavers and Spinners.

4-block huck. Both samples are light weft on dark warp.

668

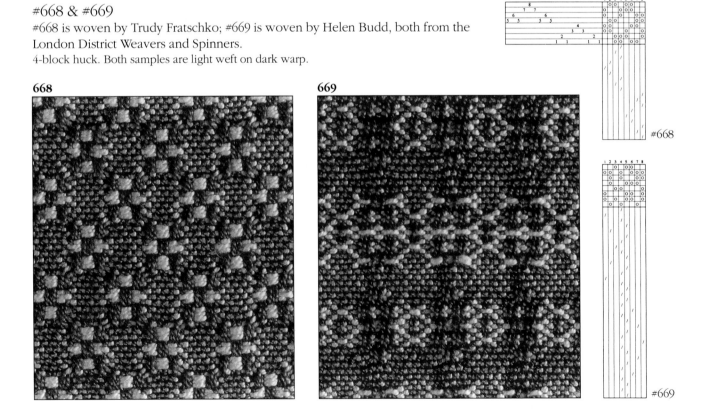

669

#668

#669

#670 & #671

#670 is woven by Donna Fleming; #671 is woven by Jean Cornish, both from the London District Weavers and Spinners. 4-block huck. Both samples are light weft on dark warp.

670

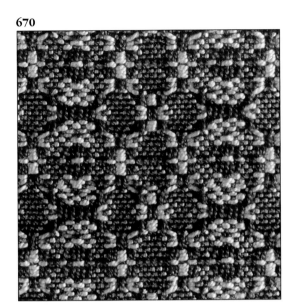

671

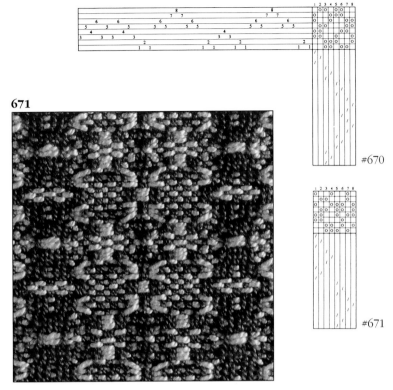

#670

#671

#672 & #673

by Norma Smayda

4-block huck. These samples are medium weft on light warp.

672

673

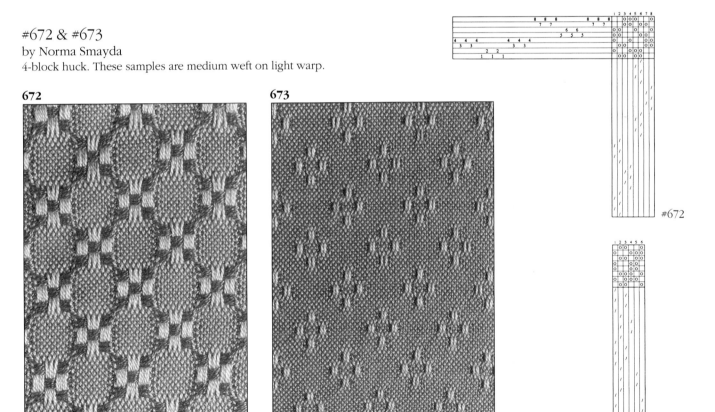

#672

#673

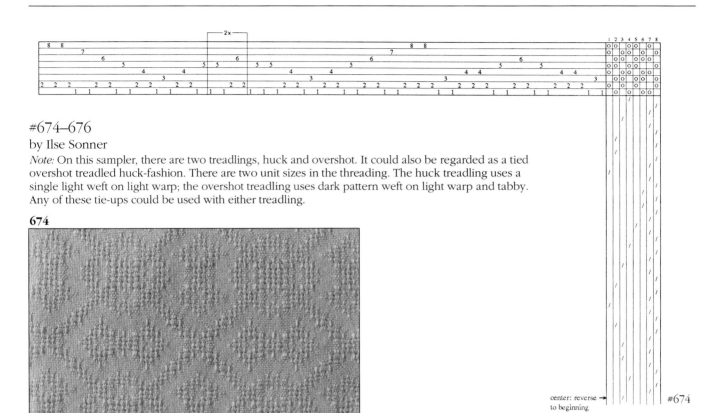

#674–676
by Ilse Sonner

Note: On this sampler, there are two treadlings, huck and overshot. It could also be regarded as a tied overshot treadled huck-fashion. There are two unit sizes in the threading. The huck treadling uses a single light weft on light warp; the overshot treadling uses dark pattern weft on light warp and tabby. Any of these tie-ups could be used with either treadling.

674

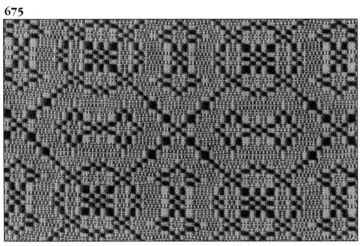

center: reverse →
to beginning

#674

675

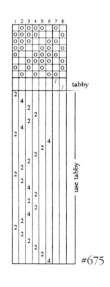

#675

676

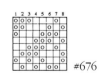

#676

Same treadling
as #675

#677
by May Kingman
8-block shadow huck.

677

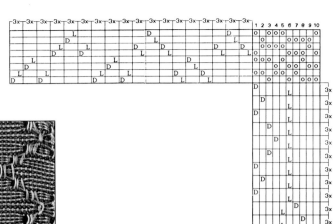

#677

D = dark
M = medium
L = light

#678
by Karen Evanson
Color-&-weave-effect "houndstooth" huck from a Marjorie O'Shaughnessy workshop.

#678

678

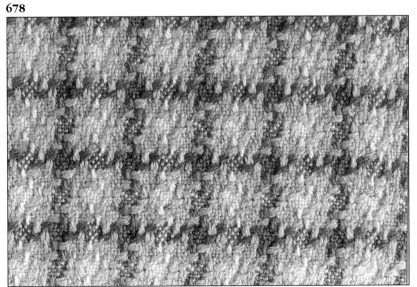

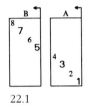

22.1

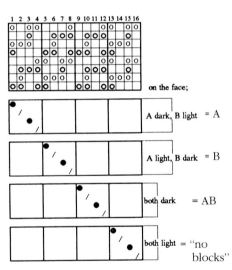

on the face;

A dark, B light = A

A light, B dark = B

both dark = AB

both light = "no blocks"

● = dark weft
/ = light weft

(Each 4-pick treadling unit weaves two picks in each layer.)

22.2

Chapter 22
BLOCK DOUBLE WEAVE

Block double weave is a structure with two sets of warp and weft. With eight shafts it is possible to weave 2-block patterns in double weave—each block containing two layers of plain-weave cloth. Pattern is formed by the layers interchanging warpwise and weftwise at block edges.

Threading

The usual threading for 2-block double weave is a 4-shaft straight draw with shafts 1 to 4 forming one block and 5 to 8 the other. Usually two colors are threaded alternately, so that odd shafts weave plain weave of one color and even shafts weave plain weave of the other color in each block (figure 22.1). (Each 4-end unit contains two ends for each layer—odds for one layer and evens for the other.) Warp sett is usually twice that required to weave balanced plain-weave single fabric in the yarn used.

Tie-up and Treadling Order

Single-layer plain weave is formed by 1-3-5-7 vs 2-4-6-8 (although plain-weave single cloth is usually warp-dominant or warp-faced because of the close sett).

Either layer can weave on the face in each block. Thus, for example, if the two colors are dark and light, options include: A dark and B light, A light and B dark, both dark, or both light (the latter two forming two separate layers all the way across the fabric). The colors are reversed on the back of the fabric. On the threading in figure 22.1, with dark on odd shafts and light on even shafts, the tie-up and treadling weaves the four options shown in figure 22.2.

Since both layers of the fabric are plain weave there are no floats. Units can be repeated at will to make either block as large or as small as desired in both the threading and the treadling. Any 2-block profile can be used, including one that weaves blocks both independently and combined.

Variations

To enlarge or reduce a block double-weave pattern, add or subtract 4-end units of threading and treadling from either block.

One major way of changing a 2-block double-weave design is enlarging or reducing the size of the blocks. Another is treadling the blocks in combination or in some other order than as-drawn-in.

Other structures can be woven on the same threading. Tie-up and treadling can be changed to use other shafts than odds vs evens for the two layers, producing basket weave or some other structure within the blocks. Or the same threading can be treated as a 2-block warp rep to be woven as single-layer warp-faced cloth with alternating thick and thin wefts. Or it can be tied and treadled to weave as 2-block twill.

Color-and-weave effect can be introduced to one or both layers (or blocks) of a 2-block double weave.

The layers of double weave do not have to be the same yarns at the same sett alternating 1:1 in threading and treadling. For example, one layer can be a yarn twice the size of the other, at half the frequency, making a heavier mesh layer against a finer dense layer.

The samples in this book give only a tiny taste of the possibilities for 8-shaft 2-block double weave.

#679–682

by Pamela Franck

Two-block double weave.

*Single layer 2/2 twill in squares with double-cloth frame.

+Warp rep—alternately fine and heavy wefts, both light colored.

679

680

681

682

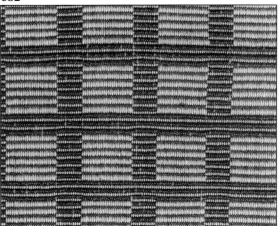

Profile draft
for #679 & #680

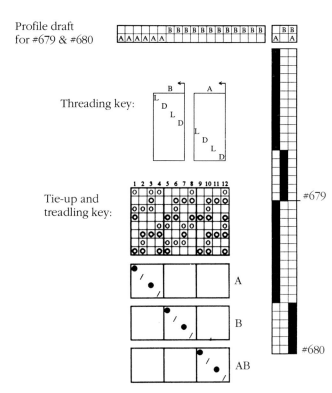

Threading key:

Tie-up and
treadling key:

A

B

AB

● = dark weft
/ = light weft

(Each 4-pick treadling unit weaves two
picks in each layer.)

Thread-by-thread
drafts for
#681 & #682

D = dark
L = light
H = heavy
f = fine

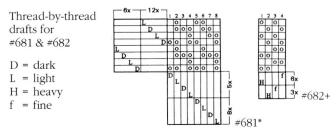

#681*

#682+

#683

by Judy Steinkoenig

This "Nine Patch" sample was designed by Carol Strickler.

683

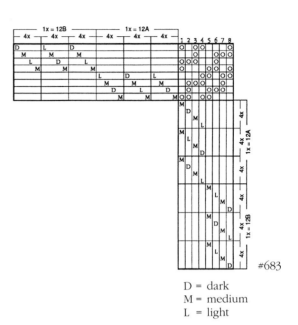

#683

D = dark
M = medium
L = light

Threading and tie-up for #684–687:

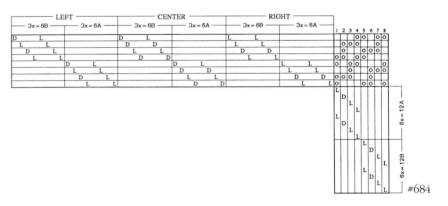

#684

#684

by Priscilla Lynch

This is a gamp of three different color orders in a 2-block double weave. The left sample is threaded with all light on odd shafts, 2D/2L on the even shafts. The center sample is all dark on the odd shafts, 1D/3L on the even shafts. The right sample is threaded all light on the odd shafts, 1L/1D on the even shafts. The color orders are the same for both blocks.

684 left

684 center

684 right

#685–687
Priscilla Lynch continued.
Same threading and tie-up as #684.

685 left

685 center

685 right

686 left

686 center

686 right

687 left

687 center

687 right

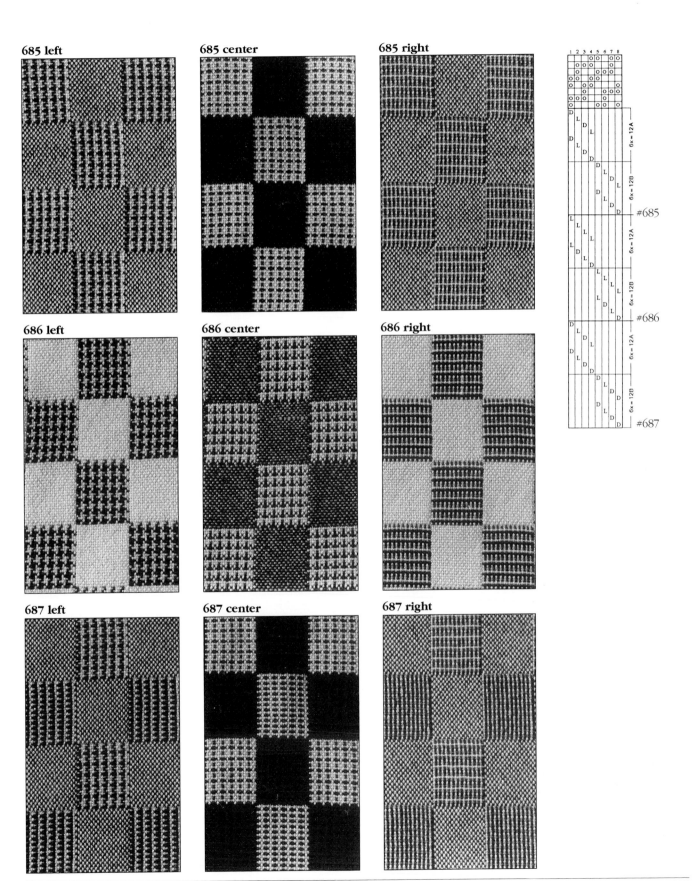

211

Chapter 23
QUILTED DOUBLE WEAVE AND PIQUÉ

In one type of double weave, layers are separate except for patterned "stitching" points that quilt them together—with or without stuffing between the layers. With eight shafts there are many possibilities for loom-controlled quilting of layered cloth, stitching the layers together by raising or lowering certain threads from one layer to the other.

In one form of quilted double cloth, both layers (face and back) are balanced plain weave in two colors of the same yarn. Warp ends from the lower layer are raised in patterned sequence to go over face wefts. These stitching points show as backing warps on the face and face-weft dots on the back. In this book, a sampler of this technique alternates dark threads of face warp on two shafts with light threads of back warp threaded in a point twill order on the other six shafts (see samples #688–691).

In *piqué* (a form of quilted double cloth), the face warp and weft weave at loose or moderate tension while the back warp is separately beamed and woven under very tight tension. The interlacement is sometimes like that of an ordinary quilted double cloth, but the tension difference between the layers makes the face layer puff and pucker between stitching points. This effect is sometimes accentuated by adding a third weft, a "wadding" weft—a large soft yarn that stuffs the areas between layers and does not interweave with either layer. In piqué (whether stuffed or not), the back warp ends can float unwoven between stitching points ("loose-back piqué", which is technically not a double weave) or can be interwoven with their own weft ("fast-back piqué", which *is* a double weave). Samples #692–694 are loose-backed (all unstuffed). Samples #695–698 are fast-backed (some stuffed and some unstuffed). In samples #699–703 the wadding weft of a figured piqué shows on the back in an overshot-like pattern.

All of the piqué samples shown here use a threading with two shafts for the plain weave face and the other six for the back warp or stitchers. All use a ratio of two face warp ends per one back (stitching) warp end. In the resulting fabrics, the face weave is always plain weave. Piqué on eight shafts *can* be drafted using more shafts for the face (at the expense of having fewer shafts for the stitching warp). Such a draft allows patterned face fabric (a point twill, for example) as well as patterned quilting. The face:back ratio can also be other than 2:1.

For more information on quilted double weaves, see *Piqué: Plain and Patterned* by Donna Sullivan, and other books and monographs on double weave.

#688–691

by Pamela Franck

Stitched double cloth with 1:1 ratio. *Note:* The face is plain weave, dark, on shafts 7 and 8. The back is plain weave with stitchers lifted in pattern, light, on shafts 1-6.

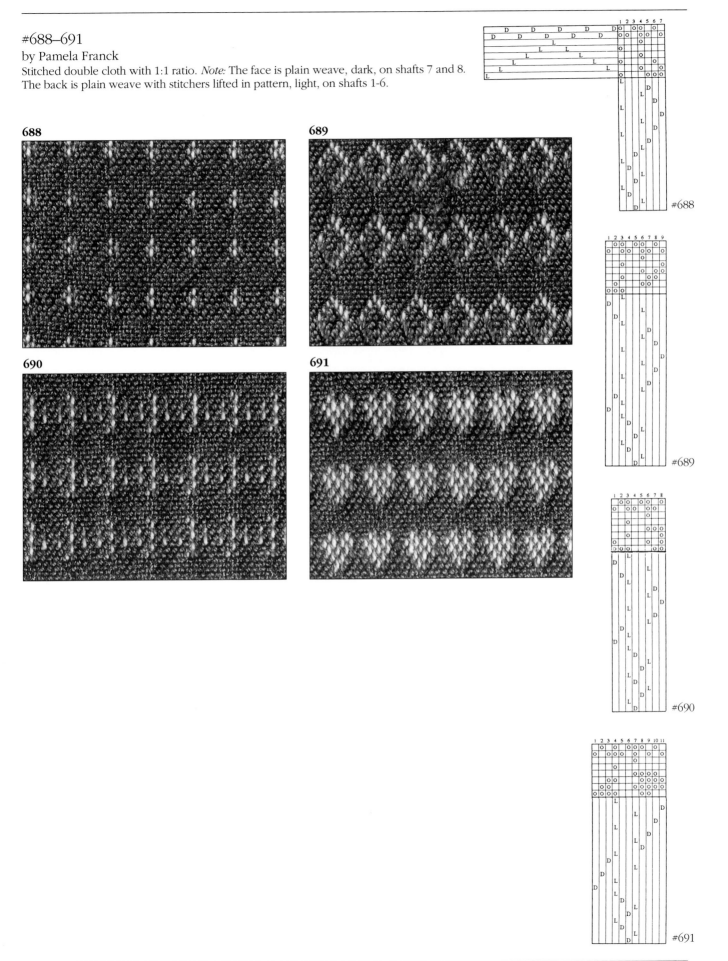

688

689

690

691

#692–694
by Shirley Jensen

Loose-back piqué. *Note:* Piqué with 2:1 front-back ratio. The face is light, on shafts 1 and 2; the backing is dark, on shafts 3-8.

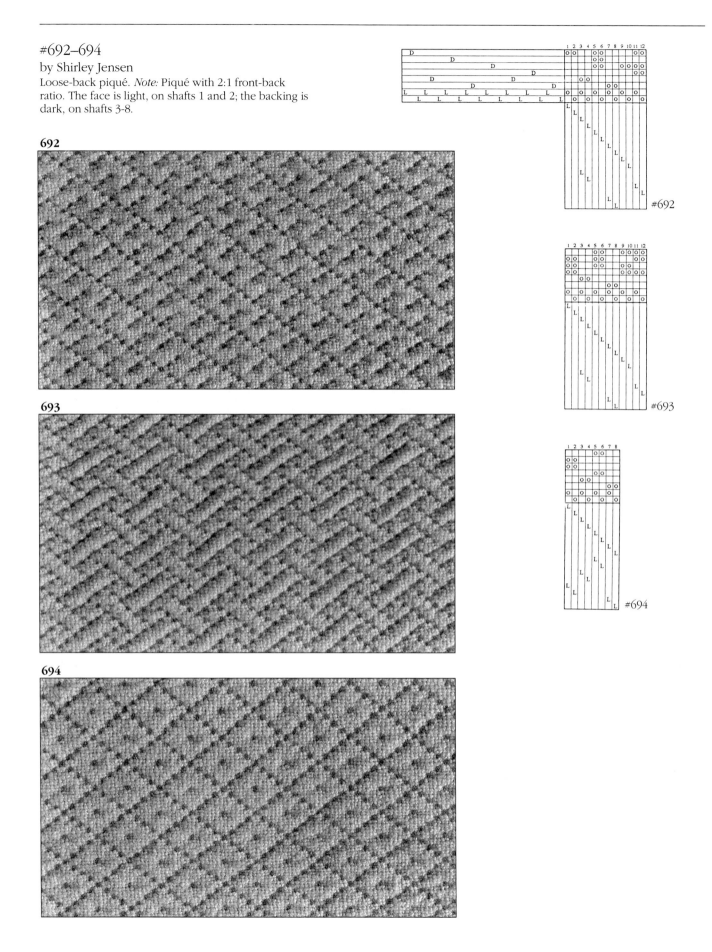

692

693

694

#695–698

by Anita Bell

7-shaft fast-back piqué from *Piqué: Plain and Patterned* by Donna Sullivan. *Note:* 2:1 face-back ratio. The face is medium on shafts 1 and 2. The backing is light on shafts 3-7. Each stitcher is sleyed with the two face ends on each side of it. Some samples have a light wadding weft.

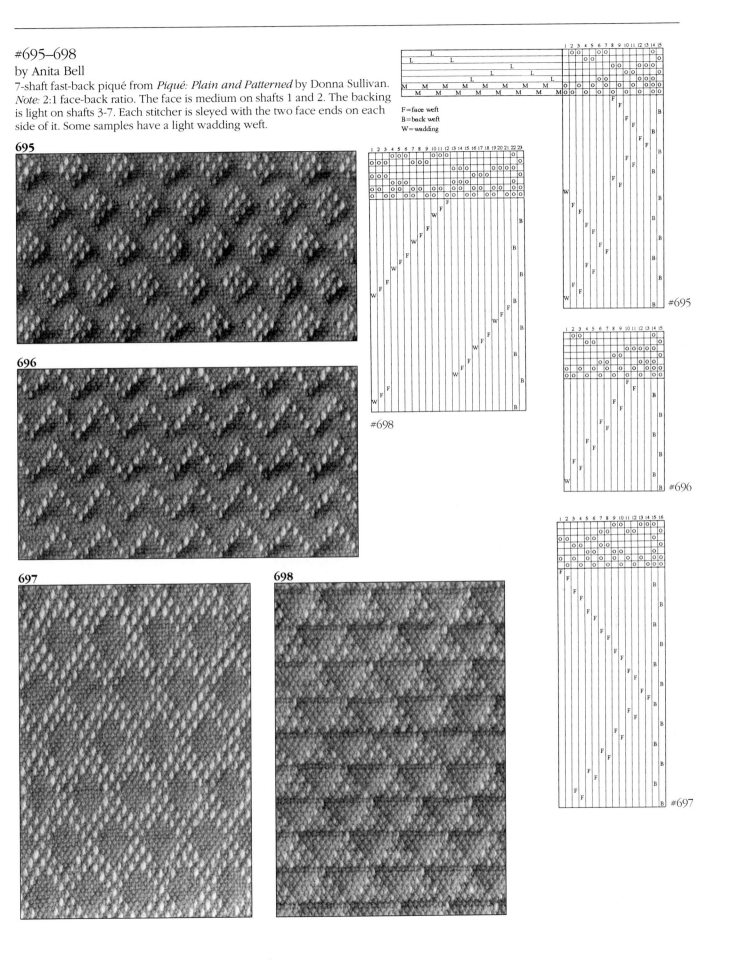

695

696

697

698

F = face weft
B = back weft
W = wadding

#698

#695

#696

#697

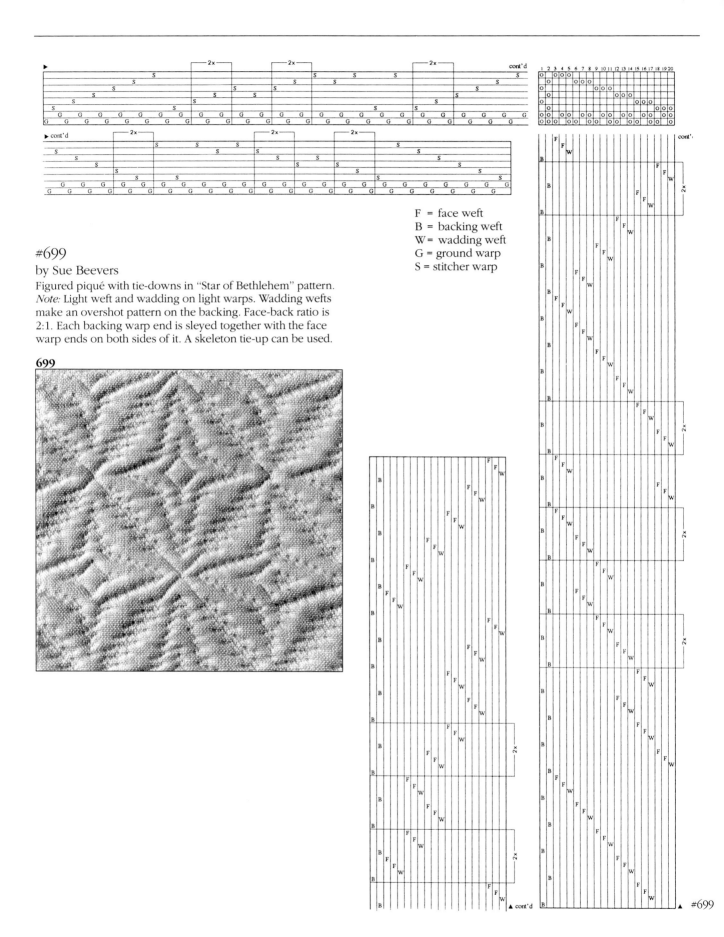

#699

by Sue Beevers

Figured piqué with tie-downs in "Star of Bethlehem" pattern. *Note:* Light weft and wadding on light warps. Wadding wefts make an overshot pattern on the backing. Face-back ratio is 2:1. Each backing warp end is sleyed together with the face warp ends on both sides of it. A skeleton tie-up can be used.

F = face weft
B = backing weft
W = wadding weft
G = ground warp
S = stitcher warp

1	2	3	4	5	6	7	8	9	10	11	12	13	14	15	16	17	18	19	20
O			O	O	O														
	O					O	O	O											
O									O	O	O								
O												O	O	O					
O															O	O	O		
O																	O	O	O
O	O		O	O		O	O		O	O		O	O		O	O		O	O
O	O	O	O	O	O	O	O	O	O	O	O	O	O	O	O	O	O	O	O

#700
Sue Beevers continued.

700

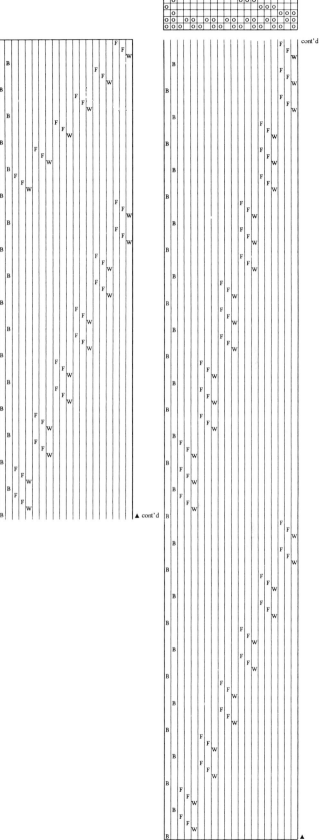

cont'd

▲ cont'd

▲

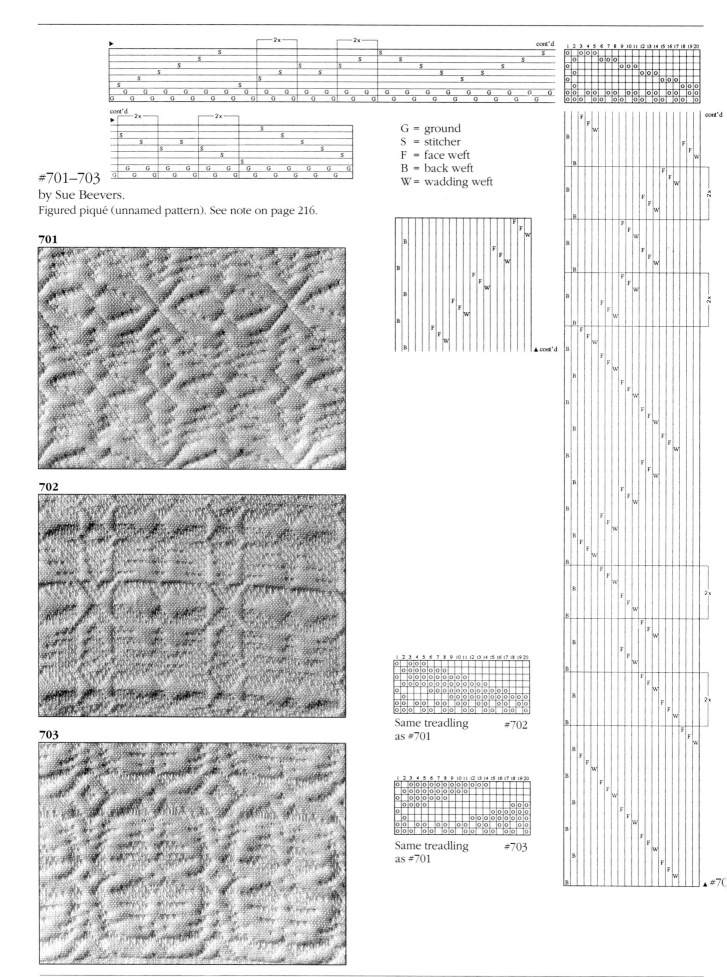

#701–703
by Sue Beevers.
Figured piqué (unnamed pattern). See note on page 216.

G = ground
S = stitcher
F = face weft
B = back weft
W = wadding weft

701

702

703

Same treadling   #702
as #701

Same treadling   #703
as #701

Chapter 24
HONEYCOMB AND DEFLECTED-THREAD WEAVES

There are some weaves in which warp and/or weft threads are deflected out of perpendicular by their interlacement. The best-known of these is *honeycomb*, in which outlining threads undulate around and between sections or "cells" of plain weave that alternate with unwoven ones.

In its simplest *4-shaft* form, honeycomb is a 2-block repeat twill on opposite blocks. To weave a cell, the two shafts of the cell being woven are raised alternately to make plain weave in the cell, while the shafts of the other cell are both raised for every shot so that all cell-wefts float below them. When the woven cell is the height desired, one or more picks of heavier outline weft are woven plain weave all the way across the fabric. If the outline wefts are laid loosely in their sheds they undulate, curving up around the cell just woven and then down into the unwoven width of the other cell. Then the second cell is woven while the first is held up—this cell filling the outlined depression left by the first. The next outline wefts undulate around *this* cell and into the *other* depression. The resulting fabric is plain weave on the face with cell-weft floats under the cells on the back (figure 24.1).

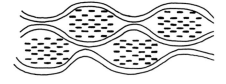

24.1 Diagram of face.

This principle of honeycomb tie-up and treadling order can be used on a number of other threadings and structures.

Honeycomb, expanded to eight shafts, offers several possibilities. Four blocks can be produced that are independent and clearly-cut because they are on four separate pairs of shafts. (If the four blocks are woven one at a time, the resulting fabric might have very long back floats where the wefts float under three unwoven cells.) Cells *can* be combined in the tie-up and treadling. Samples #704–707 are examples of 4-block honeycomb; the same honeycomb threading could be treadled with supplementary weft and tabby weft in standard 4-block overshot fashion.

Another possibility for 8-shaft honeycomb is that the cells can be something other than plain weave (as, for example, a 2-block design with each cell 4-shaft twill or rosepath). Samples #708 & #709 are examples of this.

A third possibility shown here (samples #710 & #711) is two-faced honeycomb. There are two versions here, both of which have no weft floats exposed. In one version the cells are single cloth, with the face and the back each having its own outline weft. These wefts follow the same arcing and dipping path around each cell, but on opposite faces of the cloth. In this two-faced version, the weft-wise skips of cell weft between cells are contained as a cord between the layers of outline wefts. In the other version of two-faced honeycomb, both the cells *and* the outlines are two-faced; what is cell on one face is outline on the other. In *this* version there *are no* weft skips because each cell-weft weaves alternate cells on alternate faces, and the outline wefts follow contrary paths, one dipping where the other is arcing.

Honeycomb can be varied by increasing or decreasing the size of the cells, by varying the yarn weight and the number or order of shots of outline weft between the cells, and by changing the order and/or combination in which the cells are woven. Length of weft floats on the back of the fabric should be a consideration if the honeycomb fabric is intended for a reversible or unlined end use and is not one of the two-faced versions.

The other samples in this chapter show textured and "surface interest" structures. These weaves are ideal for showcasing an expensive novelty yarn.

#704–707

by Ardis Dobrovolny

4-block honeycomb, designed by Carol Strickler. *Note:* These samples have a dark cell weft and a light heavy outline weft on a light warp.

*In this sample, the outlines are a,b, then a,b.

+In this sample, the outlines are a,b, then b,a.

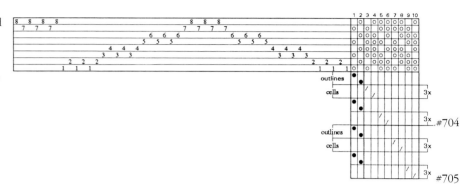

704

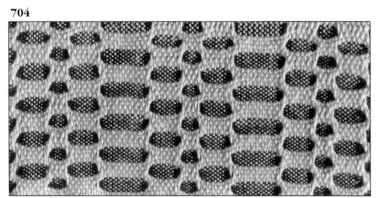

705

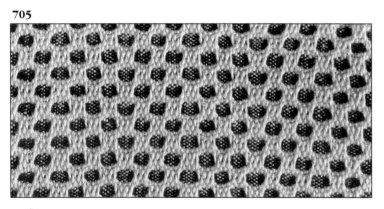

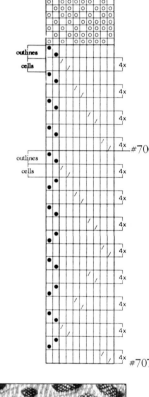

706

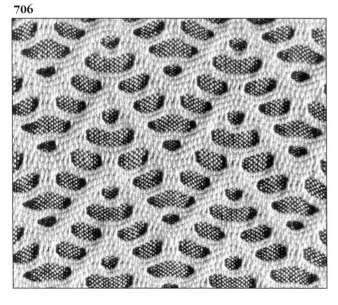

707

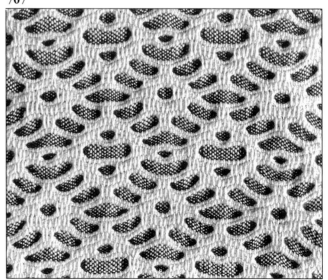

#708 & #709
by Jeanne L. Richards

This 2-block honeycomb with rosepath cells was designed by Carol Strickler.
A medium-colored cell weft and a heavy light-colored outline weft are
woven on a light warp.

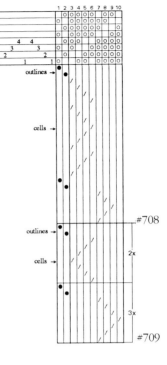

708

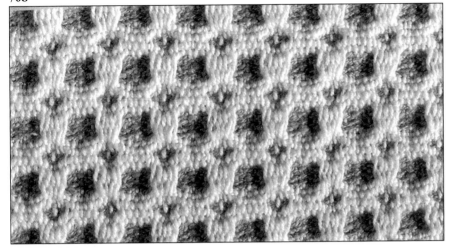

709

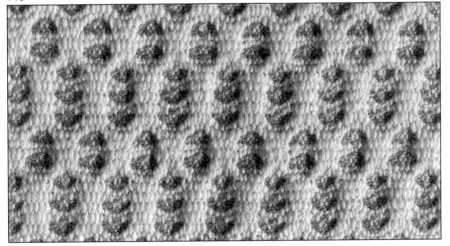

#710 & #711

by Sherron Pampalone

These two-faced honeycombs were designed by Carol Strickler.

*In this sample, the A cell weft is the same fine dark and the B cell weft is the same fine medium as the warp. Outline on the face is heavy white; outline on the back (not shown) is heavy light. The cells are block A alternating with block B and are single cloth. The face outline is on odd shafts and the back outline is on even shafts. Cell-weft skips group in the middle of the cloth, between layers of outline wefts. Only the warp changes layers.

+In this sample, dark weaves A cell on the face and B cell on the back. Medium weaves B cell on the face and A cell on the back. Face outlines are the same as in sample #710. The cells are block A alternating with block B and are double cloth (cells backed by outlines). Face outline and face cells are odd shafts, and back outline and back cells (not shown) are on even shafts. There are no weft floats. Only the cell wefts change layers.

#710*

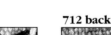

#711+

Same treadling as #710

Note: This sampler is threaded in stripes of two colors of fine yarn.
A = dark; B = medium.

710

711

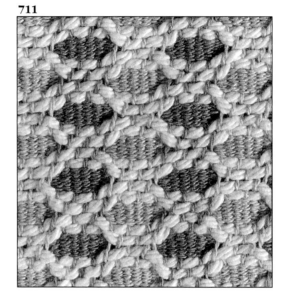

#712 (both faces)

by Cate Crissey

Deflected supplementary weft. *Note:* In this sample, the supplementary dark weft rides on the surface of the light plain-weave ground fabric, deflected and held by the warp floats.

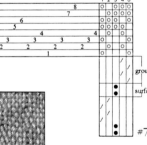

#712

712 face

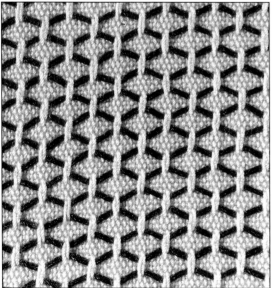

712 back

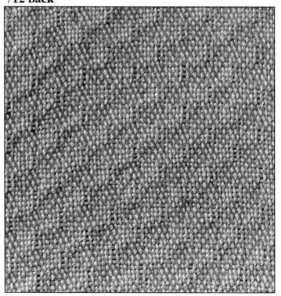

#713–715

by Yezhen Li and Linda Ligon

Note: This distorted weft pattern is similar to #712, but has a point twill ground and heavier, dark floating warps. It can be treadled to look like #712; other interlacements are shown here.

713

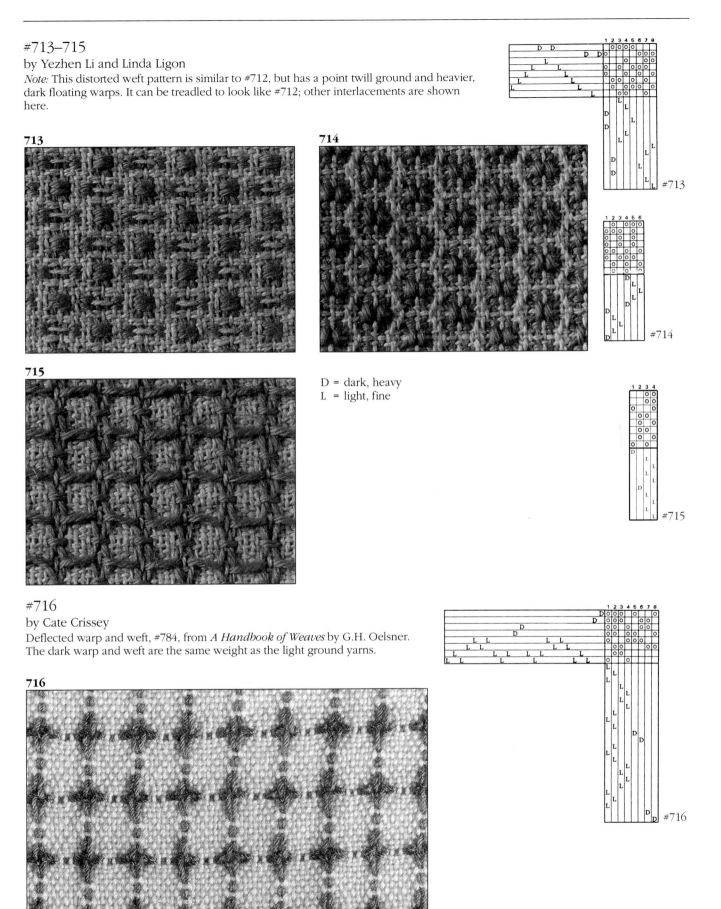

714

715

D = dark, heavy
L = light, fine

#716

by Cate Crissey

Deflected warp and weft, #784, from *A Handbook of Weaves* by G.H. Oelsner. The dark warp and weft are the same weight as the light ground yarns.

716

Chapter 25
MISCELLANY

Miscellany: A collection of various items, parts, or ingredients—in other words: "odds and ends". This chapter includes samples that just did not fit neatly into any of the other chapters. One is a 4-block "log cabin". Some are "surface interest" weaves, backed fabrics, etc.

Some of these samples are *combination twills*, threadings in which two or more different twills are sections of the draft, forming stripes or squares of different weaves. Two of the samplers use patterns designed according to Dr. Bateman's technique presented in *Multiple Tabby Weaves*, Shuttle Craft Guild Monograph 35, edited by Virginia I. Harvey.

Sometimes the term "cord" means a fabric with woven stripes or bands that are raised into ribs by threads that skip tightly straight across the back of each rib. This chapter includes samples of *warpwise cord* (which, in 8-shaft form, can be decorated by "wadding" warps that pad the ribs). It also includes one *weftwise cord* sample (which, in 8-shaft form, can be patterned in the flat bands between the cords). For more information on corded weaves, see on the industry-oriented books such as *A Handbook of Weaves* by G. H. Oelsner or *Designing on the Loom* by Mary Kirby.

There are samples in this chapter that illustrate the many possibilities for *supplementary-warp patterning* on eight shafts. These include *patterned stripes, allover supplementary-warp patterning, "turned" overshot or other supplementary-weft weave,* and *crossed warp and weft pattern.* (These weaves are often fast to weave because they use only one shuttle, compensating for the extra time and tensioning care that must be taken in threading the loom.)

One of the samplers in this chapter is an example of the possibilities of a *blended draft* (a technique in which two different 4-shaft threadings are integrated via a formula into a new 8-shaft threading). The pattern illustrated here is a blend of two small 4-shaft overshots; other weaves can be blended (for example: overshot and huck, overshot and summer & winter) as long as repeat lengths of the originals are the same. A blended draft can be woven as though it were either of the originals. Or the two patterns can be excerpted and combined into borders or new allover designs. Or the blend can sometimes be woven with an 8-shaft formula tie-up and a twill treadling order for an entirely new design. Several of these possibilities are shown here.

Many of the samples in this chapter use more than one color both in warp and in weft. All are interesting—perhaps last, in this book, but certainly not least!

#717 & #718

by Judy Steinkoenig

4-block log cabin adapted from a Marjorie O'Shaughnessy workshop., 1976, by Carol Strickler.

717

718

D = dark
L = light

#717

#718

#719

by Ardis Dobrovolny

Double-faced twill, from *Surface Interest: Textiles of Today*, Shuttle Craft Monograph 2, by Harriet Tidball. In this sample, the layers are stitched by threads raised from the bottom layer.

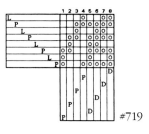

#719

719 face

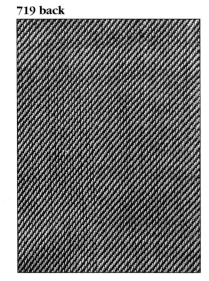

719 back

L = light (bottom layer warp, on even shafts).
D = dark (bottom layer weft, on right 4 treadles).
P = plaid (top layer, following Color Order in both warp and weft on odd shafts and left 4 treadles).
Plaid Color Order for the top layer (each thread alternating with bottom layer:

dark	22	20	4
light		4	22	20

#720 & #721

by Dorothy Lenz

"Southwest Sampler". This sampler is designed like a 6-shaft pattern with 2 shafts reserved for plain-weave tie-downs. *Note:* Use tabby after each pattern pick, with additional picks as shown.   t = tabby picks between motifs

720

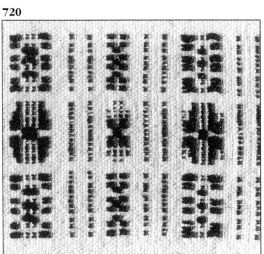

721

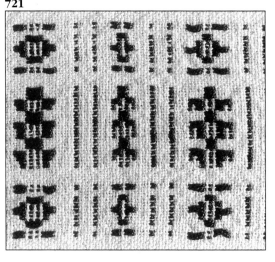

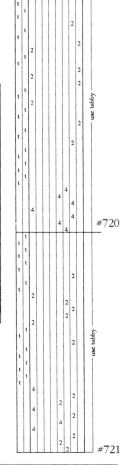

tabby

#720

#721

226

#722–725

by Jean Korus

Combination twill from *200 Patterns for Multiple-Harness Looms* by Russell Groff, page 28.

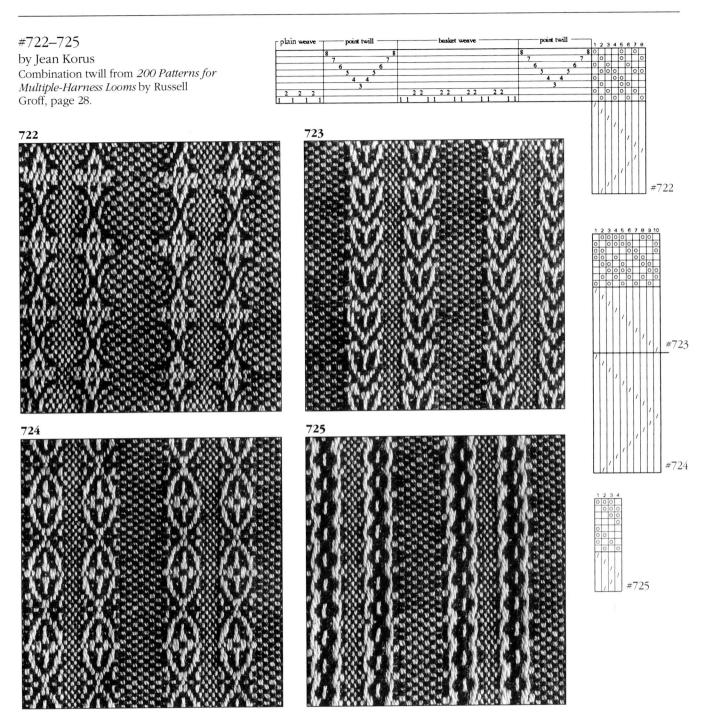

722

723

724

725

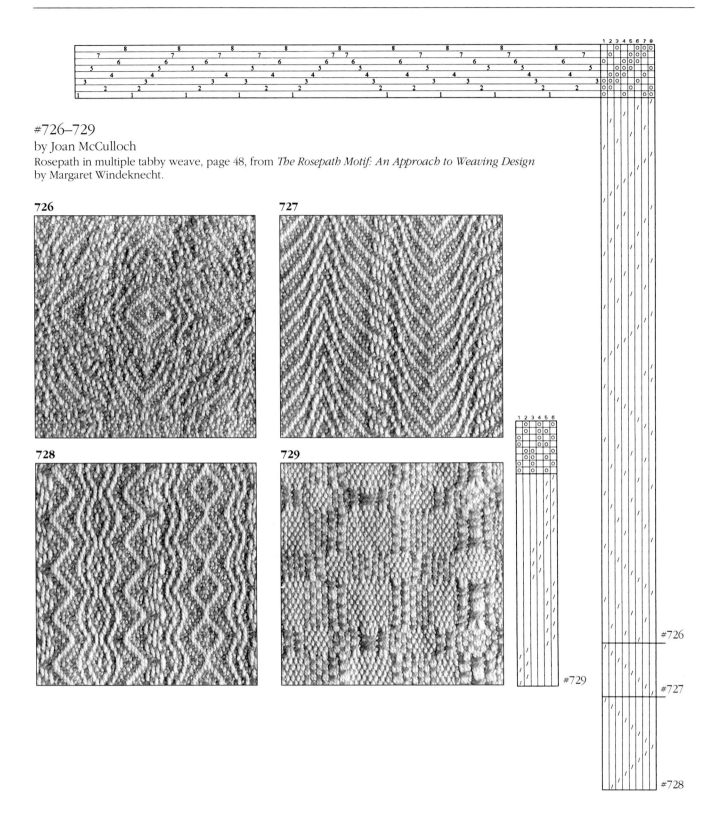

#726–729
by Joan McCulloch
Rosepath in multiple tabby weave, page 48, from *The Rosepath Motif: An Approach to Weaving Design* by Margaret Windeknecht.

726

727

728

729

#730–734
by Joyce Fisher Robards
"Many Friends" multiple tabby weave.

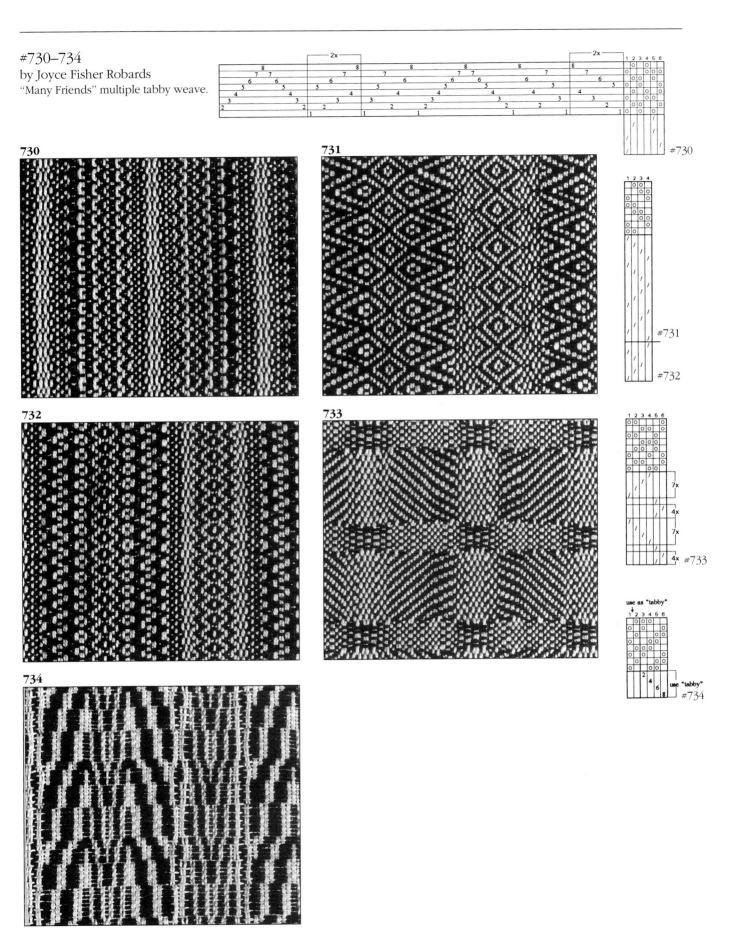

730

731

732

733

734

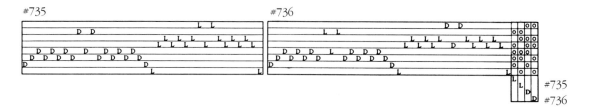

#735   #736

#735
#736

#735–738

by Jeanne Young Kudlicki
Warp-wise cord, #57, from *Designing on the Loom* by Mary Kirby.
In the threading, shafts 1-2 are the furrow, shafts 3-4 are one cord and shafts 5-6 another cord, and shafts 7-8 are padding.
These samples have the same threading and treadling: warp color orders and tie-ups differ. There is no true tabby on
this threading. Both wadding ends are sleyed with the face end they flank.

735   **736**

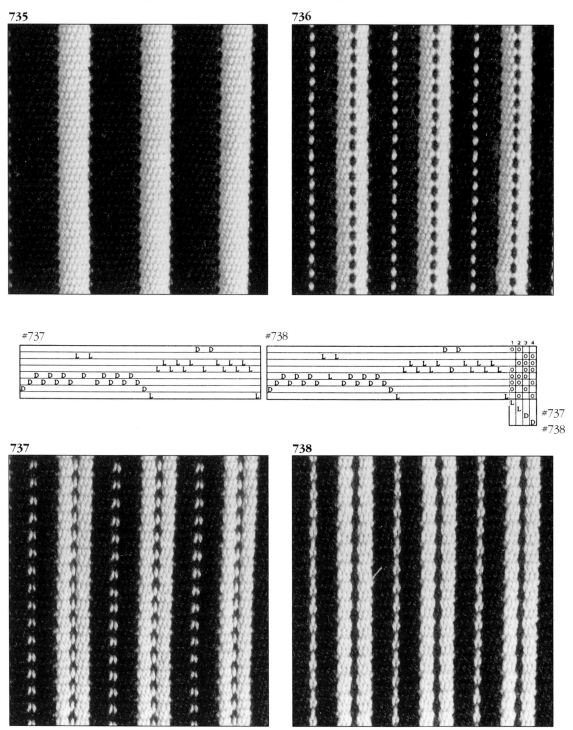

#737   #738

#737
#738

737   **738**

#739

by Esther James

Warp-wise cord. *Note:* Shafts 1-2 are one cord, shafts 3-4 are another cord, shafts 5-6 are the furrow, and shafts 7-8 are padding. This draft is the same as samples #735–738, except for shaft functions and cord sizes. In this sample, padding warps are raised to decorate the cords.

739

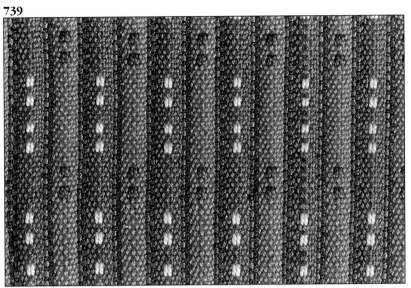

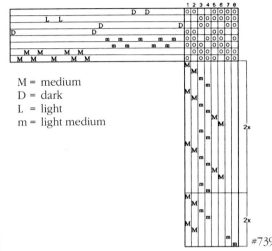

M = medium
D = dark
L = light
m = light medium

#739

#740

by Nell Znamierowski

Note: Weft-wise cord. The warp is all light. Use an especially firm beat for the first pick after the stuffer wefts. Notice that the pattern wefts make long skips on the back. Cords are weft-faced on the front.

740

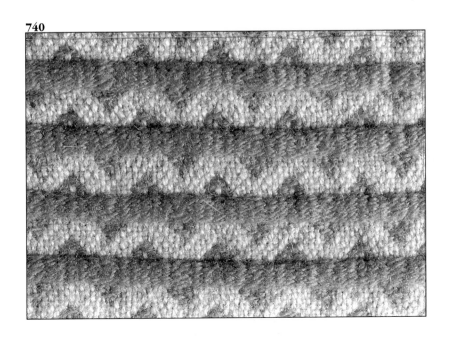

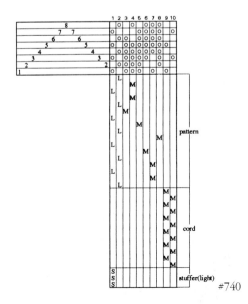

#740

#741–744

by Sallie Guy

Plain ground and supplementary warp on a straight twill profile. *Note:* Dark heavy pattern warps; medium and light warp stripes in plain-weave areas. The backs of these samples are strikingly different from the faces. A skeleton tie-up may be necessary. Sley each dark supplementary end together with its adjacent light ground end.

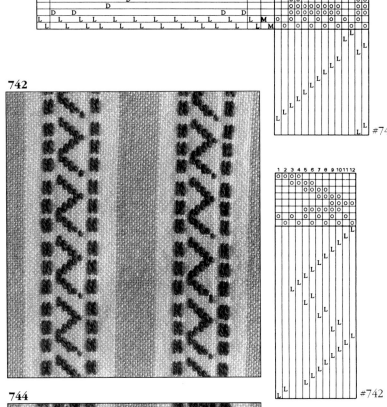

741

742

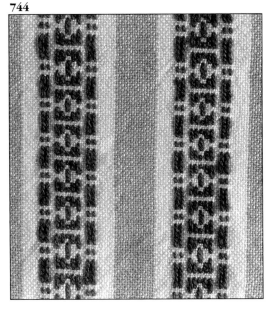

743

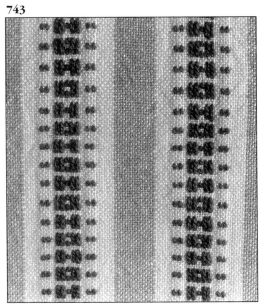

744

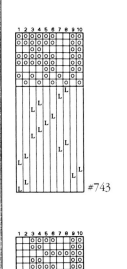

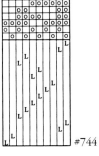

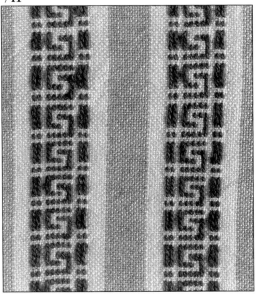

#745–747

by Judie Eatough

All-over supplementary warp from *Recipe Book* by Mary Meigs Atwater. *Note:* This sampler has a dark (heavier) pattern warp and a light ground and weft. Sley each dark supplementary end together with its adjacent light ground end. To weave all the patterns down, lift 1 vs 2; to weave all patterns up, lift 1-3-4-5-6-7-8- vs 2-3-4-5-6-7-8.

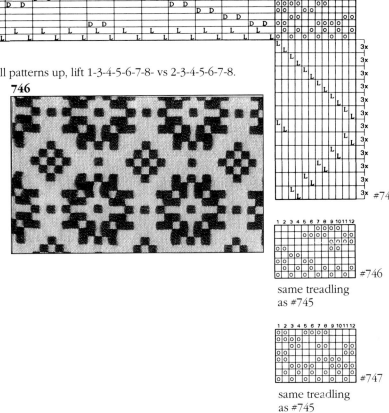

745

746

747

same treadling
as #746

same treadling
as #747

#745

#746

#747

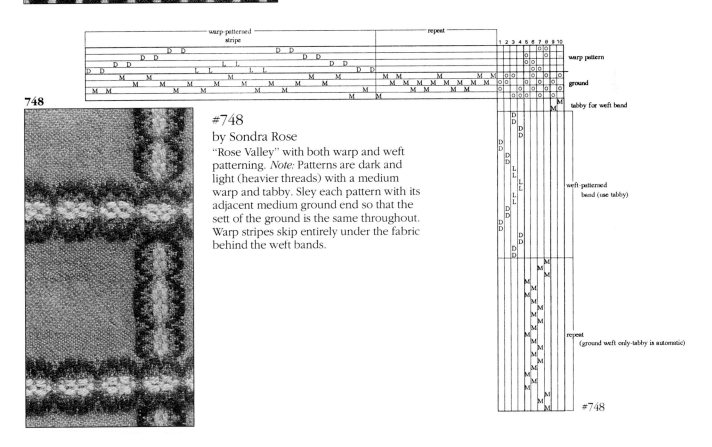

748

#748

by Sondra Rose

"Rose Valley" with both warp and weft patterning. *Note:* Patterns are dark and light (heavier threads) with a medium warp and tabby. Sley each pattern with its adjacent medium ground end so that the sett of the ground is the same throughout. Warp stripes skip entirely under the fabric behind the weft bands.

#748

#749–757

by Carol Strickler
Blended draft. Two repeats of "Star Flower"
blended with one repeat of "Star and Table".
Use tabby with all these treadlings.
*"Star Flower", woven as drawn in.
+"Star and Table", woven as drawn in.

749

750

751

752

Note: Use tabby.
Tabby is 1-3-5-7 vs 2-4-6-8.

#749*

#750+

#751

#752

#753

#754

#755

#756

#757

#753

#754

#755

#756

#757

#758

by Ardis Dobrovolny

5-shaft surface interest/cell weave. *Note:* Fine threads are medium, heavy threads are light.
In sleying, heavy threads are each in their own dent, fine threads are 3 per dent.

758

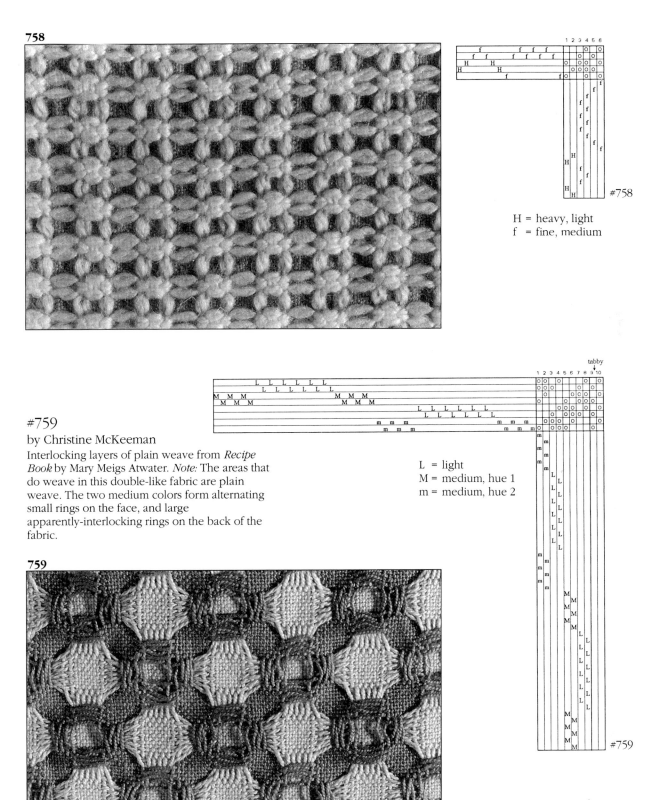

H = heavy, light
f = fine, medium

#759

by Christine McKeeman

Interlocking layers of plain weave from *Recipe Book* by Mary Meigs Atwater. *Note:* The areas that do weave in this double-like fabric are plain weave. The two medium colors form alternating small rings on the face, and large apparently-interlocking rings on the back of the fabric.

L = light
M = medium, hue 1
m = medium, hue 2

759

#760–763
by Jacquie Kelly

"Silk Brocade" from a Virginia West workshop.
Note: Threads are light, heavy and dark, fine.
The faces and backs are very different.

d=dark fine
L=light heavy

760 face

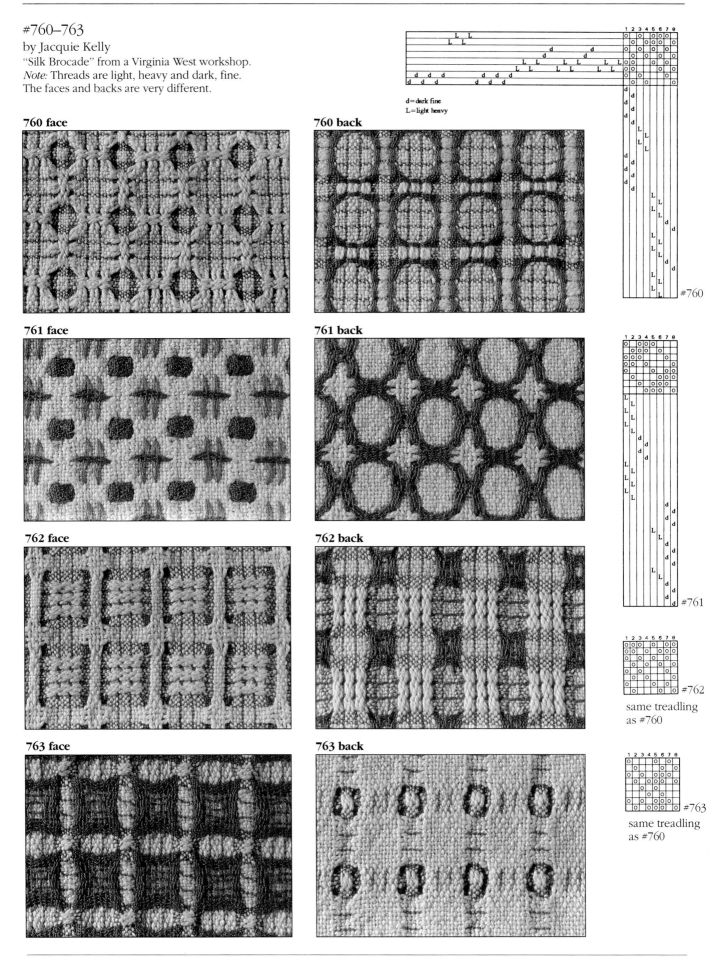

760 back

761 face

761 back

762 face

762 back

763 face

763 back

#760

#761

#762

same treadling
as #760

#763

same treadling
as #760

#764 & #765

by Ardis Dobrovolny

Outlined squares adapted by Carol Strickler from *Designing on the Loom* by Mary Kirby. *Note:* Heavy dark outlining threads skip across the back between the squares. They are sleyed together with adjacent fine ends so that the sett of the L and M ground is maintained.

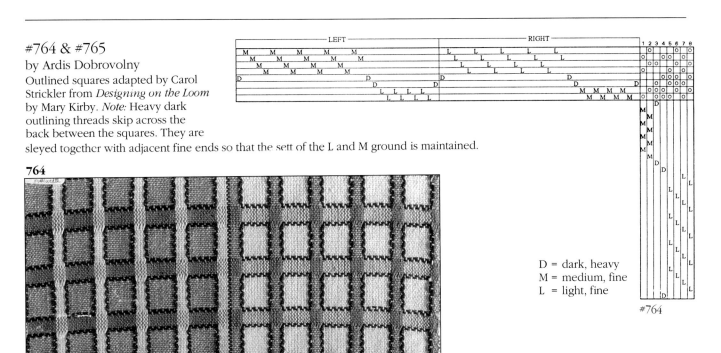

764

765

In this sample, the treadling reverses direction at * midway through the third large square.

D = dark, heavy
M = medium, fine
L = light, fine

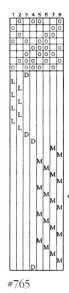

#764

#765

FINALE

This must be a finite book in a seemingly infinite world of possibilities. So the samples have come to an end, but not the options for using the patterns they illustrate. In addition to the variations suggested in the chapters, there are several ways a pattern can be changed or made into very different cloth, and there are other possibilities for doing things on eight shafts that cannot be done on four.

Color interaction with the weave structure can make a major change in a pattern (as has been shown in the many color-and-weave-effect samples throughout the book). Tie-up and treadling variations are another change that can make something quite different of a pattern. Treadling orders that often work well on other weave threadings than their own include lace-fashion, overshot-fashion (with supplementary weft and tabby weft), honeycomb, and boundweave. In many weaves, patterns can be excerpted for borders.

Yarns and sett are major factors in the appearance of a pattern, as well as in the "hand" of the resulting fabric. A strong pattern woven in very subtly-contrasting yarns can become textural rather than patterned, for example, or a lace weave woven in fine wool can develop "tracking" that subdues the design.

Some of the one-shuttle weaves (such as Atwater-Bronson lace, spot Bronson, and huck) can have their threadings "grouped". Threading border repeats of a 4-shaft pattern on shafts 1-4 and center repeats of the same pattern on shafts 5-8 makes possible a fabric with plain center and patterned border all around it. Eight shafts can also be used to weave a 4-shaft pattern double width or tubular.

And finally there's that whole other world of *weaver-controlled* techniques that can be applied to the *loom-controlled* threadings shown in this book. Discontinuous wefts, inlay, pick-up, weaver-controlled laces—the list goes on and on. How many lifetimes would it take to explore the entire world of 8-shaft weaving?

Bibliography

Some of the patterns in this book were drawn from the following books, magazines, organizations, and individuals:

Atwater, Mary Meigs. *A Book of Patterns for Hand-Weaving: Designs from the John Landes Drawings in the Pennsylvania Museum.* Hollywood, California: Southern California Handweavers Guild, 1977; republication of 1925–26 book.

Atwater, Mary Meigs. *Recipe Book.* Salt Lake City: Wheelwright Press, 1969; republication of 1957 edition,

Atwater, Mary Meigs. *The Shuttle-Craft Book of American Hand-weaving.* Coupeville, Washington: ShuttleCraft Books, 1928; reprint 1986.

Barrett, Clotilde. *Summer and Winter and Beyond,* Monograph #2. Boulder, Colorado: The Colorado Fiber Center, 1979.

Barrett, Clotilde, and Eunice Smith. *Double Two-tie Unit Weaves.* Boulder, Colorado: Weaver's Journal Publications, 1983.

Black, Mary E. *The Key to Weaving.* New York: Macmillan, 1957; reprint 1979.

Bress, Helene. *The Weaving Book.* New York: Scribner's, 1981.

Burnham, Harold B., and Dorothy K. Burnham. *Keep Me Warm One Night: Early Handweaving in Eastern Canada.* Toronto: University of Toronto Press, 1972.

Burton, Dorothy S. *Versatile Bronson,* Monograph 5. Boston: Weavers Guild of Boston, 1984.

Cherepov, Klara. *Diversified Plain Weave.* Lancaster, Pennsylvania: Klara Cherepov, 1972.

Cyrus-Zetterström, Ulla. *Manual of Swedish Handweaving.* Petaluma, California: LTs Forlag AB; distributed by Unicorn Books, 1984; revision of 1956 edition.

Davison, Marguerite Porter. *A Handweaver's Pattern Book.* Swarthmore, Pennsylvania: Marguerite Porter Davison, 1944.

Emery, Irene. *The Primary Structures of Fabrics.* Washington, D.C.: The Textile Museum, 1966; revised 1980.

Frey, Berta. *Designing and Drafting for Handweavers.* New York: Collier Books, 1958.

Goerner, Doris. *Woven Structure and Design: Part I—Single Cloth Construction.* Leeds, England: WIRA Technology Group, 1986.

Groff, Russell E. *200 Patterns for Multiple-Harness Looms: 5 to 12 Harness Patterns for Handweavers.* McMinnville, Oregon: Robin and Russ Handweavers, 1979.

Harvey, Virginia I., ed. *Bateman Blend Weaves.* Shuttle Craft Guild Monograph 36. Coupeville, Washington: ShuttleCraft Books, 1982.

Harvey, Virginia I. *Boulevard, Chevron, and Combination Weaves.* Shuttle Craft Guild Monograph 38. Coupeville, Washington: ShuttleCraft Books, 1987.

Harvey, Virginia I. *Extended Manifold Twill Weaves.* Shuttle Craft Guild Monograph 40. Coupeville, Washington: ShuttleCraft Books, 1989.

Harvey, Virginia I. *Multiple Tabby Weaves.* Shuttle Craft Guild Monograph 35. Coupeville, Washington: ShuttleCraft Books, 1981.

Hayes, Bertha G. *The Complete Book of Bertha Hayes' Patterns.* East Berlin, Pennsylvania: Creative Crafts, 1957.

Holroyd, Ruth N., with Ulrike L. Beck. *Jacob Angstadt: Designs Drawn from His Weavers Patron Book.* Pittsford, New York: Ruth N. Holroyd, 1976.

Kirby, Mary. *Designing on the Loom.* Mountain View, Missouri: Select Books, 1955.

Landis, Lucille. *Twills and Twill Derivatives: Design Your Own, Four to Eight Harnesses.* Old Greenwich, Connecticut: Lucille Landis; distributed by Unicorn Books, 1977.

Lang, Elizabeth, and Erica Dakin Voolich. *Parallel Shadow Weave.* Boston: Weavers Guild of Boston, 1987.

Laughlin, Mary Elizabeth. *More Than Four.* West Sacramento, California: Laughlin Enterprises; distributed by Robin and Russ Handweavers, McMinnville, Oregon, 1977.

Lundell, Laila. *Rep Weaves.* Sweden: ICA Bokförlag, 1987.

Oelsner, G. H. *A Handbook of Weaves.* New York: Dover Publications, 1952. (republication of Samuel S. Dale's 1915 translation)

Palmgren, S. *Vavbok.* Sweden: Norrköping. 1939.

Phillips, Janet. *The Weaver's Book of Fabric Design.* New York: St. Martin's Press, 1983.

Powell, Marian. *1000(+) Patterns in 4,6, and 8 Harness Shadow Weaves.* McMinnville, Oregon: Robin and Russ Handweavers, 1976.

Pyysalo, Helvi. *Kankaiden Sidokset.* Helsinki, Finland: Kustannusosakeyhtio Otava, 1967.

Pyysalo, Helvi, and Viivi Merissalo. *Hand Weaving Patterns from Finland.* Newton, Massachusetts: Branford, 1960.

Regensteiner, Else. *The Art of Weaving.* New York: Van Nostrand Reinhold, 1970.

Regensteiner, Else. *Weaver's Study Course.* West Chester, Pennsylvania: Schiffer Publishing, 1986; revision of 1981 edition.

Ryall, Pierre. *Weaving Techniques For the Multiple-Harness Loom.* New York: Van Nostrand Reinhold, 1979.

Safner, Isadora M. *The Weaving Roses of Rhode Island.* Loveland, Colorado: Interweave Press, 1985.

Strickler, Carol. *American Woven Coverlets.* Loveland, Colorado: Interweave Press, 1987.

Strickler, Carol. *A Portfolio of American Coverlets.* Volume 1, revised edition. Boulder, Colorado: Carol Strickler, 1980.

Sullivan, Donna. *Piqué: Plain and Patterned.* Jacksonville, Florida: Sullivan Publications, 1988.

Sutton, Ann. *The Structure of Weaving.* Loveland, Colorado: Interweave Press, 1982.

Swygert, Mrs. Luther M., ed. *Heirlooms From Old Looms.* Chicago: Colonial Coverlet Guild of America, 1955.

Tidball, Harriet. *Contemporary Satins.* Shuttle Craft Guild Monograph 7. Coupeville, Washington: ShuttleCraft Books, 1962.

Tidball, Harriet. *The Handloom Weaves.* Shuttle Craft Guild Monograph 33. Coupeville, Washington: ShuttleCraft Books, 1957.

Tidball, Harriet. *Surface Interest: Textiles of Today.* Shuttle Craft Monograph 2. Coupeville, Washington: ShuttleCraft Books, 1961.

Tod, Osma Gallinger. *The Joy of Hand Weaving.* New York: Van Nostrand Reinhold, 1964.

Voiers, Leslie. *Looking at Twills.* Harrisville, New Hampshire: Harrisville Designs, 1983.

Walker, Sandra Rambo. *Country Cloth to Coverlets.* Lewisburg, Pennsylvania: Oral Traditions Project, 1981.

Wertenberger, Kathryn. *8, 12...20.* Loveland, Colorado: Interweave Press, 1988.

Wilson, Sadye Tune, and Doris Finch Kennedy. *Of Coverlets.* Nashville, Tennessee: Tunstede, 1983.

Windeknecht, Margaret. *Creative Monk's Belt.* Shuttle Craft Guild Monograph 30. Coupeville, Washington: ShuttleCraft Books, 1977.

Windeknecht, Margaret. *Creative Overshot.* Shuttle Craft Guild Monograph 31. Coupeville, Washington: ShuttleCraft Books, 1978.

Windeknecht, Margaret. *The Rosepath Motif: An Approach to Weaving Design.* Rochester, Michigan: T. G. Windeknecht, 1987.

Windeknecht, Margaret, and Thomas Windeknecht. *Color-and-Weave.* New York: Van Nostrand Reinhold, 1981.

Worst, Edward. *How To Weave Linens.* Milwaukee, Wisconsin: Bruce Publishing, 1926.

Worst, Edward. *Weaving with Foot Power Looms.* New York: Dover Publications, 1974; reprint of 1918 edition.

Inspiration for swatches also came from these fine sources:

PUBLICATIONS

Ars Textrina; Handweavers Guild of America 1985 calendar; *Handweaver & Craftsman;* HANDWOVEN; *Interweave; Prairie Wool Companion; Shuttle, Spindle & Dyepot; Shuttle-Craft Bulletin; Weaver's; Weaver's Journal; Webe Mit.*

INDIVIDUALS AND CLASSES

Marian Powell Carpenter; HGA Learning Exchange; Marjorie O'Shaughnessy; Karen Selk; Naomi Towner; Madelyn van der Hoogt; Virginia West.

INDEX

INDEX OF NAMED PATTERNS